MACBETH

A True Story

FIONA WATSON

Quercus

First published in Great Britain in 2010 by Quercus.
This paperback edition published in 2011 by

Quercus
21 Bloomsbury Square
London
WC1A 2NS

A CIP catalogue record for this book is available
from the British Library

ISBN 978 0 85738 160 6

10 9 8 7 6 5

Typeset by Ellipsis books Limited, Glasgow
Printed and bound in Great Britain by Clays Ltd, St Ives plc

To Nick, who knows what's good for me

Contents

PART ONE

The Forging of a Kingdom

Contents

PART TWO

The Making of a King

List of Illustrations

List of Illustrations

Scotland in the time of Macbeth

NORSE

Orkney

Shetland

CAITHNESS

SUTHERLAND

ROSS

Tarbet Ness

Burghead

Nairn • Forres • Elgin • Essie

Inverness

MORAY

R. Spey

Glenelg

Lumphanan • Aberdeen

GRAMPIAN MOUNTAINS

ANGUS & MEARNS

NORTH SEA

Dunkeld

Forfar

Glamis

Dunsinane

Scone

Inverlochy

Dundurn • Perth

Forteviot • St Andrews

ARGYLL

FIFE

Stirling • Dunfermline

R. Forth

R. Tay

Dunadd

• Glasgow

Edinburgh

Berwick •

STRATHCLYDE
(British)

IRELAND

GALLOWAY
(Gaelic/Scots)

NORTHUMBRIA
(Anglo-Saxon)

CUMBRIA
(British)

The royal house of Scotland in the 9th and 10th centuries

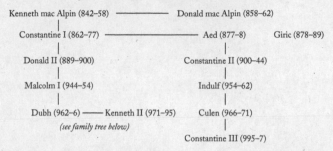

Kenneth mac Alpin (842–58) ——— Donald mac Alpin (858–62)

Constantine I (862–77) ——— Aed (877–8)   Giric (878–89)

Donald II (889–900)   Constantine II (900–44)

Malcolm I (944–54)   Indulf (954–62)

Dubh (962–6) —— Kenneth II (971–95)   Culen (966–71)

(see family tree below)

Constantine III (995–7)

The royal house of Scotland in the 10th and 11th centuries

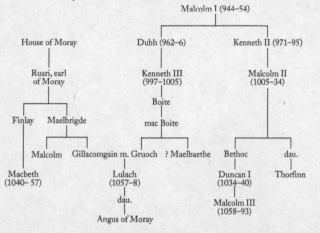

Malcolm I (944–54)

House of Moray   Dubh (962–6)   Kenneth II (971–95)

Ruari, earl of Moray   Kenneth III (997–1005)   Malcolm II (1005–34)

Boite

Finlay   Maelbrigde   mac Boite

Malcolm   Gillacomgain m. Gruoch   ? Maelbaethe   Bethoc   dau.

Macbeth (1040–57)   Lulach (1057–8)   Duncan I (1034–40)   Thorfinn

dau.   Malcolm III (1058–93)

Angus of Moray

The royal line from King Malcolm III

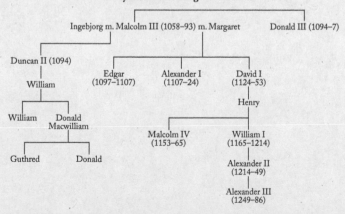

Ingebjorg m. Malcolm III (1058–93) m. Margaret   Donald III (1094–7)

Duncan II (1094)   Edgar (1097–1107)   Alexander I (1107–24)   David I (1124–53)

William   Henry

William   Donald Macwilliam   Malcolm IV (1153–65)   William I (1165–1214)

Guthred   Donald   Alexander II (1214–49)

Alexander III (1249–86)

Acknowledgements

This book has taken me back into the Middle Ages even further than I have ventured before, an experience that has been a profound relief, after years spent out of my historical depth in the modern period. It has also been frustrating, but never less than enjoyable and fascinating. For getting me interested in the real Macbeth, a king who seems now to have been always on the periphery of my vision, I must thank John Saddler, whose idea it originally was. I am also very grateful to Tony Morris for backing *Macbeth* with his customary enthusiasm and to Richard Milbank and Georgina Difford at Quercus, who have been most courteous and helpful editors and a real pleasure to work with.

Most of the first draft of *Macbeth* was written in Christchurch, New Zealand and I owe a huge debt to Ross and Pip for the use of their sofa on which to type, not to mention the rest of their lovely house during our stay. Email being what it is, I could plague Professor Dauvit Broun with questions just as often as I could have done back in Scotland. I cannot thank him enough for his patience and helpfulness in straightening out a novice, especially when he has so many other claims on his time. I am also grateful to Dr Alasdair Ross for giving me access, both in print and conversation, to his excellent insights into early Moray, while James Taylor, a bona fide Moray man, was kind enough to go through the first draft with a critical eye, much to its improvement. In the end, I have of course made up my own mind as to the story I wished to tell, and none of the above can be held in any way responsible for what has finally emerged on these pages. However, I must thank Linden Lawson, the copy editor, for helping to make the final product consistent, coherent and grammatically correct, and all with the utmost patience and kind words. I would also like to thank Kate Inskip for taking on a text full of formidably unusual names and indexing it beautifully.

There are two people without whom I doubt very much that this book would have seen the light of day. The first of these is my agent, Rachel Calder, who nurtured the original proposal until it finally blossomed into a story worth telling. I am truly grateful. The second is Nick, whose faith in my writing abilities persuaded me to leave my academic career. It was one of the smartest things I've ever done.

Finally, I would once more like to thank my mum and dad for all their support over far too many decades to mention here. And our children – Rose and Charlie, and now Finn, who told me today that he likes Scottish history. At six, he may change his mind, but it's a good start.

Introduction

It's all a strange history, and histories never end, but go on living in their consequences.

Henry James

Thanks to William Shakespeare, there can be few places in the world where the name Macbeth is unknown, and few societies untouched at some point in their histories by the kind of reign of terror over which he supposedly presided. For some, the fact that there was actually a Scottish king of that name who lived and died six hundred years before he was immortalised by the Bard will come as a surprise. But for others, Shakespeare's depiction of the terrible consequences of the reckless pursuit of power has had, and continues to have, such a powerful effect precisely because it is based on the life of a real man who once stood in places that we can still visit – the blasted heath near Nairn where Macbeth and Banquo first met the witches, the castle in Inverness (or its descendant) where Duncan was murdered, Birnam wood, whose foliage provided cover for Malcolm's army, Dunsinane, site of Macbeth's final denouement. As with the portrayal of the Scottish hero, William Wallace, in the 1996 film *Braveheart*, the factual basis of Shakespeare's story gives added authority to the universal truths with which the play deals.

Except for the fact that the Macbeth portrayed by Shakespeare bears almost no resemblance to the king who ruled Scotland between 1040 and 1057/8.* Indeed, it is difficult to exaggerate how great an injustice history has inflicted on him. As a Scot, I have always had a fondness for Shakespeare's 'Scottish play', which I studied at school, but it does not require much digging around the few known facts of the period to raise serious questions about their relationship to what is universally accepted about the man. However, this is not the English playwright's fault, since he was merely repeating, with some of his own embellishment, what was already being said about Macbeth by the Scots themselves.

Buried beneath the layers of myth, then, is another equally fascinating but entirely different story. This begs a further important question. If his life bears almost no relation to the version that we have come to know through the play, understanding how – and why – Macbeth's character was completely reinvented becomes part of the story too. But here we must tread carefully, because we are entering the realm of perception and appearance. What makes a good king? What makes a good king of Scots? What makes a good king of Scots at the turn of the first millennium? The answers to those questions change, often dramatically, depending on who you are and when you might be considering them, and they have all had an impact on Macbeth's reputation. They still do.

Let us consider, for example, the idea that, even within Scotland, views on this subject changed substantially in the

* The reason behind this apparent anomaly will become clear in Chapter 9.

centuries following Macbeth's death – moulded in part (and largely subconsciously) by a new drive for orthodoxy in religious, and eventually secular, life that began to sweep across western Europe in the centuries after 1000. Monastic reform, begun in the French monastery of Cluny in the tenth century, led ultimately to more explicit articulations of religious power and practice, a process that would soon result, among many other things, in the denigration of those continuing to do things differently. The five-hundred-year-old Celtic Church, which had once been a beacon of sophistication and civilisation throughout Continental Europe, now found itself regarded as unacceptably outmoded.

And so, too, did the Celtic peoples of Scotland and Ireland, as particular social norms – usually encompassed within the term 'feudalism' and exported, again, from France – came to be viewed as the mark of a civilised society sanctioned by powerful rulers like Louis VI of France (d.1137) and Emperor Frederick II (d.1250). Such developments were primarily associated with the growth of royal/state authority and the corresponding need to repackage attractively the role of those in the upper echelons of society who might resent their own loss of power to their rulers. 'In the twelfth and thirteenth centuries ... religious and courtly ethics, tighter inheritance customs, genealogies and heraldry, all played a part' in creating 'the defined and superior upper class of the High Middle Ages.'[1] As a result, when such superior beings encountered the very different culture of the Celts, as, for example, English knights did in 1138, at the Battle of the Standard in Yorkshire, they were quick to tell outlandish tales of bare-bottomed barbarians.

Even in Scotland itself, as Celtic culture and the Gaelic

language began to lose ground to 'Scots English'* after 1300, the gulf between 'Gael' and 'Scot' became as challenging as the mountains that often separated them. It was the kings of Scots who had presided over the introduction of the new, Continental monastic orders, leading eventually to the withering away of the Scottish Church's Celtic predecessor. These kings did not hesitate to borrow and adapt other non-Celtic social and cultural norms to modernise their own kingdom, however much older practices continued to exist alongside them. By the end of the fourteenth century, the notion that most of southern Scotland – the kingdom's new political heartland – was in any meaningful sense 'Celtic' is dubious (and would have been anathema to its inhabitants in any case). A tide of anti-Celtic feeling from within Scotland, never mind beyond, added a new dimension to the stories being told by Scotland's own historians about Macbeth, who, for reasons closely tied to Scottish domestic politics, had already been transformed from a beloved father of his people into a bloody tyrant.

But let us pause for a moment and add a note of caution. It is very tempting these days to interpret the evolution of Macbeth's posthumous reputation as a terrible Anglo-Scottish conspiracy theory, the mighty Celtic king succumbing ultimately to those who had neither sympathy for nor

---

* The Scots language still (just) spoken today is descended from the Anglo-Saxon used in south-eastern Scotland (and northern England) a thousand years ago. It is thus very similar to the Anglo-Saxon of southern England, the progenitor of modern English, sharing a common root, but developing separately. The status of Scots as a distinct language or a dialect of English is often a heated issue north of the Anglo-Scottish border.

understanding of an ancient and honourable way of life. We will have him turning blue and crying 'Freedom' soon enough if we go down that route. The idea of the noble Celt has been fashionable for some time now, even while his irredeemably backward and barbaric alter ego continues to thrive. Both views say far more about the writer than they do about the subject, and romanticising the Celt is just as patronising and derogatory as outright insult.

If we wish to understand Macbeth and the period in which he lived, we must accept that Celtic Scotland was capable of evolving and changing like any other kingdom, and that it was a fully functioning, if distinctive, member of western European society, not some idyllic, isolated and time-proof Brigadoon. Equally, we must walk a difficult line in interpreting the disparaging comments made by others about the Scots – and such insults have a very long history – recognising that Macbeth and his contemporaries were well aware of the drawbacks and downright insanity of some of their traditional ways of doing things, particularly when it came to the royal succession.

In other words, we must distinguish between the views of those who have seen the Scots, and Celtic Scots in particular, as inferior by definition – an essentially racist position that fails to accord potential equality to cultural, social and political differences – and comments on and criticisms of individual kings and aspects of medieval Scottish society, politics and culture. Of course, any such points of view come with added layers, which must be peeled off and dissected by the historian. But this all adds to the colour and texture of our story, and brings a complexity and sophistication to the so-called Dark Ages that has been underplayed in the popular mind in comparison to the violence which undoubtedly marred social relations of that period, as it has done for much of human history.

To add to this difficult mix of a thousand years of competing and conflicting perceptions, this period of Scottish history can be head-bangingly frustrating. Loose ends so often refuse to be tied up, and the range of potential interpretations of the scanty evidence can reduce the historian (or, at least, this one) to a dithering wreck. Such lacunae go a long way to explain why books about the historical Macbeth, as opposed to a fictional character hung on a few wobbly factual pegs, are extremely thin on the ground. Indeed, Dorothy Dunnett, after researching what eventually turned into her novel about Macbeth, *King Hereafter*, acknowledged that she chose fiction over non-fiction largely because of the gaps and contradictions in the evidence.[2]

So, piecing together the life of a Dark Age king about whom there is little written evidence is a different proposition from that of a historical figure from the more recent past. Such difficult material cannot provide a detailed portrait. Nevertheless, careful use of a wide and diverse range of sources does allow this remarkable man and the times he lived in to emerge, even if we cannot draw firm conclusions about him. However, to flesh out Macbeth's story more than the evidence strictly allows, as well as making use of contemporary material that helps bring the period to life, I have taken the bold step of including some fictional passages. These are clearly marked in italics and will, I hope, be taken in the spirit in which they are intended – as pointers towards potential insights and realities that would normally elude the writer of non-fictional history in this period.

Shakespeare turned this Scottish king into one of the most resonant names in history; but the real story also opens a window on the so-called Dark Ages, a complex and largely misunderstood time in European history, and on Scotland, which has for so long been seen as a poor and benighted historical subject. The period into which we are about to plunge was a crucial one,* when national boundaries were far from conclusively defined and political action was guided by the possibility of the conquest of all or part of the existing kingdoms. Those of us who are habitués of powerful state systems manipulating deeply entrenched, if contested, national identities, of a religious life reduced now to a personal leisure pursuit, of an economy that sustains most – but far from all – in the kind of material wealth that was unimaginable, in cost and implications, to our predecessors, are reaching out to another world.

However, this is the period, in British terms, when the island's constituent political parts finally emerged out of a plethora of other possibilities. Thus, although Scotland, England, and Wales survived this testing period, it would, as we will see, challenge the imagination only slightly to envisage a Norse Britain or a Scotland that stretched at least as far south as the River Tees. Such threats – and possibilities – affected the political games that were played, the way that different peoples related to each other, and contemporary views on the nature of kingship and kingdoms. They certainly played on the minds of those who lived through what were undoubtedly difficult times, though, under Macbeth, Scotland may have enjoyed better times than most.

Here, then, for your entertainment and edification, is a true

---

* Though find me a historian who does not think that their own period is crucial.

story about Macbeth. In these pages you will find a very real king presiding over a sophisticated, vital kingdom which, though situated on the margins of Europe, was still part of a dynamic Continental society. You will travel through quite a lot of his kingdom's history on the way. I have every faith that you, dear Reader, will consider Scotland's past to be as worthy of your attention as the history of anywhere else. And if we have a great Englishman to thank for bringing Macbeth to the world's attention then I, for one, am truly grateful. However, so far as our history, as opposed to our literary life, is concerned, it is only fair to acknowledge that 'No legacy is so rich as honesty'.[3]

Prologue

... in the [chapel] inscribed 'Tumulus Regum Scotia' were deposited the remains of forty-eight Scottish monarchs, beginning, as Boece says, with Fergus II and ending with the famous Macbeth.

New Statistical Account

A sturdy galley ploughs its way across the slate-grey spit of sea. A few minutes later it reaches the white sands of a sheltered bay where a group of monks huddle in silence. The few passengers stand back as the crew load a plain wooden box onto their shoulders and stagger off the boat. Once on firm ground, the new arrivals and the spectators form up into a loose procession. Seabirds cry out a hoarse requiem. The party moves quietly, heads bowed, along the track that wends north towards the scattered wood and turf buildings that form Scotland's most sacred site, the abbey alone meriting the enduring accolade of construction in stone. Many pilgrims have passed along this route, before and since.

This is Iona, home to the abbey and monastery founded by the sainted Columba nearly five hundred years before these sombre events, and the final resting place of countless kings of Scots. On this autumn day in 1058, another king is en route to join them, returning in death to the kingdom's supposed roots in the west. The man he killed

9

to become king is already here, though he too died many miles away in the east, in Scotland itself.

The king's body is lowered carefully into the ground as the head of the tiny monastic community intones a few words, reminding his listeners who the dead man is, the antiquity of his lineage and his many successes during the seventeen years that he occupied the throne. Scottish politics are only of remote concern to the monks who dare to remain on Iona among the Scandinavians who now control the region – but they know of this king's great reputation, his friendship to the Church and his sorry end, torn out of retirement for one last, fatal battle. They, like others, can only pray that Scotland is not too much the poorer for his death. Only time will tell.

The man being laid to rest is the nineteenth ruler since the great Kenneth MacAlpin who – so the scholars say – began the process of welding together the nations of the Gaels and the Picts into a new Scotland two hundred years before. But he is not of Kenneth's line.

His name is Macbeth. Murderer. Tyrant. Generous king. Bringer of prosperity. Bountiful visitor to Rome.

Which of these took his place in the hallowed ground of Iona?

PART ONE

The Forging of a Kingdom

CHAPTER 1

All the King's Men

The most erroneous stories are those we think we know best
– and therefore never scrutinise or question.

Stephen Jay Gould

Let us start our story somewhere in the middle. Five hundred
and forty-five years after Macbeth made his final journey to
Iona, an Englishman was riding at full tilt towards Scotland
as if his very life depended on it. It did not, but his future
might. As night fell on the evening of 26 March 1603, a mud-
spattered Sir Robert Carey flogged every last breath from his
horse to be first to bring the news of the death of Elizabeth
of England to her successor, thirty-six-year-old James VI of
Scotland, at the palace of Holyrood in Edinburgh.

James Stuart was delighted with the news – which was scarcely
a complete surprise – relishing the prospect of the splendid
new 'pan-British project' that would follow the union of the
crowns of Scotland and England in his own person.[1] The king
considered himself an intellectual, though others have questioned the depth of his understanding, as opposed to the breadth

of his knowledge.² There was certainly nothing wrong with his education at the hands of the great Scottish historian, scholar and austere Presbyterian, George Buchanan. King James was therefore sure that he was mentally equipped for the challenge of this 'concentration of power never seen before in the islands of Britain and Ireland'.³

The timing of his cousin's death was fortuitous, coming neither too soon nor too late. It had taken James a considerable time – perhaps until 1595, when he was nearly thirty – to wrest proper royal control of his northern kingdom back from the feuding nobles who had been squabbling over it for decades. Even by the difficult standards of Scottish minorities, 'it was a very poor beginning to his personal rule'.⁴ However, despite the fact that the king had a tendency 'to panic in a crisis', these problems were not entirely of his own making.⁵ A debilitating lack of funds, tussles with a Church set on Presbyterianism rather than the king's choice of Episcopalianism, the need to tread a delicate line with Elizabeth – neither too fawning nor too aloof – to secure the succession, problems with noble factionalism, and the whole ongoing, complicated issue of how exactly to define the authority held by a king, particularly a Protestant one, all served to perplex the man described by the French monarch, Henri IV, as 'the wisest fool in Christendom'.

He did his best and, so far as Scotland was concerned, by '1610 the two clearest symbols of the independence of local society – the bloodfeud and the bond of manrent* – were on

---

* A bond of manrent was a guarantee of support, usually armed, mutually agreed between two or more parties.

the point of disappearing into history'.[6] His government, which attempted to accommodate the detached mechanisms of an expanding state and its economy alongside the personal relationships of a feudal kingdom, has been described as 'random, fussy and intrusive'.[7] James himself was no oil painting (though many were made of him), having failed to inherit the reputed good looks of either of his parents, especially his mother, Mary, Queen of Scots.* Nevertheless, when he died in 1625 he seems to have been genuinely mourned.

In 1603, James surely felt he had been waiting a lifetime to become king of England. On Carey's arrival, the Scottish court was plunged into uproar as plans were executed for the king's swift departure, and within little more than a week James was gone, the rest of his family following later. He took care, however, to write a letter to his son and heir, Prince Henry, in Stirling, urging him: 'Let not this news make you proud, or insolent; for a King's son and heir was ye before, and no more are ye yet.'[8] He should have remembered this commonsense and very Scottish advice once he was among the courtiers of England, who were used to treating their monarchs as if they were much more exalted than the mere mortals over whom they ruled.

Although the relationship between England and Scotland had been essentially friendly since 1586 and there was no serious alternative as Elizabeth's successor, James's rather unseemly haste denoted his intention of leaving nothing to chance. But if he harboured any doubts about his reception, these were quickly

---

* James's father was Henry, Lord Darnley, his mother's cousin and a dashing young man without, unfortunately, the character to go with it.

dispelled as the royal progress through his new kingdom met with all the adulation, pomp and ceremony that Queen Bess had taught her subjects to bestow on their sovereign. London, too, despite a terrible outbreak of plague, took James to its heart, rejoicing in a new era. Above all, his new subjects were no doubt relieved that the king already had two sons – Henry and Charles – to provide the security of another generation of heirs for the English throne, a luxury that had been so conspicuously lacking throughout Elizabeth's long, barren reign.

It was one thing for the people of England to give way to wholesale rejoicing for a new king who would rarely affect their lives directly; for the men and women reliant on royal patronage, this was a more nerve-racking period. Among those who waited anxiously to see what the change of regime might bring were the Chamberlain's Men, a successful theatre company whose principal playwright was one William Shakespeare. They need not have worried; within a few weeks of James's accession they had become the monarch's own troupe, the King's Men. Shakespeare and his company were about to enter a new phase of productivity and success.

The playwright was only two years older than the new king and had been part of the 'London scene' for over a decade. A wealthy man, thanks to the success of his plays, he had moved south of the river in 1599 to be near the Globe Theatre, built by his Company in Southwark, but in 1604 he moved across the river to rent rooms in the Cripplegate, north of St Paul's.9 By now Shakespeare was in his 'tragic period', having moved away from the historical dramas and romantic comedies that originally made his name; but he had not finished with history yet.

The great tragedies that emerged from Shakespeare's quill

after 1600 – *Hamlet, Othello, King Lear, Macbeth, Antony and Cleopatra* and *Coriolanus* – are among his finest work.[10] The writer's profound understanding of how human beings tick, as well as his own experience, as an inhabitant of London, of the brutality of Elizabethan and Jacobean life, its hardships and its cruelties, poured out now through the exquisite work of a master at the peak of his powers.

Both fascinated and repulsed by public participation in state cruelty,[11] Shakespeare's portrayal of the barbarism of bygone ages in his historical plays was surely only a thinly veiled commentary on the viciousness of his own time. And at the heart of them all, he laid bare for all eternity the infinite capacity of our own nature – transcending time and place – to abandon the empathy that binds humanity together and succumb instead to the seductive exhilaration of ambition, jealousy or hate.

Though this phase in Shakespeare's writing predates the arrival of King James in London, there is no doubt that any sense of optimism inspired by the new reign was to prove no more enduring than the average West End run. All the old fears – of Catholics and foreigners, of sudden illness, crop failure, plague, animal disease, of the odd and the inexplicable – were never far from the surface. And, despite James's own enthusiasm – obsession, even – with creating a real British identity to unite his different kingdoms, regardless of 'the wave of British histories, seals, flags and coinage' with which his subjects were now bombarded, such were the suspicions on both sides of the 'happie love-knott' between Scotland and England that the regal union soon began to look, certainly from the Scottish point of view, like 'at best, an arranged marriage'.[12]

The deep-seated antagonisms lurking only just beneath the

surface of English politics erupted within months of James's accession to the English throne; the Bye Plot and Main Plot of 1603 were followed in 1605 by the even more spectacular Gunpowder Plot to blow the king and key members of his government to smithereens. All three involved Catholics disappointed that James would not grant them religious freedom, together with a degree of foreign encouragement. Rumour, panic and suspicion seized hold of the capital and the king soon had emphatically to deny that he had succumbed to an assassin's knife.

It was in this atmosphere of febrile public debate and vulnerable state security that Shakespeare – unable, through royal decree, to comment overtly on current affairs or portray the living monarch directly in his work – produced his Scottish play, *Macbeth*. Indeed, the playwright most probably began to work on his latest masterpiece in autumn 1605,[13] around the time the Gunpowder Plot was being hatched and discovered. He found the basic story in a source he was already well used to consulting, Ralph Holinshed's *Chronicles of England, Scotland and Ireland*, published in 1577.

Macbeth is Shakespeare's shortest tragedy, perhaps indicating that it was produced at great speed, but the play lacks none of the punch and polish of his longer works. Historians and literary specialists dispute the context and motivation behind its construction – certainly, the precise elements at work on and in the playwright's mind will always remain a mystery. We can surely agree, however, that James's accession provided the motivation for a play of this kind, not least for sound commercial reasons. On consulting Holinshed with a view to finding a suitable aspect of Scottish history on which to work, Shakespeare came across the story of an eleventh-century king of Scots and the rest, as they say, is history, of a kind at least.

Given that the King's Players did not necessarily perform every play in front of the court itself, and that Shakespeare can have had little or no first-hand experience of James as a person – his background, upbringing and predilections – the playwright was presumably relying on the stories about the king circulating through the capital, some of them based on the 'sensational pamphlet, *News from Scotland*, published in 1591'. It has been argued that what Shakespeare was interested in was producing a piece that would not bore his patron, a wise endeavour that may explain the dramatic supernatural presence of the three witches, given the king's known interest in the subject. 'The alternative was to put James to sleep and send the thrill-seeking crowds to rival theaters'.[14]

However – as *News from Scotland* explained – James had personal experience of witchcraft, having survived a tempest blown up by fiends when he was trying to bring his bride, Anna of Denmark, home in 1589. The king not only took an interest in the ensuing trials of the North Berwick* witches, but also soon put his knowledge to good use in his *Daemonologie*, published in 1597, noting that: 'The fearefull aboundinge at this time in this countrie, of these detestable slaves of the Devill, the Witches or enchaunters, hath moved me (beloved reader) to dispatch in post, this following treatise of mine, not in any wise (as I protest) to serve for a shew of my learning & ingine, but onely (mooved of conscience) to preasse thereby, so farre

---

* North Berwick is situated some twenty-five miles south along the coast from Edinburgh.

as I can, to resolve the doubting harts of many; both that such assaultes of Sathan are most certainly practized, & that the instrumentes thereof, merits most severely to be punished'.[15]

Though some historians argue that James was bored with witchcraft within only a few years of the publication of his book, *Daemonologie* was nevertheless reprinted soon after his move to London in 1603. In choosing to add this supernatural element to the tragic mix of *Macbeth* – the only one of his plays to do so – 'Shakespeare was burrowing deep into the dark fantasies that swirled about in the king's brain'.[16] Here was the master, playing with his audience, royal or not, shocking and unsettling as often as he amused and flattered.

Certainly the play was not shy to acknowledge the susceptibility of both 'natural' (Duncan) and 'unnatural' (Macbeth) kings to violent and premature death. And though human agency is the mechanism whereby evil deeds are committed in the play, the role of the supernatural in helping to give shape to man's darkest impulses is one of *Macbeth*'s most memorable characteristics. The king's own foray into writing about the nature of witchcraft, despite attempts to maintain a sceptical rigour, exposed a mind that fully accepted the presence of malignant spirits in the world.

The three weird sisters that Shakespeare presented to his patron in *Macbeth* were intellectually unchallenging, but the playwright had, with his usual acumen, understood the essence of the deep-rooted hold that witchcraft exerted over James's mind, and over the minds of his subjects, both English and Scottish, more generally. Such diabolical power represented every aspect of the physical world that was not what it purported to be, the stomach-wrenching but ubiquitous experience of a shifting universe, including human nature itself, that so often resists any assertion of order.

Interestingly, too, while *Macbeth* restores a natural balance to the order of human society at its end, the supernatural elements remain unpunished and at liberty to continue their interference. Despite the play's outlandish pseudo-historical setting in early medieval Scotland, Shakespeare's audience derived much pleasurable shock-value from watching their own deepest fears at work on stage. Despite the universality of the playwright's explorations of human nature, his theatre spoke volumes to his contemporaries about the social and political mores of their own time.

And indeed, it was not witches that were likely to have been uppermost in the minds of James and the rest of the audience in 1606, when the play was probably first performed. Recent, deeply troubling events were of far more pressing interest and one of the more unsettling elements of the play is therefore the possibility that it refers to the trial of Henry Garnet, a Jesuit priest who had the misfortune to act as confessor to some of the Gunpowder plotters. He was executed in May 1606 as an equivocator, for not divulging the Plot. In *Macbeth* the porter, roused from his drunken stupor on the night of Duncan's murder by a loud knocking at the door, uses this very term.

Who's there, in the other devil's name? Faith, here's an equivocator, that could swear in both the scales against either scale; who committed treason enough for God's sake, yet could not equivocate to heaven: O, come in, equivocator.[17]

Shakespeare's audience would surely have picked up on this reference to a brutal death that some, at least, had witnessed only a few months before. Not that most would have baulked at the punishment meted out to Garnet – this was a cruel world and other people's misfortunes, especially if they brought their troubles on themselves, served as a welcome reminder that, for the moment at least, death and misery were busy elsewhere. And even if we are reading rather too much into the play, Shakespeare had done his homework well, providing his audience with the kind of *frissons* of vicarious tension that were not dissimilar to those experienced at public executions. Though the enemy could be clearly defined – both in the play and in Jacobean England – he often looked and acted far too uncomfortably like you or I. The enthralled audience had no qualms, therefore, about passively enjoying the implications of the dangerous activities taking place on stage before plunging back into the ordinary dangers of their own lives.

In this respect, king and subject experienced the same shocking pleasure. Though James had no fear of starvation, unlike so many of his subjects, he was not immune to the vicissitudes of the elements and the swift, calamitous arrival of disease. Indeed, his elder son, Henry, was to die, probably of typhoid fever, only six years later. And as a focus for discontent, whether personal or on principle, the king had grown up with his own particular vulnerability. As a youth, James had been kidnapped at swordpoint, while the latest attempt by Scottish nobles to kidnap him had taken place as recently as 1600.[18] Though fascinated by violence when visited on someone else, he remained squeamish about the thought of it applied to himself.

The experience may well have enabled King James to

confront his own demons in a visceral, compelling but entirely risk-free manner, emerging triumphant, like King Malcolm, in the end. However – and Shakespeare may not have known this – he also had definite views on the sanctity of kingship, even when it was held by those demonstrably unfit to rule. In an anonymous pamphlet (but everyone knew who wrote it) entitled *The Trew Law of Free Monarchies*, published in 1598, James challenged the idea that kings were elected by their people, were subject to the law, or that even tyrants could be removed. For James VI, monarchy was a form of government that "approacheth nearest to perfection", and for a people subject to a tyrant, there was no alternative but patience and prayer'.[19]

Perhaps, now that he was relieved of the nuisance of her physical presence on earth, the king was thinking of what had happened to his mother, Mary, Queen of Scots, deposed by her own people and executed by Queen Elizabeth. It was probably just as well that *Macbeth* was set in the remote past, when one could accept that people did things differently, since by James's own argument, Macduff should never have killed the king, even on Malcolm's behalf. It was also just as well that James would never know that his son, Charles, would face execution by Act of Parliament just over forty years later, in 1649. Discussions about the role of kingship, its functions and *raison d'être*, rarely find agreement among contemporaries, let alone across time and space.

As the last wholly Scottish king, James should also have had a more complex and conflicted relationship with *Macbeth* than those non-Scots who watched it. All the kings portrayed on stage were, if not his direct ancestors, then at least his predecessors. The story, though found in Holinshed, derived originally from home-grown Scottish material. In using it, Shakespeare coincidentally gave dramatic form and substance to Scotland's particular identity and independence, however bizarrely construed, and the antiquity of its separate royal lineage, which had so recently taken over the equally ancient royal line of England.

However, James – much like the English – harboured many negative feelings towards the land of his birth. While secure in his own credentials to be king of Great Britain, he took very easily to the more overtly flattering ceremonial of English kingship, which contrasted sharply with the up-close-and-far-too-personal mores of the Scottish court. He had no time for the Celtic traditions that had – before, during and, for a few more centuries, after the reign of the real Macbeth – dominated the northern kingdom, going so far as to damn both mainland and insular Highlanders as 'barbarous'. (The question was whether they were merely barbarous or 'utterly' barbarous.)[20] In 1609 he attempted – as had many of his Stewart predecessors – to deal with the 'Highland Problem'.

The Statutes of Iona were intended, from a Lowland point of view, to bring civilisation to the Gaeltachd* once and for all by seeking to extirpate the most visible accessories of Gaelic culture, including Highland dress and the language itself. The eldest sons and daughters of clan chiefs were to be forced away from the degenerate environment of their own homes into mainland schools which would give them a civilised education in English. Further proposals anticipated a military expedition

---

*The Gaeltachd refers to the Gaelic-speaking Highlands of Scotland, though there is debate about the extent of this area, both now and in the past.

against the Western Isles, following on the heels of the unsuccessful settling of various 'adventurers' who, it had been hoped, would displace the natives and stimulate the economy. In the end, the only success stories were local ones, families like the Campbells of Argyll, the MacKenzies of Kintail and the Gordons of Huntly 'with a foot in both Highland and Lowland society', who gained in wealth, territory and influence at the expense of their fellow Gaels.[21]

This last proper king of Scots, then, was at ease with Shakespeare's version of the Scottish past, providing, as the audience expected, a glimpse of its ancient Celtic barbarity, its inherently violent, tribal nature, much of which it might be presumed – with a degree of truth but considerable disagreement in interpretation – lingered on into the seventeenth-century present. It is a helpful coincidence that the 'happy' ending of *Macbeth* is brought about in large part through English agency, though the Scots had long believed that this was the case. Though Shakespeare took a considerable risk in liberating the full dramatic potential of witchcraft on stage – and leaving it unpunished, even as the natural social order is finally restored – he does not seem to have considered it dangerous to portray Scotland itself, even in a past state, so unflatteringly to its king.

And he was right not to worry. *Macbeth* held up a mirror to the king of Scots that reflected not only a long line of his ancestors but also an element of the Scottish psyche which was well aware that centuries of distinctive and sometimes distinguished cultural, political, military and religious activity might never be good enough, precisely because it was not English. King James – in his unseemly haste to decamp to London, in his failure to return, as promised, more than once to his homeland in the remaining twenty-two years of his reign, in his desire to thrust a version of Anglicanism on a Scottish Church that leaned more than a little towards Calvinism – had no doubt about which of his kingdoms was the more civilised.

From a historical point of view the tragedy represented by *Macbeth* is not the murder of one king by another, a circumstance that, throughout history, has become mundane in its repetition. Rather, the play marks the unfortunate point at which the portrayal of Scotland – and most particularly its Celtic roots – as, at best, second-rate, at worst, 'utterly barbarous', was eloquently presented to the world by England's greatest playwright. However, responsibility for this long-standing and instinctive disregard (which must include any propensity towards romanticism) rests squarely with those who should have defended Scottish history and identity most – the Scots themselves.

It is not surprising, then, that Macbeth should have come to symbolise an ancient and glorious Celtic past among those clans who were on the sharp receiving end of Scottish royal policy towards the Highlands from the fifteenth century onwards.[22] And there is only a soupçon of irony that he should have suffered such a thorough and enduring portrayal as the epitome of unnatural government for the amusement of the last monarch to sit exclusively upon the ancient throne of Scotland.

But there comes a point in every tragedy when it is time to move on, to put the past behind us, lessons learned and amends made, as far as possible. It is time, then, for the real Macbeth, and the Scotland over which he ruled, to stand clear of a reputation which, as much as any in the relationship between history and myth, has come to the point where 'Fair is foul, and foul is fair'. The story that you are about to read concerns a very different man from the one we all think we know.

The real Macbeth is still larger than life, a tried and tested warrior, but also a man who understood the benefits of peace, conventionally pious but shrewdly aware of the advantages to be gained by aligning himself with the power of the Church – both the ancient Celtic Church of Scotland and the growing power of the bishop of Rome. His story concerns the relationship between Scotland and England, the close ties and ancient quarrels that bedevilled the two strongest and most enduring monarchies of the British Isles; but it will also take us further afield, into the politics of the Irish and North Seas, across to Scandinavia and down to Rome. As for the man behind the king, he must inevitably skulk in the wings of our imperfect knowledge, pushing his way to the front of the stage only occasionally. But we will know what kind of king he was, not by his words, which remain the preserve of the writer and the poet, but by his deeds.

CHAPTER 2

Christendom in 1050

Everyone, soon or late, comes by Rome.

Robert Browning, *The Ring and the Book*

It might seem like excessive deviation to begin a book about an eleventh-century Scottish king with a trip to Rome. However, we are in good company, because Macbeth himself journeyed to the Eternal City in 1050, the only Scottish king known to have done so. That alone is surely enough to remind us of the need to forget the man we think we know and begin the task of reinventing him, this time keeping the facts in mind.

But it is also necessary to bring Rome into the story at this early stage simply because the city maintained such a strong and vital hold over the medieval psyche. That this hold was differently construed in Scotland than in Sicily is no doubt true, but nevertheless, throughout western Christendom, Rome was a name to reckon with no matter where you lived.

The city itself was also something of a contradiction at the turn of the second millennium. In many respects, Rome was thriving as a major pilgrimage centre that could also offer visitors a flavour of its illustrious past. For all that its guidebooks struggled to understand and explain the imperial remains, no-one had forgotten that Rome was once the heart of the greatest empire the world had ever known. Many – from the highest churchman to ordinary men and women – clung to the belief that the city might one day reclaim its glorious position and that order and stability would be restored to western Europe as a result. Rome was thus a symbol of hope, of confidence in the power of western Christianity (encompassing what was known at the time as Latin Christendom) to build a better world here on earth, as well as preparing the souls of the faithful for the hereafter.

On the other hand, visiting Rome also made it abundantly clear that, even as the dawn of the second millennium came and went without mishap, this better world had not arrived yet. Indeed, some of the more dramatic architecture of the contemporary city underlined, for those inclined to apocalyptic interpretations of current affairs, that things were, if anything, getting worse. The Roman nobility were already renowned for the violence of their tempers and, as elsewhere in Italy, were in the habit of building tall towers, like the tenth-century castle of the Caetani on the Isola Tiberina, as a blatant symbol of their own power and to deter assault by others. The bishops of Rome – despite having forged a document in the middle of the eighth century stating that the Emperor Constantine (d. 337) had granted them control of the city, Italy and the entire western empire, and having taken possession of lands in northern Italy in the eighth century[1] – often struggled to exert much authority in practice. It did not help that so many popes were drawn from the ranks of Rome's noble families, thus exacerbating the rivalries that already so easily provoked the unrestrained use of the fist or the knife.

Indeed, the papacy was only just recovering from another bout of self-inflicted humiliation in 1050, when Macbeth visited. The desire for change was given significant momentum with the election as pope in 1032 of the Roman, Benedict IX, who was only a youth at the time and a particularly dissolute one at that. Benedict's conduct, which, for accusations of thuggery and sexual licentiousness would seem to put him on a par with the later Borgias, resulted in his expulsion from the city in 1036. Over the next decade three other men were elected, or bought, the papal office, resulting finally in the Holy Roman Emperor, Henry III, stepping in to put an end to this outrageously damaging situation by appointing a good German bishop as Clement II. Another German pope followed in 1048, and then a third when Henry's cousin, Bishop Bruno of Toul, was chosen to become Leo IX.

Leo was canny enough to realise that, while the papacy should rise above the self-indulgent politics of the Roman nobility, there was also danger in being too beholden to the emperor, even a reform-minded relative like Henry. So he went to Rome to be chosen formally as pope there. Only thirty years later, relations between pope and emperor broke down completely during the so-called Investiture Contest over the role that kings and princes should play in choosing and installing their own senior clergymen. No doubt when Macbeth visited Rome, the city squares and inns were still buzzing with enthusiasm over Pope Leo's rather pointed decision a year earlier to make it clear that his office was not a gift from the emperor.

However, the hottest topic of debate across Latin Christendom was Church reform. Although Christianity offered the individual the ability to negotiate his or her own path to everlasting life, its holy men continued to interpret both human and natural events on earth as a sign of Divine pleasure or discontent. At the end of the first millennium, many – and not just churchmen – were inclined to believe that God was displeased with the conduct of his less-than-faithful followers, judging by the violence that seemed so much a part of life in the petty, squabbling excuses for states cobbled together across western Europe in the centuries following the demise of the Roman empire.

The process whereby former Roman provinces became embryonic medieval kingdoms took, with the benefit of hindsight, over five hundred years.* The extent to which historians stress the dramatic and often violent change or the more constructive continuity that western Europe experienced during that period depends on what kind of history they study (ecclesiastical or otherwise), in which regions, and, perhaps, their own predisposition towards seeing a glass half full or half empty. Whether or not the turn of the first millennium was greeted in an apocalyptic vein is also hotly debated, given that the Bible explicitly banned Christ's followers from attempting to second-guess the timing of the Second Coming.

---

* To cut a long and contentious story short, this is the period between 476, when the last western Roman emperor was deposed, and *c.*1000, when kingdoms like France, England, Scotland, Norway, Denmark, Sweden, Italy, the German states, Poland, Hungary, Bohemia and so on had emerged as discernible political entities.

But there is no doubt that the demand for reform sweeping across Latin Christendom from the tenth century into the eleventh was complemented, at the very least, by attempts to interpret contemporary events within the context of the coming of the Antichrist, the immediate prelude to the Last Judgement.[2] There was a desire by people from all walks of life in western Europe for peace, a longing for the stability that they viewed, rightly or wrongly, as a prerequisite of the strong government of the imperial past.

To add to the apocalyptic mix, it must have been galling for western Europeans to look at their neighbours, some of whom were not even Christian, but who seemed to be managing this rather more successfully. Immediately to the south, Muslims from North Africa blended practical knowledge and sensual delight in the lands of Spain and Portugal which they had controlled since AD 711. The Christian God promised much to the oppressed souls of western Europe in the next life, but the Moors had already inherited paradise on earth in the gardens of the Al-hambra of Granada. Such worldliness only encouraged accusations of decadence and Christian armies had already successfully begun the process of reconquest, most remarkably under the leadership of the famous hero, El Cid (Rodrigo Diaz de Vivar, 1043–99). Nevertheless, 'Islamic influences remained all-pervasive in Iberian life'.[3]

Indeed, the west more generally was indebted to the cultural and intellectual prowess of the Islamic world, both as a repository of European texts that would otherwise have been lost, and as a touchstone of false belief (as the Christians saw it) against which European scholars were busy working out their own sophisticated arguments. There was certainly nothing in the west to compare with the *nazamiyya* (universities), particularly in Baghdad (founded in 1065), at the heart of the Seljuk empire, which stretched from Anatolia in the east of modern Turkey to northern India.

Squeezed between this impressive Muslim empire and Latin Christendom lay the greatest city in the world, Constantinople (modern Istanbul), capital of the Christian Byzantine empire. Known as the jewel of the Black Sea, she made even the most advanced of European cities look primitive in 1050. For any western European fortunate enough to see the great stone basilica of St Sofia rising almost to the heavens above Constantinople, its splendour was truly remarkable given the scarcity of stone-built castles and churches in the west. Founded by the Emperor Constantine around 330, there had been a separate emperor in the east since the death of Theodosius I in 395, and a sole emperor since his western counterpart, Romulus Augustus, gave up his title in 476.

Relations between east and west were certainly not all bad, though cultural differences were exacerbated once the east officially abandoned the use of Latin for Greek in 610. However, one of the greatest sources of friction arose in the religious sphere; from the ninth century onwards the independence of the Patriarch of Constantinople came under pressure from, among other things, increasingly insistent Roman claims to universal supremacy over the Christian Church. Indeed, Pope Leo III's decision in 800 to restore the office of emperor in the west (known henceforth as the Holy Roman Emperor), in the person of the hugely impressive Frankish king, Charlemagne, was an overt attempt to wrest the political and moral high ground away from supposedly degenerate Constantinople. By 1050, Pope Leo IX and his eastern counterpart, Patriarch Michael, could barely speak to one another except to trade insults.

Much of the impetus behind this increasingly assertive western dogmatism in religious matters came from a new movement promoting monastic reform, begun, in the tenth century, at the monastery of Cluny in Burgundy, which developed an improved version of the Benedictine rule for monastic life. It was soon frowned upon, for example, to admit children as future monks, since many turned out to be unsuitable in adulthood. Monastic wealth was also questioned, as a desire for the hermetic life described in the Bible was – yet again – officially adopted as a model for behaviour.

Support for the reformers' activities by lay rulers – especially freedom from taxation and other secular duties – provided an added incentive for increasing numbers of monasteries to follow suit. The Benedictines and new orders such as the Cistercians (founded in 1098) sought, as far as possible, to distance themselves from the sinful world, the better to contemplate its deficiencies. Most importantly, an effective administration headed by a chapter-general that would regulate and govern the lives of all the monks of a particular order helped to create institutions of pan-European influence and authority.

The effects of this spiritual dynamism over succeeding centuries were profound, influencing almost every aspect of life, from art, architecture and education through to more practical areas such as medicine and agriculture. But perhaps its most important legacy was the promotion of uniformity and, ultimately, orthodoxy. With the creation of a centralised, hierarchical structure of monastic regulation, even the smallest detail of a monk's life should be the same anywhere under the order's jurisdiction.

It was not long before the advantages of uniformity came to the attention of popes and kings as a means of promoting their own authority. In 1085, when the King of Castile (north-east Spain) captured Toledo for the Christians, the usual policy of religious toleration was abandoned in favour of enforced conversion. This did not just apply to the Infidel, since the troops recruited from north of the Pyrenees who formed part of the Castilian army were determined to enforce Roman rites and practices on anyone found to be 'improper', including those Christians who might have learned something from Islam. The acquisition of territory already chimed well with the idea of defending the Faith.[4]

Religious reform was not an unknown concept in the Church's thousand-year history. Powerful new moral forces promising peace, stability and the hand of God behind its adherents had often proved attractive to secular rulers in the past – that was, after all, how Christianity itself had come to be more than just an underground resistance movement. What helped Cluniac reform to thrive was not just the fact that it emerged at a time when kings and princes were increasingly able to provide sufficient and enduring infrastructural support for the monks' ideas. The key to the movement's success lay in the creation of unified codes of conduct and belief that transcended national boundaries and were overseen by a hierarchy of arbiters of authority reaching up ultimately to the Roman pontiff himself. Ironically, this thrust the Church into a growing reliance on secular rulers who now became God's faithful soldiers, protecting this ever more defined – and therefore rigid – version of Christianity with the sword.

Not surprisingly, attempts to impose or encourage uniformity – whether this involved the minutiae of monastic life or an acknowledgement of the right of the pope to dictate norms of religious theory and practice across Christendom – brought their proponents into increasing conflict with those who continued to do things their own way. Within the religious sphere the most recalcitrant would soon be castigated as heretics. In 1095, the First Crusade was launched against the Muslims occupying the Holy Land, resulting in the recapture of Jerusalem and the creation of the Crusader States. In 1204 the Fourth Crusade targeted not the Infidel, but the Christian, albeit Greek Orthodox, inhabitants of Constantinople. Four years later, the Albigensian Crusade was launched against the Cathar heretics of southern France, who once more championed the hermetic ideal over the worldly glories exhibited by the mainstream Church. Transgressions against acceptable codes of behaviour – the arbiter of which was now pope or secular ruler – could unleash very serious consequences, not all of which were in the interests of peace and stability.

The belief in the effectiveness of uniformity eventually began to extend into concepts of 'proper' social norms too, as most coherently exemplified by the acceptance of 'feudal' principles and culture, including the adoption of the French language by the nobility, and rules of warfare and social structures based on the hegemony of the mounted knight. Such developments certainly produced more efficient military machines and, in the hands of kings and princes, enhanced the ability of the state to enforce peace within its borders; but it also promoted an apparently insatiable desire for conquest throughout the later Middle Ages. Religious reform, then, was something of a

Pandora's box and had many unforeseen consequences, both fortunate and unfortunate, depending on who you were and where you were.

For Celtic Scotland on the north-western edge of the continent, the developing hegemony of ideas emerging out of the south from the tenth century onwards had a profound and, in the end, debilitating effect on its reputation. Despite five hundred years of vibrant and highly developed religious and political life, the Scots soon found that many of their traditions were now at odds with the new ideas viewed as essential to the development of European states and the universal Church (though opinions from England in particular were not immune to good old-fashioned neighbour-bashing, a habit that the Scots were pleased to reciprocate).

Not surprisingly, this gave new vigour to any tendency in Europe to view Scotland disparagingly. For example, according to Abbot Sampson of Bury (St Edmunds) in 1159, behaving like a Scottish monk meant keeping up an unkempt appearance, carrying shoes over the shoulder (presumably in a miserly attempt to preserve them), shaking a stick menacingly and using threatening language towards any who mocked him.[5] In 1270 King Louis IX of France, lying on his deathbed, urged his son, the future Philippe IV, to 'make yourself loved by all your people. For I would rather have a Scot come from Scotland [clearly the most outlandish idea that he could think of] to govern the people of this kingdom well and justly than that you should govern them ill in the sight of the world'.[6] It is often difficult, when judging the opinions of those in the past, to ascertain whether they arose out of experience or prejudice. We should at least admit that both are a possibility.

Not that Macbeth would necessarily have seen himself as peripheral. Certainly his kingdom could not claim the same scholarly renown as Ireland. Nor could it compete with the wealth, military dominance and bureaucratic expertise boasted by England. But Scotland could – and did – compete for the antiquity of its kingship, its physical integrity and its long history as a Christian nation.

CHAPTER 3

Light on a Dark Age

Let us, then, a fresh and unconquered people, never likely to abuse our freedom, show forthwith at the very first onset what heroes Caledonia has in reserve.

Tacitus, *The Life and Times of Julius Agricola*

Macbeth and Scotland. The two are inseparable, the dark brooding mystery of the land echoing – perhaps, rather more unpalatably, begetting – the terrible nature of the man. Such an image of Scotland would surely have sat well with Shakespeare's audiences in the south of England who were mostly reliant on hearsay, growing more outlandish at each telling, rather than first-hand knowledge of the landscape of their northern neighbour. And they would all know – or know someone who knew – one of the pestilential multitude of rascally Scots who had followed their king south into richer, more desirable England after 1603.

But this will no longer do. Twenty-first-century Scotland has a different image, marketing itself to the world in terms of the antiquity of its history, the diversity of its natural beauty, the sophistication of its arts, the new-found excellence of its food and drink, and, last but not least, the 'extraordinary' quality of its people.[1] However, such splendid positive thinking is still in its infancy and even Scotland's own tourism organisation cannot refrain from applying the word 'turbulent' to the nation's history, a term that has stuck like a knife in the back of attempts to moderate our perception of the Scottish past as more violent and less sophisticated than anywhere else – especially if that 'else' is England.

Without returning to an overly romantic view, we must try to let go of this benighted Scotland, to move on from the 'no gods and precious few heroes' school of thought that has come to dominate not just how others see the Scottish past but how many Scots see it too. The sentiment behind that evocative phrase has its place, of course, as part of a visceral, damning indictment of the poverty and hopelessness that seemed to characterise the twentieth century.

> 'Cause there's no gods and there's precious few heroes
> But there's plenty on the dole in the land o' the leal
> And it's time now to sweep the future clear
> Of the lies of a past that we know was never real.[2]

However, it does no disservice to those who, for good reason, cannot see beyond these terrible iniquities to suggest that Scotland's story has not always been like that. Of course there has been abject poverty and hopelessness, and plenty of it, in the past: pre-democratic Scotland was no different from anywhere else in enduring huge inequalities of wealth. But this does not seem to have overshadowed the national mood as it has done more recently. We are concerned here with a very different country, one whose poets felt inspired, for good or ill, to raise their voices in pride and praise rather than lamentation.

The impassioned words quoted at the beginning of this chapter were allegedly spoken by the first named 'Scot' in history – Calgacus (or Galgacus), 'the swordsman', a leader of the Caledonian tribes of northern Britain who fought, and lost, against a Roman army at the Battle of Mons Graupius in AD 84. The concept of freedom from oppression, particularly by foreigners – a popular theme in Scottish history – runs through his pre-battle speech, creating an image of a stalwart people facing the extinction of their ancient liberty at the hands of a merciless but decadent foe.

It is a pity, then, that the words were literally put into Calgacus's mouth by the Roman writer Tacitus, in his history of his father-in-law, General Gnaeus Julius Agricola, who led the Roman army at Mons Graupius. Calgacus became a useful mouthpiece for Tacitus's dismay over the corruption and greed that seemed to him now to characterise the Roman empire. The speech is thus primarily a reflection on Roman politics, but the end result is still the creation of the image of a noble 'Scottish' enemy living on the most westerly edge of the known world without 'fruitful plains, nor mines, nor harbours'.[3]

Of course, Calgacus was no Scot because there was no such thing as Scotland in the first century AD. Nor does Tacitus describe him as a king of his Caledonian tribe. The loose native confederation that fought and, despite the defeat at Mons Graupius, ultimately resisted the Romans was made up of peoples who were already resigned to handing over a proportion of their livelihood to enable their leaders to pursue their martial obsessions and extravagant lifestyles but did not yet live in embryonic kingdoms.* This was what archaeologists call a 'chiefdom society'.[4]

Racially and linguistically, there was no essential difference between the Celtic tribes of Britain, however much they marked themselves out as distinct from each other. Nevertheless, by AD 297 those inhabiting the civilised (i.e. imperial) world demarcated, for most of this period, by Hadrian's wall† and the semi-Romanised zone stretching north from the wall to the River Forth were described by the Romans generally as *Britons*. Those living beyond the Forth were *Picti* – painted ones – a derogatory term that belies both the impressive cultural heritage of the native peoples of northern Britain and the fact that they were certainly not a single tribe.

Nor did they fight alone: Roman sources often place the Picts in the company of the *Scotti*, harassing the frontier defences

---

* Admittedly their success had as much to do with the stresses and strains on the imperial war machine and treasury elsewhere in the empire as it did with the Caledonians' own ingenuity.

† This famous and enduring landmark stretches from the River Tyne in north-east England to the Solway Firth in south-west Scotland and was begun AD *c.*122. Two more lines of Roman fortifications were also built further north: the Antonine Wall (begun in AD 142) which extends across central Scotland from the River Forth to the River Clyde; and the very first one, the Gask Ridge, completed only a few years before the Battle of Mons Graupius and extending in a diagonal line from the River Esk in Angus to the upper reaches of the River Forth. This was designed to protect Lowland Scotland from those living in the mountainous north.

or making tentative 'arrangements' with imperial officers, only to break them again whenever it suited (or so the Romans complained). The term 'Scotti' is also a Latin one used to describe the inhabitants of the island of Ireland. It was long believed that contingents of Irish came across the narrow stretch of sea into Scotland at the invitation of the Picts, anxious for reinforcements against the Romans. A few hundred years later, around AD 500 – so the story goes – some of these Irish then migrated permanently to the west coast of Scotland where they created the Gaelic kingdom of Dál Riata centred on modern Argyll. This development was less to the Picts' liking.

More recent writers stress the likelihood that the creation of Dál Riata was only the latest phase in a long-standing relationship in which the Irish Sea acted as a unifying force for the peoples on either side of it.[5] The deepening of the Irish connection via Dál Riata was to have long-term consequences for the development of the kingdom of Scotland many centuries later.

Scotland, then, was never really part of the Roman empire. Apart from a few places for brief periods, Britain north of Hadrian's Wall did not enjoy the benefits of Roman law, nor the kind of infrastructure – roads, viaducts, aqueducts, harbours, baths, heating systems, coinage, all the mechanisms of urban life – to be found in the rest of the island. The Roman perception of the north, even in the words of a sympathetic writer like Tacitus, was pretty dire. This was 'the uttermost confines of the earth' beyond which there was 'nothing indeed, but waves and rocks'. Tacitus might have admired the plucky natives, but he probably thought himself fortunate that he did not have to live among them.

By AD 410, when imperial Britain was given control of its

own affairs, the north had not ostensibly changed all that much since AD 84. Between the walls and even beyond, as far as the River Tay, there were certainly impressive remains of forts and walls to be pillaged for stone. But there were still no mines, nor harbours (at least not by Roman standards), and no towns worthy of the name.

Yet such a simple picture is misleading. The influence of the empire, including the circulation of Roman treasure among the select few, stretched far beyond the physical barriers created by the walls. In Scotland south of the Tay, a market economy of sorts – limited to cheap Roman goods, but requiring the services of merchants and a local trading infrastructure – had functioned until the second half of the fourth century when the empire began to unravel at its furthest limits. Although the Picts and their allies had no wish to bend the knee to Rome, their leaders were still keen to enjoy some of the benefits of the Roman way of life, not least in order to enhance their social and economic positions. How could they have failed to see the advantages of engaging – on their own terms – with such a mighty and wealthy neighbour?

Perhaps, as a result, these northern tribes came to feel, for the first time, that they lived on the edge of the known world, as Tacitus liked to imagine. If so, any sense of inferiority was no barrier to the acquisition of power and the maintenance of the kind of military and political networks designed to keep it. It is just as likely that distance from the properly Romanised world – especially when that world began to fall apart – may have been an advantage in gaining the upper hand within northern British society.

*

With the Roman withdrawal (*c*.410), southern Britain suddenly became a land of opportunity. The story goes that lazy British kings, panicking at the thought that they were now responsible for their own defence, hit on the high-risk strategy of inviting over the Angles, the Saxons and other Germanic tribes from the Continent to protect them from the Picts and Scots (Irish). Not surprisingly, these Anglo-Saxons (as they became known) quickly exploited the potential for carving out kingdoms of their own until only Cornwall and Cumbria remained British within what eventually became England, along with Wales.

By the early seventh century, the Anglo-Saxons of Northumbria, a kingdom in northern England, had even swept across the remains of Hadrian's Wall and on into the fertile plains and good pasture lands of southern Scotland. Once again, the Britons had either to submit to their conquerors or move out of the way to the surviving British kingdoms of Strathclyde and Rheged in south-western Scotland. Northumbria – which comprised the two Anglian sub-kingdoms of Deira (based around York) and Bernicia (based around Bamburgh) – was 'the most powerful of the Anglo-Saxon kingdoms before the rise of Mercia in the eighth century and Wessex in the ninth century'.[6]

What made the successful takeover by the Angles and Saxons of so much British territory even more shocking was the fact that, for nearly two centuries after their arrival in Britain, they remained pagan, in appalling contrast to the Christian Britons. It could be argued that Rome's most enduring legacy in the islands of Britain and Ireland, as in the empire itself, was this Middle-Eastern religion, accepted throughout Rome's domains from the fourth century. Many of the tribes living north of Hadrian's Wall and south of the Rivers Forth and Clyde had adopted Christianity by the end of that same century. In the following century, we find the first Christian inscribed stone at Whithorn in south-west Scotland marking the burial place of one Latinus and his young daughter. Here was a Celtic aristocrat acknowledging the Roman roots of his new faith in his name and the language used on the monument, as well as in this public display of his adherence to the new religion.[7]

However, the Romans had difficulty in envisaging the spread of Christianity much beyond the civilised limits of their world. Conversion of heathens outside the empire was, to begin with, a by-product of ministering the Gospels to those Christians already living among the barbarians. Apart from anything else, how would it be possible to proselytise among those who knew neither Greek nor Latin, had little in the way of urban life and who gloried in the intensity of their kinship relations and vastly different attitudes to owning property?[8]

The answer, for Scotland and Ireland, was that Christianity fitted very nicely, even if – or perhaps, because – it did not develop along precisely the same lines as elsewhere in western Europe. A key element in this more gradual process of Christianisation was the role of the monasteries. Within the empire these were retreats where monks could engage in a particularly close relationship with God foreshadowed by the ascetic ideals of the Gospels – the word 'monasticism' derives from the Greek for 'the act of living alone'. Most Romans' experience of the Church was not with these otherworldly monks, but with the secular* clergy, who formed a hierarchical and territorial network from priest (based in a church, looking

---

* Secular means, in this context, not bound by a monastic rule or vows.

after a parish) up to bishop or archbishop (governing a diocese or archdiocese of many parishes).

In the 'barbarian' north, however, monasteries played a much more active and socially engaged role as teaching and training institutions, centres for book production (with all that that entailed in terms of the provision of materials such as vellum and ink) and, eventually, as major economic and political power-houses in their own right. They were overseen by abbots who, in Ireland and Scotland, were often more important (certainly in terms of political clout) than the bishops who lived along-side them in their monasteries. Half a millennium later this was still the case: Abbot Crinan of Dunkeld became one of the most powerful men in Scotland when his son, Duncan, took the throne in 1034. The top of the Celtic Church's hier-archy was thus fundamentally linked to the senior ruling classes, in contrast to the remains of the empire where churchmen tended to be drawn from the wider Roman aristocracy.

Though the Britons – living closest to the Roman world – became Christian first and there were many other, earlier saints,[9] the most famous churchman of this period of Christian missions into northern Britain was not British, but Scottish, by which we still mean Irish. Colum Cille – 'dove of the church', known to us by his Latin name of Columba – was a member of the O'Neill royal family of Irish high kings. In 563 he founded his monastery on the tiny Hebridean island of Iona, supposedly gifted to him by Aedán mac Gabráin, soon to be king of Dál Riata. Though Columba was said to have preferred the quiet life of his own monastery, he became 'a great and influential figure and the legacy of his foundation was immense, both as a centre of learning of European standing and as mother-house to a far-flung family of monasteries in Dál Riata, Ireland, Pictland, and Northumbria'.[10]

Iona is only three and a half miles long and one mile wide. The buildings constructed by Columba and his monks there were not particularly impressive – the stone church, of course, with Columba's own timber house opposite it, a refectory and guest house, and the little turf cells for the rest of the community huddled within the earthen wall that symbolised their separation from the wider world. Beyond the wall lay the barn, byre and kiln, as well as the arable fields. With their white habits, sandals and distinctively Celtic monastic hairstyles (cut from ear to ear), they practised a restrained form of interaction with the rest of humankind, ministering to those who needed it, and, on occasions, acting as diplomats between warring factions, as lawgivers and peacemakers.[11]

Part of Iona's appeal today is its otherworldly remoteness, but, in its heyday, living on 'the edge' proved no barrier to prestige and influence. The monastery's fame soon ensured that there was a constant stream of visitors, including two Anglo-Saxon princes of Bernicia (northern Northumbria), Oswald and Oswiu, who spent a period of exile on Iona before returning home to promote the spread of the Columban Church there.

Iona's visitors were not, therefore, especially intrepid by the standards of the time. We need to imagine an Irish Sea dotted with small wooden boats heading back and forth from Scotland to Ireland, as well as those from further afield, particularly Gaul,* regularly ploughing up and down it. These foreign sailors

---

* The former Roman province covering much of modern France and Germany.

brought goods and gossip to Dál Riata from at least as far as the Mediterranean. Columba supposedly prophesied that a Gallic barque expected later one year would bring news of a sulphurous rain which had fallen on an Italian city.[12] Pottery made in western France (possibly the Gironde or the Loire) around this time and found in large numbers in Ireland and western Scotland corroborates the regularity of such contact and it has been suggested that: 'It may have been a cargo of wine and western Gaulish relishes [contained within the pots] that St Columba was so eagerly anticipating', as well as news of God's retribution against the Italian city.[13]

For thirty years Iona lay, both geographically and spiritually, at the heart of the northern Church across the nations of the Gaels, the Picts and the northern Anglo-Saxons. Gaelic ecclesiastical thinking and organisation dominated northern Britain until the Synod of Whitby of 664 brought the Northumbrian Church into line with the rest of English and Continental practice. By the middle of the next century, the main issues – essentially, the date of Easter and the style of the tonsure – had been resolved across the Churches of Britain and Ireland, but in style and culture there was much that remained distinctive and renowned about Celtic Christianity.

Iona, like other Celtic monasteries, continued to act as a major European centre of religious culture. The eighth-century *Book of Kells*, which most scholars agree was probably begun on the tiny Hebridean island before being removed to Ireland, is celebrated as one of the most elaborate examples of early medieval art in western Europe.[14] Its intricate, colourful illuminations were the equivalent on calfskin vellum of the soaring cathedral architecture of the later Gothic period – a sumptuous testament to the glory of God through painstaking human endeavour and secret artistry. Equally, the unashamed magnificence of such manuscripts was also designed to impress in this world as a display of conspicuous wealth.

Columba was not the only abbot of note to grace the island. A century or so after the saint's death in 597, his biographer, Abbot Adomnan of Iona, continued to demonstrate the profound social commitment of the Celtic Church with his remarkable 'Law of Innocents' (*Cáin Adomnáin*). This laid down the ground rules for the treatment of non-combatants (women, children and the clergy) during warfare and has been compared to the modern Geneva Convention.[15] Equally impressive is the fact that Adomnan was able to persuade leading kings in both the Gaelic world (Ireland and Dál Riata) and Pictland to accept it and he was held in great affection for having liberated women, in particular, from the danger and drudgery of following their men around from battle to battle.

Adomnan's influence extended far beyond the shores of Britain and Ireland, however. His biography of Columba was read all over the Continent. So, too, was his description of Palestinian holy places, which became the main European guidebook to the Holy Land – despite the fact that Adomnan had never been there. Iona housed an extensive library containing all the main biblical texts and their commentaries, allowing another Ionian scholar, Cú Chuimne, who died in 747, to co-edit the *Collectio Canonum Hibernensis*, 'which formed the basis of church law throughout much of Europe for hundreds of years'.[16]

In addition, a plethora of other Gaelic-speaking early saints gave their names to churches, holy wells and other places scattered across Scotland (even if the use of their name does not actually prove that they ever set foot there). Nevertheless, Iona was special, and not just because of the international reputation of its monastery. By the later Middle Ages it was firmly believed, correctly or not, that all bar three of the kings of Scots down to Macbeth and his brief successor and stepson, Lulach, were buried there.[17] The particular way in which the history of the formation of the kingdom of Scotland was written ensured that the island and its founding saint continued to play a crucial role in the development of Scottish nationhood and identity, even as the monastery itself became increasingly isolated from Scottish affairs.

Aedán mac Gabráin, who traditionally gifted Iona to Columba, was one of the most successful early rulers of northern Britain, presumably thanks to the saint, who may have presided over his inauguration. If so, it was the first such ceremony in Europe.[18] He became probably the fifth king of Dál Riata around 574 in a rough line of descent from Fergus Mor mac Erc, who is more likely to have been legendary than real.* It helped that Aedán reigned for such a comparatively long time, dying as late as 608. He did not shrink from taking his armies far from home, to Orkney, the Isle of Man, and Ireland, round the coast into north-eastern Scotland, and up the rivers and across the mountains of Drumalban into the heart of Scotland around Stirling. Dál Riata was clearly looking to expand, at the expense of the Picts to the north and east and the Britons to the south-east.

---

* As we will see, there was no need or desire, as yet, for kings to succeed their fathers in a direct line of descent.

It was Aedán's father, Gabráin, who gave his name to one of the three branches of the Dál Riatan royal family and it was this branch 'from which almost all the subsequent kings of Scots claimed descent'.[19] The other two lines were the family of Oengus (Angus), about whom we know almost nothing, and the family of Loarn (Lorne), which gets only slightly more of a mention, at the time at least.[20] However, by the late tenth century, the author of a genealogical tract was at great pains to show that these other Dál Riatan families had gone on, many generations later, to spawn some of the great families of Scotland.

Of most interest to us is the assertion in this genealogy that members of the Lorne kindred migrated up the Great Glen from their original base in north Argyll to Moray, where they took over – by marriage or otherwise – from the Pictish ruling house there. Several centuries later Macbeth, the ruler of Moray, was thus seen as a descendant of this ancient Dál Riatan family, a 'fact' that, as we will explore later, seems to have been of more than merely antiquarian interest.[21]

Dál Riata was a sophisticated, well-organised kingdom in comparison with any in northern Europe at the time. The *Senchus Fer nAlban* (History of the Men of Scotland) contains the earliest (seventh-century) known census in Britain, providing the Dalriadan government with a clear idea of exactly how many fighting men it could call upon for its navy and, presumably, how much tribute, or taxes, could also be exacted. The king performed a vital role as the symbol of his people, leading and protecting them in warfare, adjudicating in their disputes and providing lavish hospitality to show off his wealth – a reflection of theirs – in the giving of gifts, particularly the fine gold and silver brooches which were manufactured within the royal citadel at Dunadd. He did not ascend the throne because he just happened to be the son of the previous king but was chosen from among the branches of the wider royal family for his proven leadership qualities.[22]

This was typical early medieval kingship, rooted in warrior culture, but showing signs of being organised by a rudimentary bureaucracy that could negotiate the needs of peace as well as war. Kingship was intensely personal, which made it all the more necessary that it should be held together by the right man chosen from within the leading family group. The emergence of Dál Riata as a powerful player in northern British politics, situated as it was on the westerly edge of Scotland and separated from the rest of the mainland by a formidable chain of mountains, underlines the fact that, as with Iona, current perceptions of remoteness are just that – perceptions. Access to such apparently far-flung places was comparatively easy at a time when sea and river routes, rather than muddy, rutted tracks, were usually the best means of moving around, whether to remind the warrior elite just who was boss at home, or to attempt to impose authority on neighbours.

The Picts, meanwhile, were also 'growing up', in political and administrative terms, in the centuries following the Roman withdrawal. While the leaders of the various Pictish peoples were doubtless already pondering with interest the organisational abilities of the royal families of neighbouring kingdoms, it seems to have been the creeping threat from Northumbria that provided the opportunity for one particular group to seize the initiative. We have kings of the Picts on record from around 580, only a few years after Aedán took the throne of Dál Riata.[23]

However, some of them are called kings of Fortriu, a Pictish province whose name comes originally from a tribe known to the Romans as the Verturiones. In 685, Bridei mac Bili of Fortriu defeated the Northumbrian king, Ecgfrith, at the crucial Battle of Nechtansmere. This halted Northumbrian expansion any further into Pictish territory, although the Anglo-Saxons still cast interested glances northwards from their territory south of the River Forth.

King Bridei made good use of his reputation as saviour of the northern tribes to create a 'loose hegemony' over the rest of the Picts. He, or his successors, even cannily appropriated the term 'Picts',* originally applied to them by the Romans but not, so far, used to describe themselves. Presumably it was a more tactfully neutral soubriquet than a name derived from increasingly powerful Fortriu. It was long presumed that Bridei's own kingdom was located in the area around Perth where the Scottish royal family would, by Macbeth's time, be based. However, this presumption has recently been turned on its head by the suggestion 'that Fortriu, in fact, lay on the shores of the Moray Firth, at the far end of the Great Glen from Dál Riata'.[24] Regional identities remained strong, not least in Fortriu itself, but there was now a growing sense of Pictishness that transcended, when required, the distinctions between these different 'nations'. The kings of Fortriu may not always have dominated the other regional kingships, but they were the most precocious of Pictish rulers.

* Sadly, this is still the Latin word – used in the surviving sources – for the Picts. We do not know the word they would have used in their own language.

If anything, the Pictish kingdom became even more sophisticated than Dál Riata, but that has not prevented one modern writer from supposing that its inhabitants lived in a 'prehistoric or protohistoric state', because there is no surviving evidence for a written culture, on parchment or vellum at least.[25] Nevertheless, the symbols engraved on Pictish stones, of which over two hundred survive from as early as the sixth century, clearly have a meaning that was designed to be understood, however indecipherable they are to us now. Indeed, it has been suggested that 'the choice of this indigenous form of written communication over, say, the roman alphabet, may in itself have been an expression and assertion of the new "Pictish" identity'.[26] There was no need for those who had resisted the might of Rome to be like everyone else in western Europe.

Like their counterparts in Dál Riata, the rulers of Pictland were also able to insist that their inferiors help maintain their deliberately ostentatious lifestyle in a coherent fashion, and supply their armies with what was required, in men and equipment, even if we do not have written evidence of the details. The kingdom of Scotland, when it emerged in the tenth century, maintained much of the organisational structure of its Pictish predecessor, including the land divisions and many of the old centres of power.[27] The kings of Fortriu also kept a navy at Burghead on the Moray coast, where a hundred and fifty ships were wrecked in 729,[28] again implying that they had a system for manning and maintaining it. No doubt there were other navies to be found in sheltered moorings scattered along the Pictish coast.

Then there was the Pictish Church. Its clergymen, some of whom trained in Ireland, could certainly read and write. Bishop

Fergus, who attended a Church council meeting at Rome in 721, was either an Irish bishop in Pictland, or a Pictish bishop in Ireland. Either way, the Irish and Pictish Churches seem to have been on close terms with Rome and with each other, at least until King Nechtan's expulsion of bishops of the Columban Church from Pictland in 717. He had been much swayed by the advice of Northumbrian Church leaders, who now denounced the stylistic differences still followed by the Columban Church contrary to Roman practices. These differences were essentially superficial, but Nechtan's real agenda was surely to assert his Church's independence from the ecclesiastical influence of Dál Riata, whose Columban missionaries had originally brought Christianity to Fortriu.[29]

Nechtan's reign also coincides with the first mention of a bishop of Fortriu, Brec, who died in 725, though it is surely no real coincidence, given the king's interest in religious matters. The monasteries at Portmahomack and Rosemarkie (probably Brec's episcopal seat) in Fortriu were key ecclesiastical sites, though they were complemented elsewhere in Pictland by other important Church settlements, including Abernethy (founded by Nechtan) and Rígmonaid (St Andrews) way down in Fife. It has been noted that these were 'coastal or near-coastal sites',[30] implying that the kings of Fortriu were not comfortable moving too far inland from the safety of their fleet when looking after their Church and generally making their presence felt in southern Pictland.

In 761 the Irish annals recorded the death, apparently peacefully, of the great Pictish king, Angus son of Fergus (Unuist son of Urguist), 'the Butcher'. It was thirty years since Angus had seized the throne in a bloody settlement of a Pictish dynastic dispute which wrested power from Fortriu, twenty years since he had finally 'smitten' Dál Riata and brought it under Pictish control after a decade of warfare, and five years since he had led a joint expedition with the Northumbrians against the British stronghold of Al Clut (Dumbarton) on the River Clyde which, unusually for Angus, had gone disastrously wrong.[31] The death of a powerful king often leads to the disintegration of his legacy among less able successors and, in the decades immediately following Angus's death, Dál Riata managed to reassert its independence and Fortriu re-emerged as the dominant region in Pictland.[32]

By now the kings of Fortriu were keen to create a higher profile for themselves in the south of their kingdom, perhaps to keep an eye on any would-be competitors. The first such king explicitly associated with the area later known as Strathearn, to the west of the River Tay, was the impressive Constantine son of Fergus (Constantín son of Wrguist), who ruled from 789 until 820. The Dupplin cross, bearing his name, 'unique in form in Scotland, owing more to models on Iona than elsewhere, originally seems to have stood on the northern edge of the lands of Forteviot in Strathearn ... It depicts a mounted warrior, perhaps a king, and ranks of foot soldiers bearing spears'.[33]

From the 820s, Constantine's brother and successor, Angus, was heavily involved in the construction of a major royal palace at Forteviot, sited on a sizeable alluvial terrace next to the Water of May, a fast-flowing stream which has by now carried off most of the medieval remains that once adorned this peaceful corner of Perthshire. The capricious River Earn winds its way through the valley a few miles away, pouring into the River Tay ten miles downstream, from where boats could sail on towards the North Sea.

Forteviot was no defensive structure, designed to protect its inhabitants from unwelcome attention – local or otherwise – but an ostentatious display of power and wealth. It was 'a veritable royal complex, a combination of royal residence or "palace", church, cemetery, assembly place and focus for ritual activities, as well as a centre for the management of agricultural production and redistribution on an extensive royal estate'.[34] The area had once been a focus for the ritual life of the Picts' prehistoric predecessors and King Angus and his advisers no doubt deliberately fostered this link with the past, reinforcing his right to rule beyond Fortriu.[35]

So too was the emphasis given to the continuing spiritual significance of the site, now expressed in Christian iconography worked in stone, most particularly the Forteviot arch. This impressive piece of sculpture, recovered from the Water of May in the 1820s, was probably a chancel arch, separating the nave from the holiest part of the church where the altar was often situated, along with any sacred relics. The intriguing frieze carved into the arch shows the king, presumably Angus, 'grasping his stave in both hands and with his back arched, capturing the very moment at which he plunged the stake into the ground and founded the church at Forteviot'.[36] He and the two clerics – perhaps meant to be St Rule and his companions who brought St Andrew's relics to Scotland[37] – are busy marking out the boundaries of the new church, dedicated to the apostle. The message catching the eye of all those passing near the arch could not be clearer: the relationship between the kings of Fortriu and their church was very close indeed.

The choice of the foreign saint, Andrew – brother of Peter, the first bishop of Rome – is also striking, especially given that Angus 'may also have been responsible for the establishment of the cult of St Andrew' at Rígmonaid, later St Andrews, as well as the dedication of churches to the saint at Kindrochit (Braemar) and Monikie in Angus. The king's thinking here may have been shrewd. Southern Pictland, unlike Fortriu and Dál Riata, had not been converted to Christianity by Columba, but by a British bishop, Nynia.[38] By dedicating churches to a saint with no problematic internal associations, Angus was – like Bridei mac Bili before him in his use of the term 'Picts' – promoting unity. He was also, of course, attempting to establish himself as an ecclesiastical benefactor with an international reputation, a desire underlined by the fact that he, his brother, Constantine, and his son, Eóganán (836–9), were all patrons of the Northumbrian Church.[39]

These were powerful kings by any standards. Constantine's very name resonates with ambition, the first king in Scotland to bear an exotic Continental moniker – in his case, that of the great Roman emperor who had allowed Christianity to take root in the western world. By 811, he seems to have been able to put his own son on the throne of Dál Riata, paying tribute to Fortriu.[40] This time there was to be no Dalriadan resurgence after Constantine's death in 820; both Angus and Eóganán could likewise place their own men – presumably members of the Pictish royal family – over the western kingdom. Pictland, under the dynamic leadership of the kings of Fortriu, was reaching the zenith of its political and cultural power. But there was not much time left to enjoy it. A new catalyst for change was already making itself felt across the islands of Britain and Ireland, the cause first of Dál Riata's disarray, then of upheaval within Pictland itself. It can be summed up in one terrifying word: Vikings!

CHAPTER 4

Accidental Birth of a Nation

... like dire wolves robbed, tore and slaughtered not only beasts
of burden, sheep and oxen but even priests and deacons and
companies of monks and nuns.

Historia Regum Anglorum

In 793 or 794, Vikings described as *Scaldingi** landed on the
island of Lindisfarne off the coast of north-east England and
proceeded to ravage its famous monastery, originally a daughter-
house of Iona. Scotland, or at least the Hebrides, was hit around
the same time. Four years later, the invaders were able to exact
tribute from the area around Dublin (Ath Cliath) in Ireland.
The sacrilegious brutality of the pagan warriors provoked horror
across these islands, though it would have taken a remarkable
non-Christian to pass up the opportunity to raid the region's
holy places of their priceless treasures. But the Norse were

---

* These were the descendants of Danish Vikings who had set up a colony
in Walcheren on the Scheld River in modern Zeeland (southern Netherlands)
(see Woolf, *From Pictland to Alba*, p. 72).

intent on securing far more than booty. Britain was in line for conquest.

Iona was first hit in 795. However, despite their best efforts, the raiders did not manage to strip the island of everything of value, particularly the shrine of Columba himself. So they returned, again and again. By 807 most of the surviving monks had decided to leave for the comparative safety of Kells, north-west of Dublin, a handful staying behind to seek martyrdom, having buried Columba's tomb. Their secret remained intact, despite the efficacy of Norse techniques for forcibly extracting the information.[1] Iona's influence, in Britain and on the Continent, would never be the same again.

To begin with, these fearful incursions seem to have had only a limited effect on the Picts. Indeed, it could be argued that the Norse did the kings of Fortriu a favour by softening up Dál Riata, allowing them to re-establish control over the west through puppet-king relatives of their own royal family. It has even been argued that there may have been some collusion between the Picts and the Norse.[2]

There were concerns, however. Although his predecessor, Nechtan, had deliberately sought to reduce the influence of the Columban Church in Fortriu, Constantine – back in control of Dál Riata after 811 – was deeply worried about the fate of Iona, most particularly that its founding saint, or at least the remaining bits of him, should not be entirely reappropriated to Ireland once the island was evacuated of all but the most resolute monks. The rebuilding of the monastery of Kells to house a number of Columba's relics from 807 may have been paralleled in Pictland by Constantine's foundation of the monastery of Dunkeld in Perthshire, even though the relics themselves do not seem to have left Iona for another fifty years.[3]

In any event, Pictland, too, soon found itself under attack. In 839, the Norse moved deep into the kingdom and were met by an army led by Angus's son, Eóganán, king of Fortriu, and Aed, the Pictish vassal king of Dál Riata. 'This battle may be one of the most decisive and important battles in British history but of its details and even its location we know nothing'.[4] Eóganán's force was routed and both kings were killed, a catastrophic defeat that had a remarkable effect in the longer term. After this disaster, Pictland descended into administrative chaos, with at least two more kings competing for, and briefly taking, the throne against a backdrop of continuing pressure from the Norse. The future of northern Britain hung in the balance. Enter Kenneth mac Alpin (Cináed mac Alpín), the Dalriadan warlord who destroyed the Picts and founded Scotland.[5]

The inhabitants of medieval Europe seem to have had an endless capacity for reconfiguring their political identities, less out of any apparent desire to experiment with alternative forms of governance than from an imperative to mess about with the existing set-up, to forge new wholes out of disparate parts. Medieval history is littered with the cycles of violence that often accompanied this imperative, justified by the identification of a 'problem' (usually other people), which could only supposedly be solved by laying down a new 'solution', namely the conquest of one political unit by another. But no sooner had a reconfigured kingdom or principality emerged than so too did the next 'problem'. Events (who did what to whom) might act as the justification for violent takeover bids, but it was ethnicity (who one group was, compared with an 'other') that apparently drove the process.

This is certainly how later writers describe the way in which the distinct peoples of Dál Riata and Pictland were forged into a new nation, the Picts supposedly enduring a violent and near-instantaneous annihilation at the hands of the Scots/Irish. The reality was different. Ethnicity played a negligible role in the creation of Scotland, as did violence (though there was plenty of it about). In other words, definitions of 'us' and 'them' as a necessary prerequisite for conquest can be as much a product of history as an explanation for it. The disparity between what actually happened and what people soon wanted to believe had taken place was a reflection of *later* medieval obsessions with the rights of kings and the precise delineation of the bound-aries of their authority, both physical and metaphysical, across Europe. Much more rigid ethnic definitions of those living within these boundaries followed on close behind.

For the warrior elites of ninth-century Pictland and Dál Riata, the acquisition of more territory was still a by-product of their perennial campaigns to collect booty; it was not yet an end in itself. Nor was their world as closely constrained by the boundaries of clan, province or even kingdom as it was for their inferiors. How could it be when their wives and daughters moved so easily across ethnic or political divides, forging new connections with each passing generation, a perennial antidote to the disruptive nature of warfare? Though a kingdom was an effective unit, its resources increasingly harnessed to provide a king with more and more power, networks of clients were as usefully built up beyond its boundaries as within it.

In such a fluid world, the ethnic background of the man in

charge – a member of a far-flung and extended royal kin group – mattered far less than his credentials as a leader and his ability to assemble the most convincing range of support behind his claim to rule. Five hundred years later such a relaxed attitude towards a monarch's racial origins was almost unthinkable. When the last Capetian king of France died in 1328, his throne was claimed by his nephew, the English king, Edward III. However, the French nobility could not bear to accept a foreigner as their ruler, especially one who was king of England, and chose a less direct descendant, Philippe de Valois.[6]

Nevertheless, for over one thousand years, Kenneth mac Alpin has been regarded as the first king of Scots and father of a long line of Scottish monarchs that could all trace their descent from him.[7] Let us unpick some of the claims made about him and his 'conquest' by succeeding generations. The first king of Scots? He was certainly not described as such at the time. Responsible for the wholesale massacre of the Picts, or at least their aristocracy? There is no contemporary evidence for this either, and it would not have made political sense. The less sensational truth seems to be that Scotland itself emerged as a continuation of the Pictish kingdom under new political and social conditions. There was no union between Pictland and Dál Riata – the western kingdom remained entirely outside Scottish control and was soon drawn into a Norse Hebridean kingdom.

There is no doubt, though, that the Gaelic language and aspects of Gaelic culture were transplanted east, along with, perhaps, several leading Dalriadan families who already enjoyed close ties with the Pictish aristocracy. For those Scots who left the insecurity of Dál Riata behind, this was ultimately a marriage of convenience which blossomed naturally out of a long-standing familiarity among those who had far more in common than might be suggested by the political wrangling that had once pulled them apart.

However, at the highest social level there does seem to have been some displacement, a development highlighted by the introduction of place-names containing the element *pit-*, which is Pictish, but usually coupled with a Gaelic second element, often a personal name. 'The apparent lesson here is that certain attractive Pictish estates were taken over lock, stock and barrel by Gaelic speakers, or, at least, by people with Gaelic names.'[8]

So, who was Kenneth mac Alpin? The honest answer these days is that we do not know, but he is just as likely to have been a member of the Pictish royal family as the Scottish (Dalriadan) one, since Fortriu had controlled Dál Riata, on and off, for over a century. One possible scenario is that he came from both Pictish and Dalriadan royal parentage, as intermarriage across the ethnic divide had become fashionable in the two kingdoms. By the ninth century, the result seems to have been a degree of overlap between their respective aristocracies which, eventually, made it much easier to create something new. Having 'mixed race' parents was also an obvious way of promoting precocious linguistic skills at a time when the aristocracy of western Europe did not share the habit of speaking Norman French, as they began to in the later eleventh century.

Perhaps it is most realistic to see Kenneth as a mixture of both Pict and Scot and, in this respect at least, one of an emerging new breed of 'Scots', though again such a view is only possible with hindsight. He supposedly became king of

Dál Riata in 839/840, probably succeeding King Aed, who died alongside Eóganán fighting against the Norse. Two years later he seized the Pictish throne from its warring Pictish factions, ruling 'happily' for the next sixteen years – surely not feasible if he had instituted a policy of genocide?[9] This was role reversal – a Dalriadan of Pictish origins controlling Pictland, with a concomitant shift in the balance of power in favour of those who spoke Gaelic rather than Pictish – but nothing else had significantly changed.

The threat from the Norse had not gone away. By the end of Kenneth's first decade as king, a new Scandinavian offensive had been launched in Ireland, where 'the Foreigners' (Gaill), as the Norse were called, gained control of the ports of Dublin, Waterford, Wexford, Cork and Limerick; they also began to take over the Hebrides, Dál Riata's insular territories.[10] In 849 St Columba's relics were finally removed from Iona to Kells in Ireland and, so tradition has it, to Dunkeld in central Scotland. The most important Columban relic supposedly housed in Dunkeld was the *Cath Bhuaidh* or 'Yellow Battler', the saint's crozier (staff), which later accompanied Scottish armies into battle.[11]

It is possible to see Kenneth's acquisition of the kingship of the Picts as an evacuation from Dál Riata in the nick of time as the Norse closed in. However, Kenneth was not safe, despite living in eastern Scotland and focusing his own attempts at territorial expansion on the south, into Northumbria. At some point late in his reign, the Norse sailed up the Tay and 'wasted Pictland to Clunie and Dunkeld',[12] perhaps even as Kenneth lay, perilously near, dying of cancer at Forteviot. He succumbed finally in February 858 and was followed as king by his brother,

Donald. These were difficult times for all the native kingdoms of Britain and Ireland.

In 866, the Danes captured Deira (southern Northumbria), including its key city of York. They took over East Anglia at the same time and reduced the midland English kingdom of Mercia to a state of dependence. 'The line of the Roman road . . . which ran from London to Chester now formed the approximate boundary between "English" England and the zone under Danish rule.' East and north was the Danelaw. Only Wessex remained a truly independent Anglo-Saxon kingdom, though even it endured a degree of Scandinavian infiltration until the reign of the remarkable Alfred (871–99), who began the Anglo-Saxon revival and the process of creating the kingdom of England.[13]

At the same time (*c.*866), Norse from Ireland attacked Fortriu itself, following up a three-year occupation there with a successful assault on the formidable British stronghold of Al Clut (Dumbarton) on the River Clyde. There was little respite from the pressure on southern Scotland either. In 875 a Pictish force was destroyed in yet another massacre, this time perpetrated by the Danish ruler of York, Hálfdan, at Dollar some nine miles north of the River Forth which was still the border between Pictland and Northumbria. The king – Kenneth mac Alpin's son, Constantine – survived, only to be killed by another Scandinavian force two years later, when 'the Northmen passed a whole year in Pictland'.[14] This was a time of turmoil and confusion, with Kenneth mac Alpin's sons and grandsons soon losing out to another unidentified royal line represented most powerfully, if ambiguously, by King Giric.

A succession crisis seems to have broken out on the premature deaths of Constantine (in 877) and his brother, Aed, who ruled after him for no more than a year and died in an internal coup presumably instigated by his successor, Giric. Both Constantine and Aed did have sons, but they cannot have been old enough to rule at a time when being an adult male was, for obvious reasons, an essential qualification for leadership. The line of Kenneth mac Alpin looked likely to disappear within only a generation of taking the Pictish throne.

Despite an extraordinary veil of silence over his origins in both Scottish and Irish sources,[15] Giric still emerges as a strong king, reigning in difficult circumstances for over a decade. Like his immediate predecessors, he seems to have confined his activities to the south, keeping the Britons at bay and extending Pictish influence, and perhaps territorial control, across the Forth into Bernicia.[16] Such efforts required organisation, the maintenance of loyal and effective lieutenants throughout Scotland to gather an army, helping, in the process, to bind this mixed bag of peoples more closely together under the king's authority.[17]

There is nothing like a joint enterprise against outsiders to bring together those who might otherwise devote too much energy to internal differences. Giric seems to have appreciated this more than most, providing another, entirely domestic, context for a solemn display of unity to add to the heady sense of collective well-being generated by taking war across the border. Gathering his great men – both nobles and churchmen – about him, Giric was reputedly 'the first to give liberty to the Scottish church, which was in servitude to the civil authorities, according to the custom of the Picts'. This might even be the first known use of the term 'Scottish' applied to the Church of this new hybrid kingdom peopled by Picts and Scots.[18]

As we have already seen at Forteviot,[19] the relationship between the Pictish crown and its Church was extremely close, the latter perhaps being viewed – by the kings at least – as little more than another, albeit important, branch of the royal administration. However, the changes instituted by Giric were probably less the result of a peculiarly Pictish tendency to keep a tight rein on ecclesiastical independence – as later historians liked to argue to justify God's apparent decision to get rid of the entire nation – than the growing assertiveness of the Church as a whole in trying to wriggle free of secular constraints. Bishop Cellach, the most senior churchman in Pictland, could presumably pile on the pressure for change as the price of ecclesiastical support for Giric's seizure of the throne.[20] Despite attempts by later commentators to write him out of history, this was a remarkable reign under a remarkable man, at a time when 'the precocity of a single kingdom of Scotia or Alba ... seems to excite little comment'.[21]

Alas, poor Giric! Later historians felt free to gloss over him because the direct male line of descent from Kenneth mac Alpin did survive, while Pictland did not. In 889 Donald, Kenneth's grandson, took the throne, presumably after a putsch.[22] Donald's father, Constantine, Kenneth's son, therefore came to be viewed as the last of the Pictish kings.* When this new king died, in 900, the Irish sources described him as *ri Alban* – king of Scotland – the Gaelic word 'Alba' having

---

* Our sources also ignore the brief and ineffective reign of Constantine's brother, Aed.

previously been used to describe the whole of Great Britain. It seems as if a new kingdom, or at least a new idea, had been born. But despite the Gaelic name and later attempts fundamentally to alter its history, Alba was still essentially Pictish and still held Pictish kingship at the very heart of its identity.[23]

Still, it did the line of Kenneth mac Alpin no harm at all that the next king proved to be one of early Scotland's most successful, and long-lasting. Another of Kenneth's grandsons, this second Constantine* ruled for at least forty years before retiring to enjoy the bracing North Sea air from the monastery in St Andrews. To begin with, his reign followed an all-too-familiar pattern, with the Norse plundering Dunkeld and 'all Scotland' in 903.[24] But God came to Scotland's rescue and the following year the Scots won a great victory against the invaders. First, though, they had to pray to Columba, promise 'to do every good thing as their clergy would best urge them' and take – apparently for the first time – the saint's crozier, the *Cath Bhuaidh*, out before them as the army's battle standard. The results for such good behaviour were predictably staggering. 'For a long time after that neither the Danes nor the Norwegians attacked them, and they enjoyed peace and tranquillity'.[25]

With the Norse dealt with for the time being, Constantine could turn his attention to putting his own house in order,

* There was a Pictish King Constantine, mentioned in Chapter 3, but, rightly or wrongly, kings of Scots are counted from Kenneth mac Alpin onwards, making this one the second Scottish Constantine even though his predecessor (Constantine I by this numbering) was really a king of the Picts. Please see the family tree.

particularly his relationship with his Church. In this he seems to have been encouraged by Bishop Cellach, Giric's old adviser. It is not difficult to imagine Cellach explaining to Constantine that God had granted him this stunning victory and in return he must now make good his promise to listen to his churchmen. If not, who knows what God might decide to do?

In 909, therefore, at a ceremony reminiscent of later royal inaugurations, king and chief bishop met at Scone, near Perth, to redraw the lines between Church and state. They ascended a small mound known now as the 'Moot Hill' but called then the 'Hill of Belief'. A crowd no doubt stood, suitably awed, beneath them. There the two men swore 'after the fashion of the Gaels to keep the laws and disciplines of the faith, and also the rights of the churches and the gospels'.[26] God would surely now continue to bless this new Scotland.

In Macbeth's lifetime, it was *de rigueur* for those wishing to take on the mantle of legitimate kingship to make the trip to Scone for their inauguration, no matter how they had managed to clear the way to the throne. This carefully orchestrated ceremony of 909, over a century earlier, was the first documented occasion when Scone was used for an important affair of state and marks the continuing development of sites in what had been southern Pictland as the spiritual and ceremonial setting for Scottish kingship and government. Forteviot, on the other hand, no longer gets a mention, implying that it had now lost its position as *the* seat of kingship and government in the region.

The reign of Constantine II of Scotland (900–944) coincided with a difficult period for the Norse, expelled from Dublin in 902, though both they and the native Irish continued to fight for control of the strategically vital Irish Sea. On the eastern side of mainland Britain, the Danes lost control of Deira, including York. With his enemies fully occupied elsewhere and having proved his own military credentials, Constantine had time to consider the future without the pressing threat of Norse armies poking their noses into every part of his kingdom.

Unfortunately, losing Dublin (temporarily) merely seems to have transplanted Norse attention elsewhere. Ragnall, grandson of Ivar, began the comeback, taking on Norse rivals on the western mainland and the Isle of Man before moving east to exploit the vacuum in Northumbria after the expulsion of its Danish rulers. He soon proved an impressive warrior and equally powerful king. In the decade after 910 'control of the trans-Pennine routes . . . may have enabled Ragnall and, after his death in 920, his brother Sigtrygg, who had re-established the base at Dublin, to rule over a kingdom that spanned the Irish Sea'.[27]

The prospect of a reinvigorated Norse presence so close to home was no doubt greeted in Scotland with foreboding, combined, perhaps, with a degree of opportunism. Constantine, fondly remembering the success of 904 against a Norse army that had included this very same Ragnall, may well have relished the chance, fourteen years later, to call out his men on behalf of the ousted Anglo-Saxon king of Northumbria, Ealdred. With hindsight, this proved to be the beginning of a major shift in Scottish foreign policy. Though previous kings such as Kenneth and Giric had dabbled in attempts to acquire territory immediately beyond the Forth, interfering directly in Northumbrian affairs with an eye to extending the Anglo-Scottish border further and further south now became a Scottish habit that lasted for over three hundred years. The potential for booty on such expeditions no doubt had recruits for the Scottish army signing up on the double.

On the other hand, it is curious that Ealdred chose to go to Constantine's court at all, rather than soliciting the help of the English king, Edward the Elder. However, Edward was currently embroiled in trying to consolidate Wessex's control over southern and middle England, including the East Anglian and Mercian portions of the Danelaw. Constantine – firmly in charge of his comparatively united northern kingdom for fifteen years – must have seemed the more likely protector.

The two sides – Scottish and Norse – met at Corbridge on the banks of the River Tyne, deep in Northumbrian territory,* and lined themselves up for battle. Ragnall had divided his men into at least four battalions, one of which was kept out of sight of the Scots under his own command. As men and spears came violently together, the Scots proved victorious, slaughtering large numbers of Norse, including some of their leaders. But then Ragnall unleashed his hidden battalion on the Scottish rear and turned the battle around, though neither Constantine nor any of his generals were killed, presumably because they were leading from the front, as kings and high-ranking nobles were expected to do.[28] In the end both sides claimed victory, though in Scotland's case this was more moral than real. Ragnall, on the other hand, was now left to enjoy the more tangible benefits of undisputed control of Deira, including, shortly afterwards, the city of York itself.

---

* It should be remembered that the border then lay, officially at least, at the Forth, rather than where it currently lies, over thirty miles to the north of Corbridge. This battle was also called Tinemore.

918 marked a watershed in British politics and helped to define Scotland's future for centuries to come, though this had little to do with the equivocal result at Corbridge. It was Edward the Elder's annexation of neighbouring Mercia in the same year that had the most far-reaching consequences. Now 'most of southern England, the richest part of the island, was in the hands of a single king ruling directly and not through autonomous sub-kings'.[29] According to the *Anglo-Saxon Chronicle*, these events soon led to King Edward being chosen in 920 as 'father and lord' by all the key rulers of mainland Britain, including the king of Strathclyde, Ragnall of Deira, Ealdred and his brothers (who probably now ruled only Bernicia, northern Northumbria), and the king of the Scots and all his people.[30] Seven years later, Edward's son, Athelstan, repeated the ceremony near Penrith, which guarded the approach to the Solway Firth, the *Anglo-Saxon Chronicle* boasting that the English king now 'governed all the kings that were in this island'.[31]

The area in which Penrith is situated, Cumbria, now imme-diately south of the Anglo-Scottish border on the west, was, in the tenth century and for several centuries after, of consid-erable interest to the English, the Norse in Deira (and else-where), and the king of Scots. Technically it formed part of the British kingdom of Strathclyde, but was far too useful to be left at that; whoever controlled the area was well on the way to commanding the Irish Sea too, so Athelstan was clearly laying down the gauntlet to his competitors in the region. The English king made another pointed gesture shortly afterwards, marching into York where he dished out treasure to his men, pulled down the Norse fortifications and formally claimed the city as his own.[32] Though Northumbria's history as a distinct entity was far from over and the Norse were not yet entirely pushed out, this moment of high drama 'has often been taken as the point at which a unitary kingship of the English was established'.[33]

The might of England, which became one of the greatest kingdoms in western Europe before going on to develop into a global power, is an aspect of history that few can be unaware of, whatever one's views on the nature of that might. And yet, such an outcome was by no means inevitable, nor does it justify the presumption that the southern portion of mainland Britain was the only major player in the politics of these islands. Despite the influence of modern national sentiment, the imprecision of any measure of comparative 'greatness' or 'strength' in this period of British history means that it is futile to attempt to rank its early political entities, including Dál Riata, Pictland, the various British and Anglo-Saxon kingdoms, as well as Ireland. However, it is certainly possible to argue that, for much of the so-called Dark Ages, those in the northern half of mainland Britain were just as well-organised and culturally sophisticated as those in the south, even if they showed it in different ways.

It is clear with hindsight that the tenth century was a key one, with the England and Scotland that still exist today both emerging in fledgling but recognisable form. Given England's 'Danish' problem, Scotland had something of a head start, partly because of the coherence and sophistication of what came before (in both Pictland and Dál Riata), partly because the encroaching presence of the Scandinavians had been contained, but also because the extent to which the new kingdom was encircled by the Norse may have led to enforced introspection.

The apparent strength of Scotland under Constantine makes it all the more difficult to understand what the Scottish king was doing, kowtowing to Edward the Elder and then Athelstan. This was the man who had defeated the Norse at home in 904 and came close to an away win in 918, the ruler for whom a poet could hardly contain his enthusiasm, calling him 'My joy, my joy!' and 'King of Kings', before adding that, during Constantine's long reign, Scotland enjoyed God's bounty here on earth:

> With fruits on slender trees,
> With ale, with music, with fellowship,
> With corn, with milk, with active kine [cattle],
> With pride, with success, with elegance.[34]

Constantine had already shown, by taking Ealdred under his wing, that he could and would intervene in Anglo-Saxon politics, with his eye on the lands lying immediately to the south of his own kingdom. Both he and Edward the Elder knew that Ragnall of Deira was a threat, but neither was in a position to get rid of him (though death soon claimed him). The 920 agreement was thus an attempt by the English king to secure his recent conquests. Ragnall was to stay in Deira and not attempt to extend Norse control back into Mercia or East Anglia. In return, Edward sought to relieve the pressure on the Norseman by getting both Ealdred and his ally Constantine to leave Deira alone.

So, what was in it for the king of Scots? Well, he received

an acknowledgement of his vested interest in Northumbrian politics and possibly now exercised effective control over at least some of Lothian, the most northerly part of Bernicia immediately south of the Forth, through his relationship with its Anglo-Saxon ruler, Ealdred.[35] The events of the 930s certainly underlined Constantine's ambitions, though this decade also saw England successfully asserting itself as the most – but not the only – powerful player, militarily and politically, among the kingdoms of Britain. In 934, Athelstan attacked Scotland directly by land and sea, in reaction to the Scottish king's continued meddling in northern English affairs, despite oaths and treaties explicitly designed to stop it.

Athelstan was particularly incensed by Constantine's negotiations, probably on the death of his old ally, Ealdred of Bernicia, with Olaf Guthfrithsson of Dublin, who claimed the throne of York now supposedly under direct English control. Having taken an English army and navy deep into Scottish territory – the first such incursion since 685[36] – Athelstan forced Constantine to accompany him back down south for a brief spell as an honoured, but presumably unwilling, guest. The Scottish king was also invited to attend a grand jamboree in the old Roman city of Cirencester planned for the following year, a 'request' that Constantine would have been foolhardy to decline.

The English king – who certainly seems to have harboured Arthurian-type visions of himself as king of all the Britons – must have been overjoyed by the sight of the kings of Scotland, Strathclyde and Wales decked out in national costume in Cirencester, proffering gifts and swearing undying loyalty to him as their superior lord. Unfortunately for him, Constantine seems to have had his fingers safely crossed during this submission ceremony, because he had no sooner shaken the English dirt from his boots before he was back negotiating with Olaf. As an ageing ruler of a kingdom unused to anyone claiming superior power over it, Constantine perhaps did not need the encouragement of any of his younger ambitious relatives to attempt to reverse the very public humiliations of the past few years.[37]

He took his preparations seriously, waiting until 937 to invade England, along with Olaf's Norse fleet and the Strathclyde Britons, whose kings, for now at least, seem to have been under the thumb of Scotland's rulers.[38] The result, however, was a catastrophic defeat in which 'hoary-haired' Constantine lost a son and innumerable others died in a 'great battle' that reverberated across these islands. Its site – Brunanburh – is unknown but likely to have been somewhere in western England, given that Olaf's boats were coming from Ireland.[39]

Ironically – as is often the way with battles that capture the public imagination – the political fall-out from Brunanburh was negligible. Athelstan himself was dead within two years and in 940 Olaf became king of Deira. Constantine survived the shock and humiliation of his dramatic defeat, a testament to the strength of his grip on Scotland. He continued as king until 944, 'long enough to see his oppressor's empire turn to dust, and this must have been satisfying'.[40] He was not finished yet, however; he entered the monastery of St Andrews, though whether he went willingly or had to be dragged there is impossible to tell. In 949 he supposedly threatened to come out of retirement to lead yet another raid on England, the final futile gesture of an old man who had been, nonetheless, one of

Scotland's most powerful early monarchs.[41] He died, finally, in 952.

The relationship between Scotland and England had changed over the course of Constantine's long reign. There was no going back to the time when the two kingdoms had occasionally rubbed up against one another, but largely left each other alone. England's rulers now had an ideal in mind that they wished to grasp and make secure: acknowledgement of their rightful position as *the* pre-eminent kings within the island of Britain.

So far as Scotland was concerned 'There can be no doubt that the kings of Alba in the tenth century on occasion promised to be the helpers of the English kings and that this relationship became more regular from mid-century'.[42] It is a moot point whether the Scottish kings would have felt obliged to take part in this 'who's the biggest king' competition (in which they gained the dubious honour of coming second), if they had not decided to intervene proactively and consistently in Northumbrian and Cumbrian politics. The English kings may have enjoyed sitting on the highest chair at a British round table of their own making, thanks to their undoubted military superiority on most occasions; but it was the Scottish kings who found themselves gradually pushing the border further and further south, at England's expense.

In 945 Athelstan's successor, Edmund, recognised his own inability to secure the north permanently by marching into Cumbria, dealing summarily with the heirs to its throne, and handing the whole lot over to the safe-keeping of Malcolm I of Scotland. Defeating armies was one thing – and the English were very good at that – but securing a lasting peace so far from their own heartland in the south was quite another. Thirty

years later, in 975, King Edgar of England formally acknowledged that the Scots were really masters south of the Forth
too, ceding Lothian to Kenneth II of Scotland 'with great
honour'. For Kenneth, attending a crown-wearing feast in
England every year and playing second fiddle to Edgar while
he was there was clearly a price worth paying.[43]

The Scottish kings were becoming masters of *realpolitik* in
this period, not least because they took a pragmatic view of
the oaths made to their English 'high king', honouring them
not a second longer than was politically necessary. Indeed, it
can be argued that, despite all the posturing, the necessary
bowing and scraping, 'the kings of Alba played a central role
in the politics of the tenth-century British Isles, containing the
expansion of the West Saxon dynasty to the south and the
Norse to both north and west'.[44]

But we should not be fooled. The English kings, together
with the rulers of Northumberland, were still capable of
snatching any opportunity to turn the clock back. The loss of
Lothian and the eastern border country to Scotland may have
looked permanent, but only time would tell if this was really
so.

As well as all these moments of high drama taking place outside
the kingdom, Scotland was settling down internally too. 'Once
Gaelic was established as the language of prestige and advance-
ment it was only a matter of time before Pictish was abandoned
completely'.[45] Given this hegemony of Gaelic culture in
Scotland, and despite the Norse presence in former Dalriadan
territory, Ireland remained a source of cultural inspiration across
the Scottish mainland. In the ninth century, the *Céli Dé* ('vassals

of God'; anglicised to Culdee) – a reformed and more rigorous form of monasticism harking back to the kind of ascetic lifestyle that Columba would have recognised – migrated across to Scotland from Ireland, having spread originally from the Continent.

King Constantine II had close connections with the new religious order. He managed to get himself written into the life of the Scottish saint, Catroe (*c*.900–71) by allegedly trying to persuade the holy man not to leave Scotland, though in the end the king acquiesced and Catroe was escorted to the border with much pomp and ceremony to become, eventually, abbot of Metz. Perhaps Catroe's example was what ultimately persuaded the king to join the Culdees on his retirement, possibly even abbot in St Andrews, though there were other major houses at Scone, Dunkeld, Loch Leven (St Serf's), Abernethy, Brechin and Monymusk. All these monasteries held lands granted to them by the royal family, and some were even founded by kings.*

Scotland's monarchs continued to take their relationship with their Church seriously. Although certainly not strangers to short-term political gain, they were also keen on acquiring longer-term celestial credits: the Culdees expected to be exempted from lay exactions, including military service from their tenants, a considerable concession for rulers determined to fight off Vikings and acquire Anglo-Saxon territory. Granting them land was not a step to be taken lightly, though fortunately, being

---

* As we have seen, Dunkeld was reputedly founded by the Pictish king Constantine and refounded by Kenneth mac Alpin. Brechin was reputedly founded at the end of the tenth century by Kenneth II.

ascetics, the Culdees did not require vast amounts. Indeed, in time, kings seem to have started to nibble away at their predecessors' gifts, appropriating Church lands with which to satisfy the demands of their military entourages.[46]

To the modern mind, the monks were equally guilty of double standards. Though they tried to lead by example away from the path of violence and warfare so fundamental to the lives of their male benefactors, donations of land, up to and including the foundation of churches and monasteries, were, in reality, about expiating past, present and future sins, rather than a genuinely held desire to mend one's ways. As the tenth century progressed, the kings of Scots were in need of some serious penance, though their churchmen were sometimes just as involved in the bloodshed that came to haunt the succession. Constantine's decision to relinquish his throne, even – especially – if he did so less than willingly, must have seemed like the epitome of civilised behaviour within only a few generations as kings and contenders began to murder each other at the first sign of weakness.

As good Gaels, the Scots had stuck to a traditional Dalriadan approach to the succession, which, technically, allowed all those within the *derbfine* – a line of male descent from a common great-grandfather – to be eligible for the kingship. In practice, however, the succession rotated remarkably regularly between two lines of the family – those descended from Kenneth mac Alpin's elder son, Constantine I, and those descended from his younger son, Aed. Sons of kings might well reach the throne, but not until an increasingly distant cousin from the other branch had occupied it first.

The long reign of Constantine II makes clear why this is so

remarkable. Surely such a powerful king, the man who had survived the catastrophe of Brunanburh intact and held power well into old age, would be able to persuade his nobility to allow his second son, Indulf, to succeed him? Instead, Constantine meekly authorised Malcolm I, the extremely patient (and mature) son of his predecessor, to take over. Perhaps Brunanburh and the death of his elder son really had made the difference, giving Malcolm the support he needed to force the old king into retirement.

The only other Gaelic kingdom to operate such a rigidly alternating system was Tara in Ireland, where two branches of the ruling family deliberately agreed to exclude other branches and rotate the kingship between them. The impasse on further consolidation of power in the hands of only one of them arose from the fact that these competing dynasties held land at a distance from each other; if one branch had tried to take the other one out, this 'would almost certainly have led to a reduction of the territorial extent of effective royal power'.[47]

So it seems likely that the descendants of the sons of Kenneth also held power in discrete geographical areas where they 'each had their own powerbase and client network'.[48] If so, where might these have lain? The evidence is mostly limited to the brief entries on Scottish kings in the Irish chronicles, which were usually, though not entirely, concerned with where they died. However, it is possible to detect a faint glimmer there of distinct spheres of interest, a concern with the north-east for the line of Constantine mac Kenneth, and the south for the line of Aed mac Kenneth.

To be more specific, although kings of Constantine's line

were occasionally killed in Moray,* they also met their deaths in the Mearns (eastern Scotland, south of Aberdeen). These two regions were situated immediately to the north-west and south of the earldom of Mar respectively. Those travelling north, into Moray and beyond, would cross Mar before making their way through the mountains via the Cairn o' Mounth, 'the most important of all the Mounth passes'.[49] Mar also included a parcel of important royal lands in the later Middle Ages known as the Garioch (pronounced Geary), centred on modern Inverurie and including the pasture lands of the area's prominent hill, Bennachie. We must keep an eye on the Garioch as our story progresses, because it may well have played a crucial role right at the very end of Macbeth's life. We cannot be sure that this was where the line of Constantine mac Kenneth had their main lands, but it is a distinct possibility. As for the line of Aed mac Kenneth, it is impossible to identify where their lands in the south might have been situated, but it is often supposed that it might have been Atholl, which was once the only identifiable Pictish kingdom other than Fortriu. Marriage would also have complicated the issue, bringing parcels of land from other parts of the country to both sides of the marital arrangement.[50]

In practice, kings from the north would have been required to spend quite a bit of their time in the heartland of the kingdom, which remained in the south, around Perth; and it was always a good idea, where possible, to indulge in noble-pleasing raids, especially across the border into English Northumbria. Despite

---

* Moray may not technically have been part of Scotland, though ruled by the Scottish king. We will deal with this interesting conundrum in Chapter 5.

the uncertainty over where exactly was home for these two royal families, we can assume that they would each have had a significant following, including the mormaers (earls) of their own provinces, waiting as impatiently as their leader for their turn in power. As Constantine surely knew, a mutually destructive civil war would be the inevitable consequence of trying to stop them.

Patience soon became a virtue in short supply in both branches of the royal family. After 962, which is the last recorded instance of a Norse attack on Scottish soil, 'the kings of Alba were left to their own internal disputes over resources and authority ... thereafter this form of "circuit" [the transfer of the succession from one branch of the royal family to the other] deteriorated into internecine strife'.[51] In other words, the external threat had kept relations reasonably civil. With that threat removed, and England once more facing a Danish invasion, the temptation to hasten the demise of the current Scottish king on behalf of his most likely successor became irresistible.

Once one such murder had been committed, the murderer could sleep safe in his bed only so long as he proved competent and popular or there was not a more competent or popular contender waiting in the wings with the perfect excuse to do the same to him. The kingship still rotated as it should, but the length of reign plummeted from a respectable average of fourteen years between 862 and 962 to five between 962 and 1005. But surely it was the height of recklessness for the internal peace and stability fostered by kings like Giric and Constantine to be squandered by the unseemly haste of their successors to take a throne that would have come to them anyway?

In effect, these two families had entered the terrible world of the bloodfeud,[52] a truly awful circumstance for Scotland to find itself in, given that kings were supposed to show a good example and regulate internal violence when it threatened to get out of hand. Though such feuding was governed by conventions which helped to restrain the natural desire to retaliate through indiscriminate killing in hot blood, those involved became extremely sensitive to perceived insults against the family's honour, which in turn could provoke more acts of violence, including rape, theft and murder. Even if a third party managed to negotiate a settlement, 'hostility [could] be reactivated, sometimes by overt incidents of affront but frequently by simple recollection of unfinished business'.[53]

It is hard to see how a king could expect to run a country, given his need to rely on his senior nobility, many of whom must have belonged to the wider kin group of the two ruling families, if they were all constantly on the look-out for provocative or retaliatory behaviour. Indeed, one can almost imagine an even more bloody and essentially farcical version of Shakespeare's *Macbeth*, with daggers around every corner, corpses on or under every bed, and women and clergymen lambasting and lamenting in equal measure (if they were not egging the protagonists on).

The sad truth is that, after 952, Scottish kings could expect to meet a violent death as a matter of course and, if foreign enemies did not get to them first, their internal ones would. However, from 995 onwards, the bloodfeud became deadly serious as one king after another was murdered by his successor. Even new kings could not rely on enjoying much of a 'honeymoon' period before getting wind of the first challenge to their throne, a challenge that might fail initially, only to become successful later on.[54]

By the end of the tenth century, then, it is fair to say that Scotland was in a political mess and there was no-one to blame but the kingdom's rulers themselves. It is true that violence was part and parcel of life across western Europe in this period: 'The relative lack of internecine strife in tenth-century England was largely due to the fact that the potential rivals were dropping like flies without a finger being laid upon them.'[55] The extent to which this quarrel among the competitors for the Scottish throne affected their ability, when they did become king, to rule effectively can only be imagined. It is certainly no wonder that the cultural life of the kingdom appears to have ground to a halt.

In 997 a solution might have presented itself naturally, with the murder near Scone of Constantine III, who proved to be the last of the line descended from Kenneth mac Alpin's younger son, Aed. Unfortunately, the feuding continued, but this time among much closer cousins, the descendants of Malcolm I (944–54) of the line of Kenneth's elder son, Constantine. The fall-out from this continuing struggle for the throne is hinted at in the enigmatic entry in the Irish chronicle the *Annals of the Four Masters* for the year 999, which states that 'Dungal, son of Kenneth, was slain by Gillacomgain, son of Kenneth'.[56]

The murder of Dungal by Gillacomgain – whoever they were – in 999 was clearly an important event, significant enough to make it into the Irish annals, which only noticed the comings and goings of great men. So this was shocking beyond Scotland's shores and surely connected to the royal house itself. The two Kenneths mentioned are, it is assumed, the late Kenneth II (971–95) and his nephew, the current king, Kenneth III

(997–1005), though whether this was an attempt to consolidate power within one branch of the royal line or to pre-empt such a move is unclear. Whatever the truth of these murky deeds, Scotland could not go on like this.

So far as we can tell, most of the murderous events associated with the royal bloodfeuding took place south of the line of mountains that separated Fortriu from what had been the rest of Pictland, but was now Alba/Scotland. Indeed, for the period between 870 and 1020 there is only one reliable reference to Fortriu/Moray (as it became) in the Scottish record. So, what happened to the proud and powerful kingdom of the Verturiones, whose kings united the Picts and took over Dál Riata? And why did Moray suddenly reappear with a vengeance soon after the turn of the second millennium?

CHAPTER 5

View from the North

The first he heard say going by:
'Lo, yonder the thane of Cromarty!'
The other sister said again:
'Of Murray yonder I see the [thane].'
The third said: 'Yonder I see the king.'

Andrew of Wyntoun, *The Orygynale Cronykil*

Anyone familiar with Shakespeare's *Macbeth* can easily be forgiven for failing to realise the importance of Moray to the story of the Scottish king. It is ironic, and not a little poignant, that this northern portion of Scotland should produce one of the most famous Scotsmen of all time, only to be unceremoniously cut out of his literary inheritance. Indeed, his homeland boasts no monuments to its notorious son.[1] The quotation above, which comes from a history of Scotland written no later than 1420, makes clear that Macbeth's position as ruler of Moray was still well-known in the early fifteenth century. A century later, it had officially been forgotten.[2]

Today, Moray is squeezed rather uncomfortably between the

bulk of Inverness-shire to the west and Aberdeenshire to the east. In the Middle Ages, though, it was a considerably more powerful proposition, stretching east along the coast from Inverness to the mouth of the mighty River Spey, then south to encompass Badenoch with its great mountains, and west through the hills and glens of Lochaber right across to Glenelg on the west coast, opposite the island of Skye.[3]

The province ruled by Macbeth and his family in the tenth and eleventh centuries was probably not much different, give or take the possibility that Scandinavians controlled the extreme western portion. Before and after AD 1000, there were certainly good communication links, Norse permitting, down into Dál Riata and across to Ireland through the Great Glen, which even today links two of the main settlements in the Highlands, Inverness and Fort William. Then there was the Moray Firth itself, the conduit through which Moray's galleys could issue forth to see and be seen by friends and enemies alike.

For hundreds of years after 1100 Moray suffered from a reputation for violent lawlessness, for being just a little bit too exciting for God-fearing and respectable Lowland folk. These days, with the cataclysmic decline of the fishing industry and a once-vibrant tourist trade, Moray is less well-known as a destination for Scots and visitors than the major cities and the west coast, despite boasting some of the best hours of sunshine in the country. As its local council* justifiably points out, the area 'offers a microcosm of the very best of Scotland: rich lowland farming; a necklace of quiet beaches, cliffs, crags and fishing

---

* This is the smallest denomination of government in Scotland, based, to some degree, on ancient regional units.

villages; rolling hills and powerful salmon rivers; and the Cairngorm mountains'.[4]

These natural features have long been admired. In 1775 the local historian, Lachlan Shaw, managed to create an image, endorsed by a range of even more venerable writers, of a northern paradise, albeit one not fully exploited, in his view, because of 'the sloth of the inhabitants'. 'Corn the earth pours forth in wonderful and never-failing abundance. Fruits of all sorts, herbs, flowers, pulse, are in the greatest plenty, and all early. While harvest has scarcely begun in surrounding districts, there all is ripe and cut down'. In essence, Moray was regarded 'as superior to any other part of Scotland for the mildness of its climate, the richness of its pastures, and the abundance of its fruits'.[5] Despite the hyperbole, there is an element of truth to this claim, given that the region is protected from severe weather driving up from the south by the great bulk of the Cairngorm Mountains; to the north, the Atlantic Drift warms its coastal waters.

These superlative natural advantages perhaps help, in part, to explain how the Verturionian chiefs of this area became the dominant kings of Pictland. Certainly Fortriu had the best of both agricultural worlds. The rich soils of the plains bordering the Moray Firth are well-suited to grain production, while the rough grazings scattered between the agricultural land, and, in summer, spread across the uplands beyond, could sustain the domestic animals – cattle, sheep and goats – that supplied not only meat but necessities such as leather and tallow.

Human endeavour had tamed this land for thousands of years; but the forests and moors that stretched into Moray's mountainous interior concealed and protected all manner of beasts that were certainly not tame. These places haunted the human imagination, their inhabitants a terrifying reminder of the limits of the civilised world. But, on occasions, they could be mastered too, temporarily at least. The hunter, only dimly aware of the noisy presence of his companions, sprang to life in this alien world, just as the warrior came into his own on the battlefield.

Moray's story begins with Fortriu, the larger kingdom out of which it emerged, in the tenth century, as the southern part. The name just means 'coastland', an apt if unimaginative description, and on its north-facing shore stood Fortriu's most important royal citadel, at Burghead. Ross, meaning 'headland', lay immediately to the north and played host to two of Fortriu's most prestigious and powerful monasteries.

According to the Northumbrian monk and historian Bede (662/3–735), it was Columba himself who brought Christianity to the Picts of Fortriu on a rare venture far from his island retreat. In an incident which has helped to create a celebrated facet of the modern Scottish tourist industry, the saint encountered and dealt severely with the kingdom's most enduring troublemaker, the Loch Ness monster. He then ventured on towards Inverness to meet with King Bridei, described by Bede as 'a most powerful king' (*rege potentissimo*).[6] Putting in yet another first-rate performance, Columba's audacious miracles, which included druid-proof singing, supposedly brought about the conversion of the northern Picts.

In truth, Christianising Fortriu beyond Bridei's court probably took rather longer, though the Pictish royal house and the Columban Church enjoyed a close relationship until King

Nechtan broke it off around 717.[7] Unlike southern Pictland, Fortriu naturally looked west (as well as north) even before its kings began to exert sporadic control over Dál Riata from the 730s. In the years after Columba's visit, Irish and Dalriadan monks retraced his steps up the Great Glen into the northern kingdom, and Pictish monks, too, played their part in Celtic Church affairs, perhaps doing some of their training in Ireland.

Monasteries based on the Columban model began to spring up, particularly at Rosemarkie and Portmahomack, now in Ross but then in Fortriu. A ten-year excavation programme at Portmahomack has revealed a major 'eighth- to ninth-century monastic workshop zone unique in Britain'. The scale and sophistication of what went on there is remarkable by any standards. In one area, objects were fashioned out of glass and precious metals including, perhaps, gold; in another, cattle hides were transformed into vellum.[8] Manuscripts held, often in colourful majesty, the information that allowed kings to control the people and resources at their disposal more extensively than if it continued to be locked up in the heads of each community's wise men. However, churchmen alone could create and decipher these documents, a powerful magic indeed. These industrial complexes seem to have been carefully planned, perhaps with some symbolic meaning. Not only that, but some of the buildings themselves were apparently constructed using 'a startling symmetry offering us more than just competence in construction.'[9]

The density of Pictish stones situated near these northern monastic settlements also pay silent testimony to the presence of artists and craftsmen confident of royal and ecclesiastical patronage, permanent reminders – should anyone be tempted to forget – of the wealth and power of Church and crown alike. Monasteries like Portmahomack were not located in some back-of-beyond wasteland. The land that provided for them was extremely fertile indeed, combining excellent soil for crops with good pasture for rearing that most advantageous symbol of early medieval wealth, cattle.

The importance of these monasteries was as much economic as spiritual, just as seats of royal government combined the mundane task of collecting the nation's resources with flaunting the mystical power of kingship, reminding subject and visitor of the reasons why God had chosen this particular man to rule. Given its political importance in northern Britain, Fortriu naturally boasted a number of important citadels, lofty hill-forts designed to be seen from afar and impress up close. Only the chosen few were granted access to their upper sanctums to conduct important meetings or perform solemn rituals that could be watched with awe by those below. Craig Phadraig commanded the northern end of the Great Glen; Dun da Lamh controlled the high passes from Badenoch into Lochaber.[10] However, Burghead, on the coast, was probably the main seat of the Pictish kings until the ninth century when Forteviot came into fashion. It was certainly the biggest, at three times the size of its contemporaries.[11]

Reinforced since the late third century AD, Burghead's massive fortifications, with walls up to seven and a half feet thick and five and a third feet high, laced in timber, dominated the harbour where Fortriu's navy could be beached, though the wrecking of a hundred and fifty of its ships in 729 provides a stark reminder of the dangers that lurked even in these estuarine waters.[12] Nurtured and protected by the symbolic power of the bull – emblem of a proud warrior people – Burghead survived for over five hundred years before being destroyed by fire around AD 900.[13] It is tempting, though unproven, to blame the Norse for the conflagration, though in any event the kings of Pictland had long since taken themselves, their families, officials, slaves and hangers-on to reside in the palaces and strongholds of the south. A century later the mighty citadel at Burghead lay more or less derelict, a victim of shifting architectural fashion and the changing status of Fortriu itself.

The story of Pictish Fortriu's transformation into Scottish Moray is one of the most mysterious in an already obscure period of history. The problem is not merely a lack of evidence, exasperating though that is. We must also deal with the deliberate fabrications and distortions inflicted on the documentary record by both Scottish kings and historians in the centuries after Macbeth. The object of that exercise was to damn in the eyes of posterity, and hopefully of their contemporaries, the claims of the ruling house of Moray to govern Scotland, a claim that Macbeth had made good, but which his successors, with the exception of his short-lived stepson, Lulach, failed to achieve. We must be even more careful than usual in choosing what to believe.

What happened to Fortriu? By the eleventh century, historians were asserting that members of the Cenel Loarn, a branch of Dál Riata's royal family, headed up the Great Glen into northern Pictland, presumably around the same time as Kenneth mac Alpin was making his assault on the Pictish throne in the south. We should not necessarily believe this assertion, but nor can we disregard it. At the very least we must accept that this was what was believed. It was certainly as easy to travel through the Great Glen into Fortriu as it was to cross against the grain of the mountains of Drumalban into the eastern plains around Perth, as Kenneth did.

Briefly to sketch in their pre-Scottish background, the Cenel Loarn ruled Dál Riata in the first half of the eighth century, having temporarily ousted the Cenel nGabrain (Kenneth mac Alpin's forebears) from the throne of the western kingdom.[14] Their powerbase – remembered today in the area of northern Argyll known as Lorne but also including Ardnamurchan and the islands of Colonsay, Mull, Tiree and Coll – lay just to the south of the Great Glen, providing them with an obvious route through which to get to know – presumably first as enemies, then as allies and ultimately as family – Fortriu's royal house. Within a century, however, northern Pictland lay reeling from the catastrophic death at the hands of the Norse of Eóganán, the last Pictish king to come from Fortriu (839), along with his brother and many of his nobility. Dál Riata's king died along with them.[15]

We can also conclude beyond much doubt that Viking attack had already proved disastrous for at least one very important institution within Fortriu. Three of the monks buried in the graveyard at Portmahomack had been sliced right to the bone by a blade, though at least one survived the assault. Another, who was killed, looks to have been attacked from behind, succumbing ultimately whilst on his knees. The monastery complex was largely destroyed by fire, the stone walls of the church and at least four enormous stone crosses cast down and the pieces scattered around the ground between 780 and 820.[16]

The threat showed no signs of going away. Around 847, the

Norse of Ireland were on the prowl again in the Irish Sea, targeting Dál Riata's island territories around 847. Though the Hebrides probably remained at least nominally under Dalriadan control for another century, those best placed to leave their homeland had both the incentive and the opportunity to look for a new start at the other end of the familiar route into the north.[17] Perhaps members of the Cenel Loarn did indeed leave the sea lochs and steep-sided peaks of northern Argyll for the broad mountains and plains of Fortriu.

These were not peasants picking their weary way through tussocky slopes and treacherous bogs with their few precious belongings. This was Loarn's élite, its men of action and their well-connected wives, come to rejuvenate Fortriu, now that Pictland's throne was occupied by those who had no links with the northern heart of the kingdom.* Perhaps the newcomers made their move even before Kenneth mac Alpin launched his formal bid for the Pictish throne. For Kenneth himself, such a development may well have proved fortuitous. An alliance with a rejuvenated Fortriu led by distant relatives, who, like he, were as much Picts as Gaels, would surely strengthen his bid to sit in state in the halls of Forteviot.[18] One thing we should not presume is that these Gaels brought with them into Pictland the ancient enmity between Kenneth's Cenel nGabrain and the Cenel Loarn. That was ancient Dalriadan history.

When Kenneth died, in 858, he was described in the Irish annals as king of the Picts in Latin, not king of Fortriu in Gaelic, as Eóganán and his two predecessors had been.[19] He

---

* After Eóganán's death, the Pictish throne passed to a line of short-lived kings from the south before Kenneth mac Alpin swept them aside.

was not, of course, a king of Fortriu and, as far as we can tell, the new king never ventured into the north, so it makes sense that the Irish chroniclers used the broader, less geographically specific term. Nevertheless, Kenneth was careful to maintain an interest in the ancient heartland of his kingdom, presumably appreciating the historic nature of its relationship to the Pictish whole. It made sense for the king to bring about the promotion of Tuathal, abbot of Dunkeld – whose church he was busy sponsoring as *the* centre of Columba's cult in Pictland – to bishop of Fortriu as well, even though the northern Church had not been part of the Columban family since the early eighth century.[20] The fact that he chose to keep Fortriu's main bishopric, probably based at Rosemarkie, as the pre-eminent episcopal seat for the whole of Pictland makes it clear that Kenneth's kingship reached across the Grampian mountains, even if he personally did not.

For Fortriu, on the other hand, this was the end of a long and august chapter in the region's history. Its leaders' apparent equanimity over losing control of the kingship might suggest that Kenneth was astute enough to treat them with respect and, perhaps, that they themselves straddled the increasingly blurred political divide between Dál Riata and Pictland, just like the king. However, they soon had a far more pressing issue to deal with than the niceties of their relationship with the new dynasty.

Within only a few years of Kenneth mac Alpin's death in 858, Fortriu faced the prospect of a Norse colony on the doorstep as a highly successful warband led by Olaf the White, ruler of Dublin, swept across the Irish Sea into the northern Scottish mainland around 866. These particular intruders were bought off three years later with the promise of tribute and the giving of hostages,[21] but the terse descriptions of the events in the Irish chronicles surely belie the terrible uncertainty that the northern Picts must have felt as they tried to figure out the enemy's intentions. Was this an attempt at permanent annexation through the establishment of longphorts (trading colonies with direct access to the sea), as had already happened in Ireland? What would happen to Fortriu's remaining monasteries at the hands of a pagan invader? Would Pictland's ruler, far away across the mountains, lift a finger to help those in the north, or would the region's nobility have to look entirely to their own defence?

The king, Constantine I, Kenneth mac Alpin's son, did indeed avenge the attack on Fortriu, though entirely coincidentally. Soon after Olaf had successfully brought down the mighty British fortress of Dumbarton in 870, the restless Norseman headed into Scotland once more; but this time, perhaps having realised that Fortriu no longer saw much, if anything, of the king, he took a hundred ships and headed for central Scotland. Though the Norse 'wasted' Pictland and stayed a few months there, Olaf had finally overreached himself and Constantine managed to defeat and kill him. This was not the end of the story, though. A decade or so later the Pictish king was himself overwhelmed by the Danes of Northumbria at Dollar, some ten miles north of the River Forth, before finally dying at the hands of another force (either Danish or Norwegian) which landed at Inverdovat at the mouth of the Tay in 877. This last battle's most serious consequence was the doubt it cast on the new dynasty's ability to protect the kingdom, unleashing the

ambitions of rival claimants to the throne in a contest that
Giric won, temporarily at least.[22]

In the past, historians might well have been tempted to
conclude that this new challenger came from Fortriu, with its
long-standing interest in the kingship. However, there is a hint
that Fortriu's leaders, far from being involved, were none too
pleased with the latest twist and turn in Pictish politics. Of
course, if they had nailed their colours to Kenneth mac Alpin's
mast, then this is entirely understandable. But there is strong
circumstantial evidence to suggest that Giric had a Gaelic background too, not least in his determination to give the Pictish
Church the same freedoms as its Dalriadan counterpart.[23] It
is possible that the new king was himself a grandson of Kenneth
mac Alpin, through his mother, who was perhaps Kenneth's
daughter. He might also have been a member of the third
branch of the Dalriadan royal family, the descendants of Angus,
whose powerbase, the island of Islay, was invaded by the Norse
in 847.

Of all the Dalriadan families that supposedly came with
Kenneth and went on to 'found' Scottish provinces,[24] only the
house of Angus gave its name to the later Scottish creation, a
name that the region still bears today. It would be only natural
if Giric placed his own trusted friends or relations in this crucial
zone north of the Tay, especially if he were intent on a rather
more serious Gaelicisation of the Pictish kingdom than either
Kenneth or his immediate successors had wished, or dared, to
embark upon.

In 889 Giric ended his days in the ancient hill-fort of
Dundurn, situated in a narrow glen in the province of Strathearn,
thirty miles west of Perth. There is a slim chance that he died

peacefully in his bed, but the *Prophecy of St Berchan*, a notoriously garbled chronicle of the late eleventh century, asserts that it was the men of Fortriu who killed him.[25] It is not difficult to imagine Kenneth's young grandsons, Donald and Constantine, fleeing north or perhaps to Ireland, where their aunt had married into the powerful Tara dynasty, once Giric had taken their throne. Giric's own death was surely a counter-coup and it is not surprising that the return of the mac Alpins was made possible, in part, by the support of the men of Fortriu, if they had indeed helped Kenneth forty years before. Donald now became the first named king of 'Alba', followed by the long-lived and highly successful Constantine.

So, despite a thousand years of history telling of the inexorable rise of the house of mac Alpin, mighty forefathers of the Scottish kings, the truth is that they, like others before and after them, were swept in and out of power on the strength of the personality of the next potential king and of the alliances that they were able to make across the kingdom. Fortriu, on the other hand, no longer had a direct stake in this troublesome competition; its rulers may have become king-makers, but they were no longer kings.

As a result, those writing history seem to have lost interest in Fortriu and, for the hundred and fifty years following Olaf's occupation in 866, the province scarcely gets a mention, even when its southern part came to be called 'Moreb', or Moray, in the sources. But this does not mean that nothing was happening. On the contrary, Moray's lords were busy adjusting to a changing political landscape. Over the course of the tenth century, their world was drawn ever closer into a Norse orbit, and they needed strength, vigilance, cunning and the subtle arts of diplomacy to prevent the kingdom's northern frontier from haemorrhaging away to an enemy that, by AD 1000, was clearly here to stay.

The northern mainland of Scotland had its own charms for the Norse as a potential source of booty, slaves, essentials such as timber, suppliers and customers for their European trade, and, eventually, land with which to keep their men in a suitably amenable frame of mind. The region also offered those Scandinavians now settled in Ireland a vital element of strategic control over the northern approaches to the Irish Sea as a riposte to the growing power of the Norse lords of the Western Isles, who would eventually acquire them from Dál Riata.[26]

Unfortunately, the dramatic hyperbole of the Scandinavian Sagas leaves us with very little firm information with which to assess Norse progress in taking and holding even their eventual heartland in Orkney, never mind parts of the northern mainland of Scotland. Giric was fortunate that Norse aggression from the Hebrides seems to have ground to a temporary halt in the aftermath of Olaf the White's death, though the fact that it started up again as soon as the Scottish king was dead suggests that he may have had some kind of 'arrangement' with them. If he had come from out of the west – from Islay in particular, as the descendants of Angus supposedly did – then he may even have offered them a swap – an island that they were going to take anyway, for peace and quiet, while he got on with claiming the Scottish throne.

According to the Sagas, Olaf's son, Thorstein the Red, did carve out an impressive empire for himself in the Western Isles, before going on a conquering spree across northern Scotland in the company of Sigurd of Orkney.[27] Sigurd himself was reputedly buried around 893 at 'Ekkialsbakki', or Cyder Hall, on the north bank of the Dornoch Firth (the Oykell [Ekkial] estuary) in Sutherland, after an epic battle with a Scottish earl named Maelbrigde 'Tooth'* (so called because he had a very prominent incisor which ultimately brought about Sigurd's demise).[28] However, even the Sagas admit that, despite their claims of a Norse empire across northern Scotland, as late as *c.*900 there was still a Scottish earl of Caithness, named Duncan, who was married to a daughter of Thorstein the Red.[29]

That there were violent encounters between natives and Norse, up to and including battles in which both sides might engage in devious tactics and downright treachery, cannot be denied. But even the people of Easter Ross seem to have grown used to a Norse presence in their waters, within sight of the Moray coast. Indeed, it is remarkable that the monastery of Portmahomack, so catastrophically sacked around 800, appears to have leapt back into industrial production almost immediately. It is true that the monks had gone, but there were plenty of other clients – Pictish, Scottish *and* Norse – to keep them busy, albeit making much plainer fare than their tonsured masters had required. A hoard buried around AD 1000 contained, among other things, 'coins of English and French kings of the ninth–tenth centuries and a number of silver arm-rings – the

---

* The story goes that Sigurd tricked Maelbrigde in battle and killed him, cutting off his head and attaching it to his saddle, whereupon the dead man's protruding incisor cut into Sigurd's leg, giving him fatal blood poisoning (*The Orkneyinga Saga*, pp. 203–4). The real Maelbrigde must have perished before 997 when the line of Aed mac Kenneth died out, since he seems to have had no aspirations to the throne of Scotland, unlike his brother, Finlay.

ring-silver of the Norse who used them as money'. The conclu-
sion is striking. 'We can see now that this was a smith's hoard
waiting to be converted to the commission of the next warlords
– be they Viking or Mormaer'.[30] But for all that these metal-
workers seem to have flourished even as the monastery and the
surrounding monumental landscape lay abandoned all around,
this particular smith was not able to come back for his treasure.

This phase of the story of Portmahomack indicates that there
was a positive side to the Norse presence off Scottish waters.
Their penchant for long-distance trade (which probably explains
the Frankish coins in Pictish/Scottish hands) made them attractive to those fortunate enough to be engaged in an industry
for which any Dark Age warrior would be prepared to pay.
Large cargo ships ploughed their way up and around the Scottish
coast, with Orkney acting 'as a hub of routes for the Atlantic
trade, a nexus for a network that stretched from Dublin and
York to Norway, Iceland and Greenland', even if it were not
yet a distinct Norse earldom.[31]

It is easy to overplay Norse success in acquiring territory in
this period. When they were pushed out of Ireland for around
forty years after 880, they did manage to cast their net around
the Irish Sea world for alternative bases and a salve to their
wounded pride, focusing their efforts on Cumbria (the southern
part of the British kingdom of Strathclyde), as well as the
Hebrides and, eventually, the former Danish kingdom based
on York.[32] Fortriu was certainly attacked again, in 904,[33] but
the Norse were beaten off and, so far as we can tell, did not
come back until the tail-end of that century. Even in Orkney,
the Norse presence was still probably restricted to scattered
settlements interspersed among native communities. Some might

have been traders but most seem to have divided their time between farming and that most pleasant pastime of summer plundering. There is no contemporary evidence for the steely authority of a Norse earl of Orkney before the later tenth century.[34]

So, for much of the later ninth and early tenth centuries, the Norse could best be described as a complicating factor, a sporadic nuisance or useful sideline in the quarrels of Pictland's – then Scotland's – kings and provincial rulers. Nevertheless, whatever the true magnitude of the threat from the north, and, given that the members of Pictland's elite were warriors first and foremost, there was considerable political capital to be made out of scaring abbots and farmers with the thought of a Norse invasion. Certainly, it may have been the initial phases of Viking raiding, the newcomers' fearsome reputation spreading like a summer storm ahead of them, that drove Fortriu's leaders to instigate a great leap forward. This involved no less than a complete overhaul of the administrative mechanisms that underpinned the entire agricultural system and the corresponding assessments of who should hand over what in order to sustain the kingdom's warrior elite. In essence, the land was now rationalised into units later known in Gaelic as *dabaig* (anglicised to davoch), whether or not the landowner was a layman or the Church.

These were the property of a tenant farmer, or perhaps farmers, if more than one son had inherited the land. In addition to the turf dwellings which they would have shared with their animals, a conglomeration of smaller buildings nearby housed their unlanded servants and unfree serfs, who could not leave the property to which they were attached. However, their lives were ruled less by the edicts of distant rulers than by the constraints of the agricultural cycle.

It is a testament to the power, not to mention the imagination, of these Pictish kings that they were able to transform the landscape, certainly within Fortriu, in such a coherent and efficient way. Each davoch was made up of everything that the farmer needed, from fishing and timber rights to arable and pasture land, including, on occasions, summer grazing some distance away because nothing more convenient lay to hand. When those responsible for the reorganisation ran out of compact units, they lumped leftover bits together, so that everyone had everything, but some of it might be somewhere else.[35]

To pull off such a remarkable piece of planning required a systematic understanding of the resources available: in effect, exactly the same kind of information as was so effectively recorded in the *Domesday Book* more than two hundred years later. And to justify collecting the data and working out how it all fitted together, not to mention sorting out the allocation of land to people (though presumably they would try to keep the status quo as much as possible), the Pictish kings needed an extraordinary threat. Though it is far from clear when these changes took place, the early ninth century might be a good guess – it was certainly the period when other kingdoms in western Europe, most notably Charlemagne's Frankish empire, were doing very similar things. It would be hard for anyone to argue against making the most efficient use of the kingdom's resources to support the king and his warriors in their patriotic struggle against the forces of the infidel Norse. The end result, whether or not the kingdom came under attack, was a richer, more powerful warrior class sustained by an efficient taxation system, albeit one based on raw materials – grain, meat, dairy produce and so on – rather than hard cash.

Naturally, the kings of Fortriu paid particular attention to the lands surrounding their own castles, carving out 'a unique and distinct cluster of multiple-[davoch] lands in the immediate vicinity of Inverness', as well as Dun-da-Lamh, some fifty miles to the south-west. No doubt the home-farms surrounding Burghead were equally well provided for, but, sadly, all trace of these arrangements has disappeared.[36] Though the archaeological evidence suggests that ninth-century kings of Fortriu, like Constantine and his brother, Angus, no longer lived in lofty fortresses such as the one at Inverness that Columba had visited two hundred years before, they may not have moved very far into timber palaces on the plains, which are notoriously difficult to identify archaeologically.

This new penchant for low-lying, inland residences, following the model of the latest, state-of-the-art monastery-cum-palace at Forteviot, may partly explain the abandonment of Fortriu's citadels by AD 900, as does the threat of Viking war-galleys making a shock appearance, though the general insecurity in the region may also have prompted its kings to spend more time in the south. At the same time, any reorganisation that Constantine – the most likely candidate – instigated in Fortriu may also have given him the extra financial security to construct Forteviot.[37]

So far as everyone else was concerned, life had to carry on, preferably much the same as it always had, or at least for as long as each short-lived generation could remember, punctuated by moments of terror when the hill-top beacons blazed their warning that the enemy had been sighted. Those not quick enough to get out of the way of even a hit-and-run raid on the coast – no matter their status, their age or their sex – ran the risk of being taken into slavery and shipped off to Norse colonies in the British Isles or further afield. But these were still unusual events and the affairs of kings and nobles, who came and went on the fickle tides of political power, were of only passing interest to those engaged in the constant battle against the vagaries of the seasons and the tyranny of disease.

The day began and ended with the sun's rise and fall – only the very privileged would make use of candles for any length of time. The year, meandering its way inexorably through the seasons, brought periods of intense labour punctuated by interludes of relative idleness. The Church might preach that man stood at the head of the chain of being encompassing the rest of the natural world, but the toilers on the land knew full well the control that nature exerted over their lives. If their rulers were able to mediate successfully with the Divine powers that governed weather and fertility, then that was greatly to their credit, but it should not be relied upon.

The local warband had its uses, of course. No leader could hold power for long if he failed to protect those on whom he relied for direct support, and, by extension, the rest of the social and economic networks that put food on the table and surpluses on the market to pay for the weapons, horses and expensive jewellery that distinguished, at a quick glance, the warrior from the tiller of the soil. Most people probably had more faith in the local saint, though, whose presence in the area, however many centuries ago, was still remembered as if it were yesterday.

The holy man's miraculous record against some of the immediate dangers that haunted their lives – childbirth, crossing a river, the hailstorm that could destroy a whole crop – was often far more impressive and useful than the drunken boasting emanating from the lord's hall, and he was, of course, the reason for holy days and fairs, when local people could officially down tools and enjoy some partying of their own. The more recent saints, as well as many of the living monks who might occasionally be seen working hard at their devotions, were *Céli Dé* – 'Friends of God' – disciples of the reforming movement that had arrived in Scotland from Ireland from the ninth century onwards.[38] Like their royal benefactors, the Culdees do not seem to have ventured into Fortriu, presumably because the monasteries of Portmahomack and Rosemarkie were too well-established, too vulnerable to sudden attack and, more pertinently, now too far away to attract royal patronage.

Intriguingly, it has been argued that, for the first three hundred years of Alba's existence, 'Moray was not ... regarded routinely as part of Scotland, and there is place-name evidence which suggests that the people of Moray in turn did not regard themselves as "Scots"'.[39] Unfortunately, after 904 they were not called the men of Fortriu either. Another chronicle reference to that same 904 event (an invasion of Fortriu by the Norse in which Imar, grandson of Imar was killed) records the death of *'Ead ri Cruithentuaithe'* (Ead, king of the Picts), which may be an Irish attempt to deal with the problem caused by the new use of the term 'Alba' for the lands south of the Mounth, leaving those to the north to be described (on this one occasion) as *'Cruithentuaithe'*.[40]

Such a split – together with the tantalising reference to the otherwise unknown Ead as king of the northern region – might then lead us to suppose that Moray and Ross were going their own way, effectively independent of the kingdom of Scotland. We could also point to the emergence of southern bishops as the premier ecclesiastics in the new Scotland, in contrast to the apparent unity in the Pictish Church promoted fifty years previously when Kenneth mac Alpin kept the bishop of Fortriu, based at Rosemarkie, as primate of his kingdom.[41]

If this scenario really does represent reality, it is likely to have been true for only a short period of time, perhaps during Giric's rather revolutionary reign (878–89). We could even speculate that it had been Ead who led the men of Fortriu against Giric in 889 on behalf of the mac Alpins (in the person of Donald, son of Constantine, 889–900), though his own royal title would not necessarily have precluded him from acknowledging Donald as king of Alba thereafter. This is the only reference to such a kingship. What makes all this even more curious is the fact that Donald was killed, allegedly 'because of his daughter', in Forres, situated nearly thirty miles east of Inverness in the heart of coastal Moray.

So, here we have Donald killed by the very people who supposedly helped to put him and his family back on the throne. This smacks of agreements ignored or broken, perhaps involving marriage if the reference to his daughter is true. Moray disappears during the long, eventful reign of Donald's cousin, Constantine II, but the memory of his death almost certainly did not. When Donald's son, Malcolm, eventually took the throne in 944, one of his first acts could easily be interpreted as revenge, bringing the name of 'Moreb' (Moray) into the history books for the first time.

As ever, the laconic description of this event in the near-contemporary *Chronicle of the Kings of Alba* begs more questions than it answers: 'Malcolm proceeded with his army into Moray, and killed Cellach'.[42] We do not have any real idea who this Cellach was. He may have been the region's ruler, though we should not discount the possibility that he was a churchman.[43] Having dealt with the long overdue matter of his father's death, the king then turned his attention to more important affairs, especially once Edmund of England had entrusted him with Cumbria. Malcolm seems to have been killed in 954 by the men of the Mearns at Fetteresso, near Stonehaven, at the far south-eastern end of the Mounth (though some chroniclers did attempt to blame the men of Moray once more). This was clearly a ruler capable of making his presence felt the length and breadth of Scotland and beyond; as the *Prophecy of St Berchan* says, 'he will have nine years in the kingdom, traversing their boundaries'.[44] However, such indefatigability did not necessarily make him popular.

When Malcolm was killed, the crown passed, as usual, to the other branch of the mac Alpin royal family,[45] to Indulf, Constantine's son, before eventually coming to Malcolm's own son, Dubh, in 962. However, Dubh – who earned the revealing nickname of the 'Vehement' or 'Impetuous' – was immediately faced with a rebellion led by Indulf's son, the equally hasty prospective king, Culen. Though Dubh won that battle – possibly fought near Dunning, south-west of Perth and involving the men of Atholl, who were probably Culen's supporters – he was 'driven from the kingdom' a few years later and eventually killed in 966 'by the Scots themselves'.

In fact, just like his grandfather, Dubh seems to have met his death in Forres and is at least as likely to have become surplus to requirements within his own family as to the man who had expelled him, the current king, Culen.* But it is striking that he is said to have gone into exile outside the kingdom (of Scotland), Moray perhaps acting as neutral territory in which Dubh hoped he would be beyond Culen's reach. Though both Donald and Dubh came to sticky ends there, it is still possible that these descendants of Constantine mac Kenneth had family ties in Moray, perhaps in the female line and, in Dubh's case, his death may not necessarily have been caused by the same people as had given him refuge.

Dubh's brother, Kenneth, had an uneasy start to his reign, taking over after Culen's death in 971, but facing a challenge from the latter's brother, Olaf (probably because of an unsuccessful expedition against the Britons of Strathclyde) which was settled when Kenneth killed Olaf six years later. This tendency in the later tenth century for brothers to attempt to slot themselves into the succession can only have exacerbated the crisis that was already threatening to take the throne of Scotland in its bloody grip. With Kenneth's demise history repeated itself: he met his violent end at the hands of 'his own men' at Fettercairn, less than twenty miles from Fetteresso, where his father, Malcolm, had been killed. Both are situated in the Mearns, Kenneth supposedly dying through the treachery of a daughter of the region's mormaer (Angus) whose son he had killed.[46] One thing that seems certain is that there was no

---

* The two branches were, respectively, the descendants of Constantine mac Kenneth, and Aed mac Kenneth (see Chapter 4, p. 85).

love lost between the line of Constantine mac Kenneth (to which both Malcolm and Kenneth belonged) and the family that controlled Angus and the Mearns. Once again, if this branch of the royal family were based in Mar, immediately to the north over the mountains, then their animosity was directed against near neighbours.

It is worth considering briefly the relationship between the crown and the rulers of the provinces into which Scotland was divided. By the end of the tenth century, the mormaers and their family trees had been amalgamated into a story of how their roots connected to that of the royal line, meaning that they all, ultimately, could trace their descent back to Erc, the legendary father of Fergus Mor, who brought the Gaels to Dál Riata from Ireland. However, this scholarly understanding provided some with a closer relationship to the Cenel nGabrain than others. The mormaer of Strathearn's family was deemed to be most recently related to the royal family, followed by Gowrie and Fife; then came the northern portion of clan Conaing (possibly Buchan); finally, quite a long way back, came Moray and Angus.[47] Whether or not the precise details of these family trees bear any relationship to reality, the implications for Scotland's senior families of their comparative proximity to the crown in terms of blood must have played a crucial role in politics.

These genealogies have little to say about the more recent relationships created through marriage in particular, connections that, as we will see, could bring members of regional families perilously close to the throne. Finally, we must remember that the line of Aed mac Kenneth – the southern branch of the royal family possibly based in Atholl – died with Constantine,

Culen's son, in 997. As a result, the political and territorial map of Scotland may have been redrawn when the remaining royal family, based in the north, split into two and perhaps appropriated royal lands in the south belonging to their former rivals.

None of this takes us much closer to understanding the politics of Moray itself. Neither wholly in nor defiantly out of the orbit of the kings of Scots, the ambiguity of the region's situation can be found in both the contemporary annals and in more recent histories. Modern commentators tend to the view that the region was not independent, at the same time acknowledging that it probably was not considered a part of Scotland itself.

Making sense of this conundrum requires a mental leap away from later medieval and modern notions of nationalism and identity of the one kingdom, one nation variety. The people of Moray almost certainly acknowledged the lordship of the king of Scots.[48] In that respect, they were no different from the inhabitants of Lothian. But the region's fundamental importance to the history of Pictland meant that the bond between Moray and Scotland was bound to be much closer and more complex, with intermarriage and political alliances helping to obscure some of the distinctions between them, rather like the relationship between Pictland and Dál Riata two hundred years before.

We can surmise, then, that the rulers of Moray retained a *de facto* detachment from the dictates (infrequent as they probably were anyway) of the king of Scots that was greater than that enjoyed even by the most powerful mormaers within Scotland. By the mid-tenth century, we might also suppose that

Macbeth's great-grandfather, Donald, was a leading member of Moravian society, if not its ruler. However, it was only with Macbeth's grandfather, Ruari, that the family raised its head above the parapet of Scottish history.

Ruari plays no direct part in this story, though if things had worked out differently for Macbeth, he might well have emerged from the shadows of historical indifference to become the founding father of a long line of Scottish kings. He had at least two sons, the elder of whom was Maelbrigde, and the younger, Finlay. He might also have had another son, Donald, who, along with Malcolm, Culen's son, granted the lands of Biffie to the monastery of Deer in neighbouring Buchan.[49] Is this grant evidence for a family relationship between the southern royal house of Aed mac Kenneth (Culen's family) and the house of Moray? Atholl lay directly south of medieval Moray, which included Badenoch in those days, though it was not easy to cross from one to the other by horse. In any event, somewhere along the line between Macbeth's great-grandfather, Donald, and his grandfather, Ruari, there must have been a marriage with a daughter of the house of Aed mac Kenneth.* Ordinarily such a union would have been unlikely to influence the course of Scotland's history, but, when that line died out in 997, the significance of his maternal ancestry was not lost on Ruari's eldest surviving son, Finlay.

As the second millennium began its disquieting approach, Ruari's sons had more to worry about than their relationship

---

* This girl could have been a daughter of Culen mac Indulf (966–71), Indulf mac Constantine (954–62) or, at a stretch, Constantine mac Aed (900–44) (see Woolf, 'The "Moray question"', pp. 154–5).

with the royal house of Scotland. Far to the north, a new power was rising out of the remnants of an impressive Pictish past and more recent Norse raiding and trading concerns. The Norwegian earldom of Orkney was now making good the long-standing Norse potential to destabilise the far reaches of the Scottish mainland.

Sigurd Hlodvisson may, as the thirteenth-century *Orkneyinga Saga* asserts, have been the latest in a long line of Norse *jarls* – royal lieutenants – of Orkney – or, as the contemporary evidence suggests, the first.[50] The credit for turning the rather footloose Scandinavian presence on the Orcadian archipelago into something much more effective should probably be given to the powerful Danish monarch, Harold Bluetooth, grand-father of the even mightier Cnut. Earl Sigurd, nicknamed *digri* ('the Stout'), was presumably known to the king as someone with all the attributes associated with an imposing physical presence and was therefore just the man to be promoted to *jarl* of Orkney in the 970s or 980s. King Harold was already Christian, but the tales about Sigurd strongly suggest that he was not, until, as the traditional story has it, King Olaf 'the Good' of Norway forcibly converted him in 995.[51]

Sigurd – and his youngest son, Thorfinn, after him – proved an enthusiastic political manipulator, keen to play off any and all of the surrounding political factions, whether they were Scandinavian, Scottish or Irish, to his own advantage. His influ-ence reputedly extended west across to the Hebrides, where he set up an earl of his own, named Gilli in the Sagas. Towards the end of his life he was courted by both the crown of Scotland and the famous Irish high king, Brian Boruma.[52]

As ever, the precise details of Sigurd's heroic exploits the length and breadth of the Irish Sea, as well as across the northern Scottish mainland, remain shrouded in baffling hyperbole. The earl did not control 'Ross, Moray, Sutherland and Argyll'.[53] However, Sigurd does seem to have made great efforts to extend his own territories into Caithness, the far north-eastern portion of the Scottish mainland. Not surprisingly, this provoked a reaction from the native earls, such as the otherwise unknown Hundi and Melsnati, who, on occasion, must have included the rulers of Moray.[54] Even the notorious battle with Maelbrigde 'Tooth' may actually be misplaced by a century and refer to Macbeth's uncle, though the latter was not responsible, even posthumously, for Sigurd's death. As we will see, this was not the last battle fought between the earl of Orkney and the earls of Moray.

At the same time, warfare was only one method of promoting the interests of both sides: the Sagas state on more than one occasion that Scottish kings were prepared to countenance members of the Orcadian ruling house as earls of Caithness under their jurisdiction.[55] But as the new millennium came and went, it became more and more likely that the kings of Scots referred to in the Norse Sagas – and the Irish chronicles – were members of the house of Moray rather than the southern-based descendants of Kenneth mac Alpin.

In 997, the death of Constantine (III) mac Culen, the last descendant of Kenneth mac Alpin's son, Aed, brought to an end the one element of stability in the otherwise volatile Scottish succession process, the perpetual rotation of the crown between that family and the descendants of Kenneth's elder son,

Constantine. However, the mere fact that a royal bloodline had died out on the male side was unlikely to cause much of a dent in the ambitions of those who had been card-carrying members of the Aed mac Kenneth entourage. All they needed was another powerful branch of the family onto which they could fix their allegiance. There was not much time since another candidate must be found through the female line and enough support gathered around his claim before the death of the current king, Kenneth (III) mac Dubh.

As already mentioned, Finlay of Moray's mother or grand-mother was probably a daughter of either Indulf mac Constantine or Culen mac Indulf, kings from the line of Aed mac Kenneth. Finlay would have been known to the mormaers of Scotland but was not one of them, a potentially useful attribute. Here, then, his supporters claimed, was the next king of Scots, a man capable (in theory at least) of maintaining the crucial balance of power between north and south.

This was the tense and volatile world into which Macbeth was born.

PART TWO

The Making of a King

CHAPTER 6

Murder as Usual

> Art thou afeard
> To be the same in thine own act and valour
> As thou art in desire?
>
> *Macbeth*, Act I, Scene vii

In medieval Scotland – as in most places for most of history – the birth of a son inspired much rejoicing. For the woman in labour, the last searing moments of childbirth were followed by a final few agonising seconds as she waited to see if her husband would turn away, tight-lipped, at news of a girl, or come running to praise her efforts in giving him a boy. It was the woman's role in life to provide sons and, though daughters might come to be loved – for their beauty, their noble spirit or their obedience – it was their brothers whose appearance in the world was naturally prized.[1]

Finlay of Moray was no doubt overjoyed to hear of the birth of his son. Perhaps, like any expectant father, he had spent the previous hours pacing his hall, stale and silent without its usual wild company. Or, returning from yet another expedition, had thrown himself off his horse, mud-spattered and stinking with sweat, to demand news of his wife. Sadly, but not entirely unexpectedly, the identity of the lady herself is unknown.[2]

We do not know exactly when Macbeth was born, but it is feasible, if somewhat poetic, to imagine that his arrival coincided with that of the new millennium, give or take a few years either side of it. Nor do we know where. The lands belonging to the rulers of Moray seem to have 'stretched from Inverness southwards to Strathspey' and, while they could certainly have called on the hospitality of members of their nobility, their wives would probably have preferred to go into labour in their own stronghold.[3] We can be sure that Finlay's lady would not have arranged to spend her confinement in the citadel of Burghead, destroyed by fire a century before and symbolic of a royal Pictish past long gone. Perhaps it would be overly romantic, too, to read much into the name of a fortification called *Caisteil Finlaib* – Finlay's castle – situated a few miles downstream from Nairn, on the northern side of the hill of Geddes not far from Cawdor, with its own Macbeth associations.[4] This was once a hill-fort with timber-laced walls, very old* but, like Craig Phadraig further west, still used by the rulers of Fortriu and probably Moray centuries later.

Such a castle did not need to be an imperious eyrie, so long as it was essentially defensible, and preferably not too near the coast so that passing Viking raiders would be unlikely to stumble across it. It did not need to occupy a large floor space either, since its architects could easily build upwards, to create a timber tower of the type more usually associated with Macbeth's

* i.e. Iron Age, and therefore more than two thousand years old.

successor, Malcolm III, in Dunfermline. The internal apart-
ments would have been small but cosy, the light of a fire
brightening the smoke-clouded walls.[5] The surrounding country
was pleasant: gentle hills, well-stocked rivers overhung with
alders, and a rich, loamy soil. This is as good a guess as any at
the kind of residence frequented by Finlay of Moray and his
family in the eleventh century.

The worry of childbirth over, the newborn must now be
given a name. Macbeth means, literally, 'the son of life', and
was not particularly common.[6] We might wonder if the birth
of this child was the result of years of prayer, his parents more
than happy to offer their grateful thanks to the Almighty by
remembering His son every time they addressed the boy. The
prayers would not stop with the successful delivery, however,
given the likelihood that even a high-born child might succumb
to any number of diseases or conditions. Fortunately, this one
proved robust. His mother, having done her duty, could rest
now. It was not customary for highborn ladies to breastfeed
their own offspring, but to entrust the task to a wet-nurse,
presumably a sturdy, well-practised local woman. Even before
he was weaned, though, Macbeth was probably sent away to
live with foster parents, standard practice within Gaelic society.

As news of his birth spread across the country, noble families were no doubt soon vying with each other for the honour
of bringing up Finlay of Moray's son. Such a bond affected
both sides deeply. The boy was obliged to honour and, eventually, protect his surrogate parents just as he would his own;
in return, his foster father and brothers would watch his back
for the rest of their lives. They would also teach him how to
be a man, but not just any man: 'Not as a churl looks to the

heritage of his children, not between flag-stone and kneading-trough, nor from the fire to the wall'.[7] He must learn to be a leader of men, in war and in peace, far beyond the narrow confines of home and hearth.

The child's education began early, for he had much to learn. First, of course, he must acquire the skills of the warrior: speed and dexterity with spear and sword, bow and shield, control and poise on a horse, the muscle to take a turn on the oars – but also mental attributes, including the 'gift of prudence until his warrior's flame appeared'. This military prowess was not merely a source of power. His privileged position, the reason why the farmer and the labourer toiled to feed him and his family, he owed to the protection that he must offer to those in need. 'I am a shelter for every poor man, I am a rampart of fight for every wealthy man, I give comfort to each wretch, I deal mischief to each strong man.'[8]

This was only the start for the budding paragon of noble virtues. The child also needed knowledge: of the past, which explained who he was and justified how things were in the present; of the law, the myriad of local customs and (still rare) royal pronouncements which he would be responsible for administering; of poetry and music, the better to praise those who deserved it and appreciate what was offered to him; of games such as draughts and other manly diversions to while away the long winter evenings; and of the complex rules of hospitality, the ability to sustain nights of feasting so that his reputation grew with the tales of them. He must learn how to praise without flattery and admonish without offence. Last but not least, he needed to acquire the ability, through long, hard practice, to drink prodigiously.

*

The abbey of Iona has a long and distinguished history as a major centre of Christianity, despite being situated on a tiny island in the Irish Sea.

Burghead, Moray. An enormous Pictish citadel once stood on this headland, guarding the Moray Firth.

Dundurn. This hill-fort, situated in a narrow glen stretching east from Loch Earn, was where Giric, who was probably responsible for the creation of the kingdom of Alba/Scotland, died.

The Ring of Brodgar. The landscape of Orkney is littered with enduring prehistoric monuments, compared with the less visible remains of the Norse presence in the Middle Ages.

Glamis. The residence now of the earls of Strathmore and Queen Elizabeth, the Queen Mother's childhood home, Glamis was the site of King Malcolm II's final battle. The place is also associated with Macbeth in later tradition, since it is the first of the new honours that he acquires on his way to the throne.

Dunkeld, refounded supposedly by Kenneth mac Alpin to house the relics of St Columba that were due to come to Scotland from Iona once the island had become a Norse target. King Duncan's father was abbot of Dunkeld and the monastery may have remained antipathetic to Macbeth, hence the story of the nearby Birnam wood in Shakespeare.

Cawdor, Nairnshire. More recent tradition has it that Macbeth became thane of Cawdor before taking the throne. However, the earliest versions had him become thane of Cromarty instead.

View towards Pitgaveny from Spynie castle. Pitgaveny is the site of the battle that took place between Macbeth and King Duncan. Spynie Loch, which can also be seen, has been drained in modern times, but used to give direct access to the sea.

Elgin Cathedral. After the battle at Pitgaveny, King Duncan's body was supposedly buried here, though tradition also asserts that it was taken, as was usual, to the island of Iona.

The Brecbennoch of St Columba, which was kept originally at the abbey of Dunkeld. Its abbot in the 1030s and 1040s was Crinan, father of King Duncan, who was defeated after rebelling against Macbeth in 1045.

St Serf's island, Loch Leven. The Culdee monastery there was given lands by Macbeth and his queen, Gruoch.

St Andrews Cathedral. The remains of the medieval cathedral stand on the site of the much earlier Culdee church. Bishop Maldovine of St Andrews was probably one of Macbeth's key advisers, particularly in relation to his pilgrimage to Rome.

Monte Mario, a small hill giving the pilgrim the first ecstatic view of the Holy City of Rome huddling below along the River Tiber.

Dunsinane. The remains of a prehistoric fort can still be seen on the top of the hill, which commands an excellent view both north and south. Tradition has it that this is where Macbeth met Siward's army in 1054, though the Scottish king survived to fight another day.

Essie, Aberdeenshire. Situated in the hills to the east of Moray itself, Macbeth's stepson, Lulach, who was now king, met an army of Norwegians fighting on behalf of Malcolm, son of King Duncan. There may have been some treachery, but there is no doubt that Lulach was killed.

Lumphanan peel. The remains of a later medieval castle can still be seen at Lumphanan, which is the site of Macbeth's final battle against King Duncan's son, Malcolm, and his Norwegian allies.

Macbeth's well. Local tradition has it that the Scottish king took a drink from this well just before he entered the fray of battle against Malcolm.

A medieval axe found at Lumphanan.

Sword dance. Still a staple of the Scottish country dance circuit, the dance was supposedly invented by Malcolm III immediately after killing Macbeth.

Orson Welles as a particularly moody Macbeth. The play is always being updated and reinvented but its essential message still resonates with modern audiences.

While his son was away learning the intricacies of his noble calling, Finlay must surely have become increasingly embroiled in the politics of Scotland, in pursuit of his claim to its throne. Macbeth can only have been a few years old when the kingdom – or at least the retinues, clients and hangers-on of the royal family – suffered the trauma of yet another violent end to one reign and the beginning of another.

A young man rides onto an expanse of flat ground at the head of a party of armed men. Monzievaird, plain of the bards. With a steady gaze he searches the surrounding hillsides, full of shaggy cattle, for signs of an ambush. Somewhere nearby the River Earn, broad and handsome, rushes across stones and boulders towards the loch that bears its name. Someone shouts. Malcolm holds up his hand and his followers stop behind him. Across the other side of the plain another small army has appeared. The young man can just make out the banner of his cousin, King Kenneth, among those of his kin and followers. He sighs grimly, breathing in the cool, clear air. Messengers are sent back and forth, but there is nothing to discuss. He has wasted too many years in exile in the far west since his own father, another Kenneth, was killed ten years ago.

It is time. Malcolm signals that his men should dismount. He smacks his own beast sharply on the rump, sending it careering off, back the way it had come. There will be no retreat from this battle. He and his men take their positions behind a bright line of shields. He can just see his adversaries marching across the plain, slowly turning into individual faces, grim-set, poised and ready to fight, Scot against Scot, kin against kin. Then the battle begins and the world beyond this place and this moment fades away. Malcolm hears only the harsh rhythm of his own breathing, sees nothing but the king's banner. Here, today, their futures will be decided and God alone knows which one of them has a future at all. Steel meets muscle, then bone. Their eyes lock for a moment. The older man knows at last that today death has sought him out but, even as the light fades, still he fights against it.

Malcolm seizes the banner and, as the red heat of battle begins to cool, he orders the old king's body to be placed on a litter. Soon it must be taken to its proper resting place, on Iona. But now he must make his own plans to go to Scone to become king. As he leaves the bloody plain, he cannot help but recall the look in the old man's eyes. Now he knows that Kenneth dreamt often of that moment, had imagined its coming in a thousand different ways. And he knows, too, that those sleepless nights and waking dreams are his now. Unless he can find a way to break the cycle.

In 1005, Malcolm, son of Kenneth (II) mac Dubh, returned from exile, possibly with his mother's people, the Uí Dúnlainge, whose kingdom lay on the Liffey in Leinster in eastern Ireland.[9] At Monzievaird in Strathearn, he met and killed the current king, Kenneth (III) mac Malcolm, pre-empting any possible bid from the regrouped line of Aed mac Kenneth. Finlay of Moray and his supporters in Atholl must have been aghast at this missed opportunity but there was not much they could do about it. Not yet anyway.

However, the chance to challenge Malcolm soon presented itself. In 1006 the new king decided to put his stamp on Anglo-Scottish affairs by pursuing some outstanding grievances that had sprung up since the Scots had taken control of the former Northumbrian province of Lothian.[10] The 'opportunity' probably stemmed from the fact that the bishops of Lindisfarne (now operating, for safety from Norse activity, out of Durham) held lands north of what was now, technically at least, the border between England and Scotland. The Scottish king, eager to prove who was master of these lands, devised a plan to march south into England, presumably to force the bishop to relinquish them. Apart from anything else, the opportunity to go pillaging across the border was bound to prove popular with his men and any potential supporters still unsure about the latest change of ruler. Unfortunately for Malcolm, he met his match in a young man 'of great energy and highly skilled in war', Uhtred of Northumbria.

The current earl of Northumbria was actually Uhtred's father, Waltheof, but he preferred to shut himself up in his mighty sea-fortress at Bamburgh rather than deal with the Scottish problem. So Uhtred, outraged by tales of the Scots making mischief with 'fire and slaughter' on their way south, gathered together a large force and attacked the intruders, who had now settled into besieging Durham. Malcolm only just escaped with his life, but he was one of the lucky ones. Most of his army ended up with their heads fixed on stakes around Durham's ramparts, their hair carefully braided, then washed by women who received a cow each for their trouble.[11]

This was not the way for a new king of Scots, especially one who had taken the throne by force, to maintain the confidence even of those who had supported him only a year before, never mind those who had their doubts. Indeed, Malcolm must have displayed some force of character to survive this disaster. It was surely now, when the king had little strength to resist him, that Finlay proclaimed his own rights as king.

It might seem extraordinary that a king of Scots could stand to relinquish so much of his painstakingly accumulated power and allow a region that already seems to have been semi-autonomous to free itself from his rule. But is that not a prejudice of our own time, the tendency to assume that those kingdoms which, in the end, survive and can therefore be categorised as successful, do so because they put on weight – the state acquires more power and the kingdom itself expands – steadily and constantly? A single king, particularly from a sole dynasty, was not the inevitable means of organising political power in much of Britain or in Ireland, however much kingship itself had come to dominate the political life of the nation.[12]

The idea that one man had dominion over all others far beyond his own family's territory took some getting used to, not least for those who found their own similar positions downgraded as a result. The rhetoric – largely provided by the Church – was all there, of course, but the long-drawn-out process of bringing it about remains obscured behind the actions and, eventually, the writings of those who ultimately succeeded. For the victors, that success was inevitable: a single, centralised monarchy ruling over a unitary political unit was the 'natural' institution of government and they were its true and righteous office-holders.

However far Scotland, continuing where Pictland left off, had proceeded towards centralisation – and it had clearly gone some way – the extent to which its kings held a monopoly on kingship still haunts the history of this period.[13] This is particularly true for those regions that acknowledged the jurisdiction of the king of Scots, but were not a part of the kingdom of Scotland. Since there are no death notices – nor, indeed, any notices at all – in the Irish annals for the rulers of Moray before

1020, we do not know whether the Irish viewed them as kings or as mormaers. All we do know is that when Finlay died, they described him as *ri Alban* – king of Scotland.[14]

Malcolm would certainly not have agreed to his rival staking a claim to his throne if he had had any choice in the matter. Perhaps, in practice, the deal made little difference; Moray and Scotland were already effectively two discrete power blocs with their own different outlooks and ambitions – the north fixed on Norse encroachments and relations with the Gaelic west, the south devoting much time and energy to southern and western expansion. This was also not the first time that Scotland had endured both a king and a 'king in opposition'. But these power-sharing 'agreements' represented a potentially dangerous development, one which could destabilise the already volatile succession even further for the simple reason that the rulers of the north were just as likely to desire a single Scottish kingship vested in themselves as their southern counterparts. Most Scots beyond the immediate family and friends of King Malcolm and King Finlay were no doubt hoping that the next transfer of power would be some time in coming.

In the meantime, Macbeth was growing up. The young man, his blonde moustache beginning to show, probably returned to his father's household as an adult member somewhere between 1010 and 1015. Finlay had plenty of work for his son to do, tasks that would put his years of training to the test. The most pressing problem for Moray remained Earl Sigurd. The Orcadian had his eye on Caithness, taking expeditions out every summer to go plundering in the northern Scottish mainland. These trips – like Malcolm's foray into England – unleashed the usual havoc and mayhem as the Scots fled out of the way, quite probably in the run-up to harvest, knowing full well that they would return to find their houses and crops in flames, their animals driven off.[15] Sigurd's empire also now seems to have extended across into the Hebrides, giving him a strategic grip on the northern routes through the Irish Sea.

Not surprisingly, Finlay – like other northern leaders before him – resolved to do something about the perennial Norse nuisance. Though the accounts are garbled as usual, his first move may have been to send an army into the Dales of Caithness (modern Strathnaver),[16] which was defeated, giving Sigurd greater control over the region. The Scots 'were vexed with their defeat',[17] so Finlay decided to challenge Earl Sigurd personally, agreeing to meet at Skitten Mire (Skidmore), north-west of Wick on the far northern coast of Scotland.[18]

Sigurd took this challenge seriously, worried about the numbers that Finlay was reportedly bringing against him. In the first instance, he did what any right-minded warrior would do: he consulted his mother, Audna, who, conveniently, was a 'wise woman' blessed with supernatural powers. Unfortunately she turned out to be short on sympathy for him, sneering that 'I would have reared you up long in my wool-bag if I had known that you would wish to live forever'. However, she did feel sufficiently maternal to give him a magic raven banner, which 'will bring victory to him before whom it is borne, but death to its bearer'.[19] Wound up by his mother's words, Sigurd left to try to assemble a decent-sized army, but the only way he could persuade the Orkney men to fight was by giving them full hereditary rights to their lands. This was the difference between being ruler of a province like Moray, with its well-established infrastructure, and the first *jarl* of Orkney, more used to leading a small-scale raiding party of trusted warriors.

Given the distance and nightmare conditions of travelling overland, the men of Moray probably took their galleys out of the Moray Firth and north along the coast of Ross before landing in Caithness, taking care to steer well clear of the 'Swelkie', the dreadful whirlpool that guarded the entrance to the Pentland Firth separating the mainland from Orkney.* Having presumably found somewhere to camp some distance from Skitten Mire, Finlay perhaps decided that this was a good moment to let his son flex his leadership muscles and Macbeth was despatched as commander of a small force. He can only have been in his mid-to-late teens at most. The young man led his army into a fierce, but inconclusive, battle against the Norse, whose leader was killed. The stage was now set for a battle between the two earls.

The engagement itself seems to have been a disorderly affair, in terms of any discernible tactics. As Sigurd's mother had predicted, the earl's standard-bearers did not last long, all three shot down by arrows one after the other beneath the deadly banner. However, as she had also promised, the victory ultimately went to the Orcadians. This whole episode sounds remarkably like Earl Sigurd's final battle in Ireland in 1014, suggesting that Skitten Mire did not take place all that long before, and has been confused with it, or that it did not take

---

* The whirlpool lies at the north end of the island of Stroma. According to Viking legend, it was caused by a sea witch turning the mill wheels that ground the salt to keep the seas salty. 'Swelkie' comes from the Old Norse word for 'swallower'.

place at all. In any event, the Scots seem to have lost control of Caithness far more comprehensively than ever before in the early decades of the eleventh century and its revenues were surely now making their way north to Orkney. This was not an auspicious start to Macbeth's military career and one can only imagine the long silences between father and son on the long journey home.

Fortunately for the Scots, the mighty Orcadian now diverted his attentions to the explosive politics of Ireland. For some decades now Brian 'Boruma', originally a petty king from County Clare in the far west, had slowly been working his way towards becoming king of all Ireland, a position traditionally held by the O'Neill family. He succeeded in 1002, much to the chagrin of more established dynasties, including the Uí Dúnlainge of Leinster. Over the following decade Brian managed to force all his fellow kings to acknowledge him as their overlord, though no sooner had he done so than the old hands, led by the Leinster king, Maelmorda, began looking around for allies as a prelude for war. Maelmorda's nephew and neighbour was the Norse king of Dublin, Sigtrygg 'Silkenbeard'. Sigtrygg, in turn, was keen to forge connections with Earl Sigurd, whose growing control over the Hebrides complemented the Dubliner's own interests in the Irish Sea. The affairs of Ireland and its waterways were not just an Irish concern, but of direct interest to every nation within the neighbouring islands of Britain. As this episode also makes clear, the politics of the region had advanced far beyond a straight fight between natives and Norse.

The showdown finally came in April 1014, at Clontarf to the north of Dublin. The battle was a long and bloody affair, warriors on both sides cut down 'like a field of oats'.[20] When sword, bow and spear were finally put aside, the dead included Brian, his son and grandson, Earl Sigurd of Orkney, Maelmorda of Leinster and the Scottish earl of Mar, Domnall mac Eimhin.[21] As a result, the O'Neill could resume their monopoly on the high kingship, temporarily at least. For Moray, the death of the earl of Orkney – forced eventually, by a lack of standard-bearers, to carry his raven banner himself[22] – was probably the battle's most significant outcome, in the short term at any rate.

Malcolm II, as we have noted, was related through his mother to the Uí Dúnlainge of Leinster who opposed Brian Boruma at Clontarf, along with the O'Neill, other native families and their Norse allies. While the alliances associated with one particular encounter do not prove lifelong friendship, the Scottish king's Irish relatives were, nevertheless – in 1014 at least – in cahoots with Earl Sigurd. This becomes all the more interesting when one considers that Malcolm of Scotland supposedly married off one of his own daughters to this very same earl of Orkney, probably around the time that he took the Scottish throne.[23] Given that Finlay of Moray was busy trying to stop Earl Sigurd from taking over Caithness and pushing further south, it appears that Malcolm and Finlay were not operating in separate spheres of influence, one below the Mounth, the other beyond it, and that Malcolm at least was actively pursuing a policy that – intentionally or otherwise – was bound to cause problems for Moray.

The complexity of Scottish politics is nonetheless underlined by the presence of Earl Domnall mac Eimhin of Mar on Brian Boruma's side at Clontarf. This is most interesting, if

Malcolm II's family really did come from Earl Domnall's part of Scotland, since the king's mother's family, the Uí Dúnlainge, as well as his son-in-law, Earl Sigurd, were both on the opposing side. In that context, Earl Domnall's support of Brian Boruma makes it highly unlikely that his presence was either encouraged or sanctioned by Malcolm II. However, the situation may be more complicated and it is possible that the Scottish king could even have been hedging his bets. Brian had supposedly been able to exact tribute from both sides of the Irish Sea, including parts of western Scotland that formerly comprised Dál Riata – the same area where Malcolm II of Scotland reputedly spent his years of exile and took tribute. It may be that Malcolm and Brian found they had quite a lot in common, especially when it came to raising money at the expense of the Dublin Norse, and that the earl of Mar was the Scottish king's agent in the Irish Sea region.[24]

With Earl Sigurd dead and his sons squabbling over their inheritance, the pressure on Moray, from Orkney at least, was removed for the time being. The pressure from the south, on the other hand, was becoming more intense. Malcolm II, having survived the disastrous beginning to his reign, was maturing into a wily and effective monarch with his fingers in numerous pies across Scotland and beyond. In the first instance, he sought to make use of his young grandson, Thorfinn, his daughter's child by Earl Sigurd, now being brought up in Caithness.

In 1014, Thorfinn was reckoned to be only five years old, though we might forgive the Sagas a degree of poetic licence in this, as in most other matters; he may have been slightly older, perhaps only a few years younger than Macbeth himself. In any event, Malcolm now conferred the earldom of Caithness and Sutherland on his ugly little grandson,[25] a move clearly designed to provoke the ruler of Moray, who presumably regarded the territory to the north as his, even if it was not a part of Moray itself. This would have been a good time for Finlay to exert himself, to try to regain control of Caithness and its revenues while the Orcadians were busy with their own affairs and the ostensible mormaer of Caithness was still a child. Perhaps Malcolm's shrewd move over Thorfinn had wrong-footed the Moravian. In any event, Finlay did little or nothing to redeem himself in the years after Skitten Mire, a failure that contrasted all the more strikingly with the powerful and confident kingship now practised by Malcolm II. Macbeth must have been watching his father closely, learning not just what he should do but what he ought not to do, if he wanted to rule both well and long.

Macbeth was a man now. Though we have no direct evidence to work from, it is intriguing that the earliest version of his curriculum vitae, as related by the three weird sisters in Andrew of Wyntoun's chronicle (*c.* 1420),[26] notes that his first 'job' was as thane of Cromarty.[27] The thane was an important man in medieval Scotland, though whether he was a royal official or a landowner controlling an estate of five hundred to six hundred acres in his own right is still the subject of debate.[28] In either case, he was responsible for that estate's administration, for making sure that justice was done on and for its inhabitants, for leading out the able-bodied men in time of war, and, now and again, entertaining the king and his household in his own home. This was a vastly expensive undertaking, something only a wealthy man could contemplate; indeed, the ability to entertain the king oneself was the very thing that differentiated a noble man from a base one.

Did Finlay send his teenage son across the Moray Firth to practise his skills as a land manager? It is an intriguing thought and, certainly, becoming a thane was as good a training as any for the young Macbeth to learn diplomacy (sorting out perennial squabbles between neighbours), as well as astute governance (pulling off the delicate task of extracting a proportion of the year's hard-won produce in taxation). These were exactly the skills he needed to take his place at Moray's helm once his father was gone. On the other hand, the evidence from Portmahomack suggests that Scottish control even of southern Ross was extremely tenuous and it looks as if the people there were largely left to their own devices. Cromarty lies on the Black Isle, immediately south of the peninsula on which Portmahomack is situated at its northern end. If Macbeth cut his teeth there, then the experience was surely a challenging one.

This period of Moravian military ineffectiveness coincides with brief, tantalising snippets of evidence that suggest that all was not well within Moray itself. The catalyst for change almost certainly took place rather further afield, as Malcolm II launched yet another attack on Northumbria in August 1018, presumably hoping to wipe out the memory of his catastrophic defeat twelve years earlier. The omens were good. A comet had spent a month riding the skies above northern England, a sure sign – though admittedly only in retrospect – of impending misfortune for its inhabitants. Then there was the rather more mundane, but crucial, fact that Earl Uhtred of Northumbria – the unequivocal victor of 1006 – had been murdered two years earlier at the instigation of the new king (since 1016) of England,

Cnut of Denmark, who did not like Uhtred's power and influence in the north. The current earl, though restricted now to Bernicia,* was Uhtred's brother, Eadwulf, nicknamed 'Cudel' or Cuttlefish, a man who does not go down in the annals of history with glowing tributes, for reasons that will become obvious.

Malcolm prepared well, making an alliance with the British king of Strathclyde, Owain the Bald, whose territory was often on the receiving end of attack from the Northumbrians. Their two armies probably met at Caddonlea (Selkirkshire), where the road south from Scotland met the road coming west from Strathclyde. This joint force then headed south across the border, only to find their route barred by a Northumbrian force at Carham, between the River Tweed to the east and the Cheviot Hills to the west.

Eadwulf seems to have been expecting retaliation for the 1006 episode now that his brother was dead and may have spent the summer raising men the length and breadth of Bernicia. Such a large force would have been impossible to gather if the first notice of this invasion had been the sinister sight of smoke spreading along the hill-tops, coming from the beacons lit hastily by the march-wards posted along the border once the Scots had mustered at Caddonlea.[29]

Carham was a 'great' battle, though not one that proved of sufficient interest in the south of England to merit a mention, never mind a description, in the *Anglo-Saxon Chronicle*. Malcolm won and was suitably grateful in victory, doling out gifts both to individual churchmen and churches.[30] He must have been

---

* Cnut's man, Erik of Hladir, now controlled Deira, the southern portion of Northumbria.

feeling very pleased with himself, now that his military reputation was restored.

Eadulf, who survived the battle, reportedly 'surrendered the whole of Lothian to them [the Scots] by a firm treaty'. Since the Scottish kings had officially held the territory south of the Forth for over forty years, this cannot be right.[31] However, Eadulf could have been 'persuaded' to give away more land – the territory between Cheviot and Tweed, perhaps, though this did not become permanent until the twelfth century.[32] Alternatively, he may have agreed to give the Scottish king full control over the lands of Lothian, effectively reneging on previous grants to, among others, the church of St Cuthbert, now in Durham. No wonder Bishop Aldhuin of Durham supposedly died of a broken heart on hearing the news of this terrible day. Eadulf himself did not live for much longer, though no-one is sure whether his death was from natural causes or if he, like his brother, was murdered. It is not hard to imagine, in the circumstances, that foul play was involved.[33]

Malcolm's reputation as a successful and pious ruler was now spreading far afield; he was known even in France for being 'powerful in resources and arms, and (what was most efficacious) very Christian in faith and deed'.[34] There is no doubt that Carham did wonders for his image and put him in an extremely strong position back home. Even Cnut, master of Denmark and Norway, but not particularly powerful in the north of his new English acquisition, must have been worried about the security of the border with Scotland. Erik of Hladir, the new earl of Deira, was Cnut's son-in-law and an excellent lieutenant to date; but he was reaching the end of his illustrious career and no more was heard of him after 1023.

Malcolm was not alone in viewing the Anglo-Scottish border as fair game. Owain, king of Strathclyde, who also won at Carham, seems to have acquired territory on the western border as a result. If he managed to extend his control into Cumbria, then this would directly challenge English access to the Irish Sea, on which the southern kingdom's security had long been seen to depend. With both Scotland and Strathclyde encroaching on his kingdom, Cnut needed to secure his own position in the north as soon as possible.

The new king of England was, of course, one of the most impressive rulers of eleventh-century Europe. Without wishing to diminish his attributes, Cnut was also the scion of a precocious Danish dynasty. His grandfather, who had given his kingdom coherent shape and the Christian religion, was the same Harold Bluetooth (*c.*958–87) who straightened out the Norse earldom of Orkney in the 980s.[35] His father, Svein Forkbeard, continued the good work, killing the Norwegian king, Olaf, in 999 and restoring Danish hegemony over its northern neighbour before turning his attention to the abundant wealth of England.

After ten years of warfare, Svein had effectively conquered England when he died at York in 1014. His younger son, Cnut, was chosen to secure his father's conquest and, despite initial setbacks, became sole ruler of England in 1016, at the age of eighteen. Two years later, the youngster succeeded his elder brother as king of Denmark as well. He proved a powerful and astute leader, able to negotiate the complex politics of a great empire united by little more than the force of his own personality. Remarkably pious and committed to fulfilling his obligations to those in need, Cnut also had no qualms about fleecing the English people in taxation to pay for the army and the fleet. The levy of 1017 'was the heaviest single levy of taxation which has ever been exacted from them'. And although he did not redistribute the land of England on the scale of William the Conqueror, his supporters certainly got their reward, in gold and in property.[36]

However, as the many conquerors of England all knew, the key to controlling the kingdom was London and the south. The situation in the north should not be allowed to get out of hand, but it was not a priority. The Scottish king's victory at Carham cannot have amused Cnut one jot, but he was in no position to do much about it. A well-informed source on the Continent claims that he was forced – for the moment at least – to adopt a pragmatic policy towards the king of Scotland. Military efforts had failed and so now 'he entirely laid aside all ferocity, for the love of God; became gentle, and lived in peace'. It is even alleged that Cnut stood as godfather to Malcolm's son, though this child – otherwise unknown – cannot have lived for long.[37]

But it would be foolish to imagine that the English king was satisfied with all this billing and cooing of friendship towards a man whom he must certainly have regarded as his inferior. Even as he appeared to be focusing on a myriad of competing claims on his attention, Cnut was clearly giving some thought to what – or whom – he might use to keep Malcolm II much more firmly in his place, preferably behind a rapidly retreating border. Unfortunately, the answer was not yet obvious.

In Moray, news of Carham would no doubt have been greeted with an ironic round of applause. Though a defeat of the English was always welcome, it would have been hard to work up much enthusiasm, given that a Malcolm trawling the depths of ignominious defeat would be much easier to deal with than a Malcolm riding the crest of a celebrated victory. Indeed, there surely were one or two young men exchanging meaningful glances across the hall as Finlay sought to brush off the implications. The ruler of Moray was probably forty or fifty years of age by now, quite an old man by the standards of the time. He had experience, of course, though his track record was far from glorious. He had a son too, but Macbeth was still relatively young, perhaps not quite experienced enough, however promising the signs. If Malcolm II was effectively trying to put an end to Finlay's claims to kingship, then some may have been unsure that Moray would be able to resist him.

The victor of Carham's next move did not involve calling out an army, but its implications sent shockwaves through the political communities of both Scotland and Moray nonetheless. Malcolm, like Finlay, was moving through middle age towards the dangerous territory of venerable antiquity. The king knew very well what happened to ageing monarchs, given that he himself had been responsible for despatching the last one. He knew, too, that if he wanted to safeguard his own position, now was the moment to strike. His political standing after the momentous victory against the Northumbrians could not have been higher among those senior nobles who had taken part, their coffers now bursting with English treasure, their pastures full of English cattle and their new tales of valour taken out and polished daily. They might therefore be amenable to listening to their leader's radical idea about the succession.

Spreading the burden of providing male heirs among a number of branches of the royal family had ensured that the kingdom always had an experienced adult male at the helm. That was its strength in troubled times. Its weakness, as we have seen, was the temptation this dangled before the tanist (the designated or presumptive heir who was not a member of the current ruler's immediate family) to hasten the transfer of power, leaving the country vulnerable to feuding across the royal houses. Primogeniture (descent from father to eldest son) was likely to resolve the feuding issue, but did severely increase the likelihood that the heir would be under-age, and raised the spectre of a failure of male heirs altogether. However, this was precisely the system that the rulers of western Europe began to view as commensurate with their increasingly exalted view of kingship, given that the winning family would take all and rise far above the rest of the warrior elite.

Malcolm was in a perfect position to give primogeniture a try. A strong, successful and – even in 1018 – comparatively long-lasting monarch, he looked as if he could wipe the floor with any rivals. There was just one problem. Despite all his obvious qualities of leadership, his tenacity and political astuteness, he lacked the only real prerequisite for a dynastic approach to the succession: sons. If the king had finally been blessed with a boy, comparatively late in life, in the years immediately following Carham, then his joy was short-lived. It was time to make some decisions as to the succession before someone else did it for him. Fortunately his eldest daughter, Bethoc, had done her duty, producing at least one son, perhaps around 1010, with her husband, Crinan, the abbot of Dunkeld. This child's name was Duncan.

Perhaps Malcolm got together his most senior noblemen – men like the mormaers of Angus and Strathearn – within a year or so of Carham, treated them to a major bout of feasting and gift-giving (no doubt courtesy of the good people of Northumbria) and, when they were feeling sufficiently mellow, dropped his bombshell. His proposition was that his grandson, Duncan, should follow him onto the throne. He knew that what he was suggesting would catapult his own branch of the family into permanent possession of the crown, creating a dynasty based on an alien system. Keeping the throne in the family would, hopefully, put an end to the bitter rivalry among his own wider kin group, but only if he could tidy up some loose ends first.

Malcolm was, for obvious reasons, entirely sanguine about transferring his own right to rule to his grandson through the female line. Descent through a woman was not a trend that had so far proved fashionable within Gaelic society, presumably because the current system was already awash with potential successors in the male line. However, if the king was successful, then the role of marriage became not just about the procreation of children to take the husband's family into the next generation; it might also engineer the possibility, now or in the future, of changing the status quo through power inherited from the wife's family.

On the other hand, keeping the crown within one dynasty by definition excluded other branches of the royal family from exercising their rights to the throne. Not only was this likely to make the potential heirs under the old system and their supporters unhappy, it was also bound to make them feel vulnerable. If Malcolm wanted to designate his own grandson as heir, then he was not going to wait around to see if those he had disappointed were prepared to resort to violence on behalf of a traditional claim. He was bound to strike first. Scotland's senior families no doubt went home determined to keep a watching brief on these developments, some for the possibility of good things to come by hitching their fortunes to this rising dynastic star; others in dismay that they and their allies were being written out of royal history and, quite possibly, eliminated altogether if they could not make themselves sufficiently powerful.

Finlay would not have been invited to the formal unveiling of Malcolm's dynastic ambitions, but he would soon have heard of them. This was not good news. Despite being the obvious heir to the line of Aed mac Kenneth, the royal blood that flowed through his veins would mean nothing if Duncan managed to follow his grandfather onto the throne. It is unlikely that either king viewed the division of Scotland into two parts as permanent; both would surely have wanted to see Alba and Moray come together again, either within their own lifetimes, or that of their successors. Malcolm clearly had no intention of resolving the issue by passing the throne on to Finlay or his son. In that case, the southern king was likely to want to reunite the kingdom by force. What strategy was Finlay going to devise to stop him?

The house of Moray, like its royal counterpart in Scotland, was a sprawling, complex affair. As we have seen, Finlay seems to have had an elder brother, Maelbrigde, who had sons of his own. As the prospect of a permanent stake in Scotland's kingship, grasped by the Moray family after 1006, began to fade away in the face of Finlay's mediocrity and Malcolm's dynamism, it is likely that the next generation resolved to take matters into their own hands. At some point in 1020, Finlay was murdered by his nephews, Malcolm and Gillacomgain, Maelbrigde's sons. We do not know where or how exactly, but the event was significant enough to be noted in the Irish chronicles.[38]

This dramatic outbreak of feuding within the royal house of Moray might imply that there was some sort of curse plaguing anyone foolhardy enough to take too close an interest in the throne of Scotland. Malcolm, the elder of the two parricides, assumed his uncle's position as king, causing obvious confusion both for contemporaries and subsequent generations, given that both kings of Scots now had the same name. No doubt the older Malcolm reacted grimly to the news, recognising this latest political assassination as, if not a declaration of war, at least an intimation that Moray was still willing to take the field. Finlay's erstwhile friends and supporters could surely be persuaded that his death was ultimately in their best interests, whatever their personal feelings. But for his immediate family, his wife (if she was still living) and, particularly, his son, the slings and arrows of outrageous fortune had shattered the fragile assumptions of their old lives for ever.

CHAPTER 7

Kings in Waiting

> To be thus is nothing
> But to be safely thus.
>
> *Macbeth*, Act III, Scene i

The death of a father, a presentiment in gentle times of one's own mortality, is difficult enough. To know that his departure from this earth was premeditated – perhaps to have only just escaped the same fate – by those who share the same blood and heritage is soul-destroying indeed. And yet history and literature is littered with such vipers in the nest – wicked uncles, sisters, stepsisters, nephews and cousins.* It is no wonder that a reliance on one's kin, a practice viewed as both normal and natural in early Gaelic culture, was already under severe strain

---

* To name but a few, Richard III and Hamlet, 'The Twa Sisters' (a Scottish ballad), Cinderella, Mordred (in King Arthur) and, in a modern-day saga of an orphan who is saddled with despicable relations, Harry Potter. The universality of this theme is also echoed in, for example, the story of Krishna's murder of his cousin, Kansa, who had seized his throne.

in Scotland and Moray, with the realisation among those in high office that loyalty might prove more binding by inducement than by blood. Indeed, the system of fostering a noble child among those who were unconnected to him suggests an understanding of the wisdom of placing the precious egg in an unrelated basket.

Given how little we know about the circumstances prevailing in Moray, it is not certain that Macbeth would immediately have followed his father in high office anyway. Our only guide – the kingship of Scotland itself – suggests that his cousin Malcolm may well have been the expectant heir, his actions a product of unseemly haste, most likely precipitated by an external threat, rather than an ambition to which he was not entitled. Murder, in these circumstances, had become a political tool, one that added – along with the warfare that gave the nobility their status – to the brutalisation of those whose lifestyles could have cushioned them from the everyday tragedies of their inferiors. They would not starve, these men of violence, but their lives might prove as short, their deaths as disquieting a prospect as it was for those who did.

Finlay's murder was surely not the only one committed on that fateful day. His own bodyguard, at the very least, would have perished with him, whether the final denouement was an ambush in some shaded glen or – as was so often the case – the careful entrapment of the victim in his own hall. The effects were the same: a number of grieving families denied the support and protection of a mature adult male. A new clutch of young men was now pushed to the head of their families, whether or not they were ready. The future rested with them, including responsibility for avenging their fathers' deaths. If this was truly the beginning of a bloodfeud within the house of Moray,* focused on the dead king's son, then the fire of Macbeth's righteous anger was surely kept alive by the many others directly affected by it – retainers, neighbours or clients, many of whom might be relations too.

Ever since Cain killed Abel, human relationships have been irresistibly shaped by the demands of the bloodfeud, generating insistent calls-to-arms over many generations not to expedite a particular political purpose or even satisfy the whim of a tyrant, but to fulfil the complex demands of family honour. Perhaps our ancestors thought twice about unleashing these blood-soaked hydras, but once a bloodfeud had begun, the conventions designed to keep it within socially acceptable bounds did little to end the violence.

They were not designed to. The warrior, or at least his ideal, cultivated in western European society, as elsewhere, was one who did not act in hot blood, but kept account of the scores to be settled with chilling restraint. That was his duty, and even his own death merely passed on that responsibility.[1] Perhaps this was the unconscious promotion of an even more basic biological imperative to ensure that only the fittest survived. Eventually the state harnessed the violent impulses of its young men on its own behalf, dispensing in any meaningful sense with the ties of kinship that had previously governed loyalty and betrayal. The results, to be fair, were even more catastrophic. It is only in the very recent past that peace has become the prevailing condition throughout western

---

* For all we know, Finlay could have killed his brother, Maelbrigde, father of Malcolm and Gillacomgain, and been murdered in revenge.

European society, rather than merely an interlude between bouts of violence.

The young man who would transform his natural grief at the death of his father into something more formal and enduring was at least twenty, and surely accustomed to leading men in war as well as peace. But he was in no position just yet to do anything other than safeguard his own situation, perhaps even his life. In the immediate aftermath of the murder, Macbeth is most likely to have fled into exile, leaving his family behind. The women would be safe enough, though no doubt the sudden withdrawal of the privileges enjoyed in a royal household would take some getting used to. Macbeth was old enough to have been at least in the process of getting married, but perhaps the chaos that now descended upon his life made it impossible to continue negotiations for a bride. Though this was to prove fortunate in the long run, it must have been worrying at the time.

Who knows where this troubled young man might have fled to safety? The best guess is Ireland, entailing a treacherous sixty-five-mile journey through the Great Glen, then on, probably by boat, down Loch Linnhe, past the island of Mull and out into the Irish Sea. In later life Macbeth seems to have had some kind of alliance with the powerful king of Leinster, Diarmait mac Maíl na mBó, whose family, the Uí Chennselaig, eventually took power from Malcolm II's relations, the Uí Dúnlainge, in the area around Dublin. In the 1020s, however, both these young men could still only dream of the glorious future that they might one day enjoy. Perhaps Macbeth was related in some way to the Uí Chennselaig. The truth will always remain obscure, but the family interconnections between

Scottish and Irish society – at this level, entirely indistinguishable from politics – certainly makes it a possibility.

Meanwhile, back in Moray, Malcolm, aided by his brother, Gillacomgain, had work to do in order to make his murderous acquisition of his uncle's throne look like more than just vaulting ambition. What the two Moravians needed was allies, particularly in the south, where Malcolm II was still basking in the kudos of his Northumbrian adventure. The old king's Achilles heel – potentially at least – lay in his determination to see his grandson, Duncan, inherit the throne. That had, perhaps, precipitated the extraordinary events in the north, but it also affected other noble families, particularly those who, like Malcolm II himself, were direct descendants of Malcolm I.

Among these was yet another young man who had good reason to feel extremely vulnerable. His name was Maelbaethe[2] and his credentials were impeccable. That was, indeed, the problem, since he was the heir in the senior line of descent from Malcolm I through his father, Boite, brother of Kenneth III and son of King Dubh. Like Malcolm of Moray, his nervousness stemmed from the fact that Malcolm II intended to ignore his claim to the throne, even though the current king was, in fact, descended from the junior branch of this family (Malcolm's father, Kenneth II, had been Dubh's younger brother). This young man would know that the eventual transfer of power to Duncan would most likely be 'facilitated' by the removal of those who were viewed as unlikely to give up their own well-founded rights. He only had to consider the recent history of his immediate family to know exactly what fate might be in store for him, since he was probably a cousin of the

Dungal who was murdered, perhaps by Malcolm II's brother, Gillacomgain, in 999.[3]

If Malcolm of Moray and Maelbaethe joined together, agreeing to support each other as kings north and south of the Mounth – an unfortunate necessity – then this might well prove a sufficiently formidable alliance against Malcolm II. Maelbaethe himself may have had a connection with Fife, the south-easternmost corner of Scotland above the River Forth,[4] which would have placed him very close to the main royal power centres of the south. As the 1020s progressed, the wisdom of such an alliance became ever more apparent and at some point in that decade Maelbaethe's sister, Gruoch, was given in marriage to Gillacomgain of Moray (presumably because Malcolm was already spoken for). The couple soon produced a son, Lulach, cementing the relationship between the two families, their destinies now firmly intertwined.

There was one other player to whom this northern alliance* could turn for support. As ruler of Denmark, Norway and England, Cnut would have found their plans interesting. Moray politics was intricately bound up with the Norse world focused most particularly on Orkney. Though Denmark lost control of Norway (Orkney's overlord) between 1015 and 1028, this was still very much an issue – like the Anglo-Scottish border – that Cnut had merely placed on hold. Given his concern to neutralise any potential threat to his own position across his empire, the

---

* Given the difficulty of identifying two sides led by kings with the same name, and even though Maelbaethe may have had a connection with Fife, I will describe the Malcolm of Moray/Gillacomgain/Maelbaethe axis as the northern alliance.

conjunction of interests that came together in Orkney, including its earls' involvement in the politics of Ireland and the western British seaboard, made the area ripe for political manoeuvring. Making an alliance with the Moravians, who had a long history of attempting to contain Orkney's influence as well as a current helpful difference of opinion with Malcolm II, must have appealed to Cnut, not least because they might be persuaded to do much of his dirty work for him.

Malcolm II had already shown his hand here, promoting his grandson, Thorfinn, as earl of Caithness under his own jurisdiction, a useful challenge to Orkney's Norwegian overlord, Olaf (II) Haraldsson, but a worry also for Cnut. Of even more concern to the English king would be the likelihood, alluded to in the *Prophecy of St Berchan*, that the Scottish king had been making his presence felt in the Western Isles, securing tribute from the area as the 'voyager of Islay and of Arran'. Indeed, it has even been suggested that Malcolm II managed to create a kingdom for his brother, Suibhne, who was described at his death in 1034 as king of the 'Gall-Gáedel', the Norse-Gaels who operated as an independent force outside Ireland and eventually gave their name to Galloway in south-west Scotland.[5] This Scottish king could give Cnut a run for his money in terms of his ability to manipulate the complex politics of Scotland's northern and western fringes.

In the first instance, the English king made a similar attempt to intervene in the west, appointing Hakon, son of his new earl in Deira, Erik of Hladir, as king of the Isles perhaps as early as 1016–17.[6] Both Cnut and Malcolm II were clearly taking advantage of the turmoil still reverberating through the region in the aftermath of Clontarf. The politics of Britain were a minefield of overlapping and sometimes downright contradictory alliances and loyalties, interconnecting one with the other in a thickening plot that – so far as Cnut was concerned – stretched from Norway down into Normandy, from Ireland across to Poland, with Scotland right in the middle.

In the years immediately following his seizure of power, Malcolm of Moray must have thought long and hard about his own position. The alliance with Maelbaethe made sense, a perfectly harmonious conjunction of interests bent towards a common purpose: their own safety and the promotion of their aspirations through the destruction of their mutual enemy. Getting involved with Cnut, on the other hand, was playing with fire, however potentially impressive the results. Malcolm should have harboured few illusions about any interest that the Dane might show in his schemes; equally, his own usefulness to Cnut would rely on the formulation of a definite campaign of action against Malcolm II.

Both the Norse Sagas and the *Anglo-Saxon Chronicle* relate that three kings from Scotland – indeed, more specifically, from Fife – approached the English king around 1025, offering their submission. This was portrayed in both the English and the Scandinavian sources as a great show of magnanimity by Cnut, who graciously 'laid aside for them his anger, and gave them all the lands that they had previously had, and great friendly gifts besides'.[7] The proof of this generosity may be the hoard containing coins of Cnut's reign dated to *c.*1025 discovered at Lindores in Fife, reputed to be a seat of the region's medieval earls.[8] Its deposition and subsequent abandonment does, of course, suggest that its owner came to an untimely end.

The third king mentioned in the *Anglo-Saxon Chronicle* was

named 'Iehmarc', which historians presume is a crude attempt to make the Gaelic name 'Echmarchach' intelligible to an English audience.[9] Echmarchach mac Ragnaill was another contestant in the convulsive politics of Ireland centred on Leinster and Dublin. It is not clear what he was up to in the 1020s, but in 1036 he emerged from this obscurity to seize the kingship of Dublin which he held, on and off, until 1052 when he was squeezed out by none other than Macbeth's friend, Diarmait mac Maíl na mBó. 'Through him [Echmarchach] Canute was to regain his security in the west, blocking the ambitions of the earls of Orkney for over a decade and extending his reach even further into the Norse-Gaelic world.'[10] The three young 'kings' who presented themselves before Cnut were clearly men on the make, prepared to be exposed to the machinations of a much more powerful player as a price worth paying for the highest stakes in their own particular political spheres.

Malcolm II would not have been content merely to sit back while his enemies strengthened their position. There may have been some ego-massaging – present-giving and, perhaps, discussions of marriage – to be done among the Scottish nobility so far inclined to be loyal to him, though he must have felt reasonably secure in the breadth of support he currently enjoyed. It is likely that he had already confiscated Fife from the errant Maelbaethe, a predictable gesture that would have serious repercussions for both the king and, ultimately, Macbeth.[11] In the meantime, Fife's broad, fertile lands would no doubt prove useful as a reserve from which to reward his own supporters. It is worth adding at this point that the lands of Bolgyne (Bogie) near Kirkcaldy were said to belong, a few decades later, to 'the son of Thorfinn'. Perhaps the king's Orcadian grandson, a very useful ally against the pretensions of a northern alliance based in Moray, was one of those to benefit with a Lowland retreat easily accessible by galley.

Key to Malcolm's own 'party' was his son-in-law, Abbot Crinan of Dunkeld, Duncan's father. Dunkeld had long played a vitally important role in the spiritual identity of the Scottish kingdom and, even though St Andrews now tended to assume the lead in ecclesiastical affairs, its abbot still wielded spiritual and political power thanks to his monastery's legacy as the Scottish successor to Iona. Situated less than fifteen miles north of Perth in a wooded glen on the main route north to Inverness, Dunkeld lay within Atholl, once the main Pictish kingdom south of the Mounth and perhaps the heartland of the former royal family of Aed mac Kenneth, whose line was now represented by the house of Moray.

Malcolm of Moray and his allies certainly seem to have believed that Dunkeld was both fundamental to Malcolm II's devilish plans for the succession and vulnerable to attack. Abbots of the Celtic Church did not necessarily eschew the violence inherent in medieval politics, as Columba would have liked. Indeed, Crinan was later to prove the very model of a warrior priest, suggesting that he had not been an advocate of peace in the run-up to his son's accession to the throne. In 1027 the Irish annals quietly lamented that 'Dún Caillen [Dunkeld] in Scotland was totally burned'. This was surely the work of the northern alliance, encouraged by Cnut's support and tangible proof of their commitment to action. Perhaps Duncan, the heir, was the one being targeted, in which case the attack failed. It did nothing to halt Malcolm II's plans either, but the king must have been shocked to realise that his enemies were prepared to bring an army so far from Moray deep into the heart of Scotland.

Shortly afterwards, Cnut put the final piece of his own complex plans in place to sew up control of the sea routes around the British Isles: he installed Hakon, son of Erik of Hladir, as his deputy in Norway (after the expulsion of Olaf II), to add to Erik's long-standing strategic roles as king of the Isles and earl of Worcester in the south-west of England. Malcolm II would have been painfully aware that a host of enemies now threatened to surround him. At the very least, these worries must have disturbed a hard-earned old age.

Fortunately for Malcolm II, his enemies were just as likely to be cruelly mocked by fortune, which could leave their careful schemes in tatters within a short space of time. In 1029 Malcolm of Moray, 'king of Scots', died.[12] There is no hint in the annals of any violence associated with his demise, but there is no doubt that it was all downhill for the alliance's plans from now on. A year or so later, a ship carrying Hakon Eriksson, the lynchpin of Cnut's North Sea/Atlantic strategy, fell foul of the notorious 'Swelkie' in the Pentland Firth, and 'he was swallowed up in the depths of the whirlpool, with all his company' en route to his wedding in Norway.[13] Cnut must now have been hoping that Gillacomgain and Maelbaethe in Scotland and Echmarchach in Ireland could continue to hold the line against Malcolm II and Thorfinn of Orkney.

The 'mighty' and 'noble prince' Thorfinn, whom we last met as an infant earl of Caithness, may, like Kenneth mac Alpin, owe much of his reputation to the fact that he was the progenitor of a long line of Orcadian earls rather than strictly to his own achievements. Nevertheless, he was a determined and forceful character, even if his 'empire' may not quite have lived up to the hyperbole of the Sagas. In his youth, while still under tutelage, he is portrayed as attempting to 'persuade' King Olaf of Norway to help him to secure at least a third of the Orcadian earldom currently held by his older stepbrothers; he used the threat of seeking help from his grandfather, the king of Scots, with all that that might imply in terms of giving Scotland suzerainty over the Northern Isles. In reality, this ploy only brought Orkney more explicitly under Norwegian control. However, the change of regime in Norway in 1028, when it succumbed to Denmark, gave Thorfinn the go-ahead to manoeuvre himself into a greater share of his father's earldom and in 1030 he seized control of all of it, ignoring the rights of Rognvald, the son of his dead brother, Brusi, to at least a part.

The other great event in Thorfinn's early life concerns an epic sea battle against a Scottish king, Karl Hundason, who has bothered and bewildered Scottish historians ever since. The Norse chronicle, the *Orkneyinga Saga*, makes much of Thorfinn's youth in this first glorious encounter, which only served to enhance his military prowess. In truth, the whole episode may owe more to fiction than to fact, but if there was a confrontation between the young Orcadian and a Scottish force in this period, then it surely involved the Moravians. The story goes that the Scottish leader had just taken over from a king called Malcolm, so 1029/30 – when Thorfinn would have been in his early twenties and Gillacomgain had just succeeded his brother – is as likely a time as any. The pressure from Cnut may have been weighing heavily on Gillacomgain, as well as the know-ledge that neither he nor his brother had made significant inroads against Malcolm II. Ignoring, for the moment at least, the complicated politics of Scotland for a potentially easy victory against an inexperienced Norse commander must have been very tempting indeed.

The confrontation flared up out of Scottish (or Moravian) attempts to re-establish control over Caithness, for which Thorfinn was now refusing to pay any tribute and which Karl (Gillacomgain?) wanted to give to his sister's son, Moddan. This Moddan supposedly gathered men in Sutherland but was forced to return 'to Scotland' when Thorfinn marched against him with a force from both Caithness and Orkney. King Karl now took direct charge of proceedings, sailing out from the Moray Firth with eleven warships which ultimately headed towards Orkney in pursuit of Earl Thorfinn. The Scots managed to surprise the Orcadians at Deerness on the south-eastern tip of the main island, and the two sides prepared for battle, fastening their ships together to form an unsteady platform upon which to fight. The Sagas delight in Thorfinn's hypcractive leader-ship, jumping from quarter-deck to fore-deck at the head of his men before, finally, King Karl decided that discretion was the better part of valour, cut the ropes and sailed away back to the Moray Firth.

This was not the end of the matter, though: merely an interlude while both sides gathered more men. Moddan even managed to negotiate some troops from Ireland (perhaps sent by Echmarchach in support of their mutual antagonism towards the Orcadians). The two sides met, finally, at Torfness (Tarbert Ness) in Ross, which lay on the border between

Norse and Scottish territory. The fighting was once again incredibly fierce, this time on land, Thorfinn cutting a fine figure in his gold-plated helmet, 'a sword at his belt, and a spear in his hand'. Needless to say, he led from the front. King Karl personally brought his standard into the fight against the young earl but, after yet more intense fighting, he was forced to flee:

> *Well the red weapons*
> *Fed wolves at Tarbat Ness.*
> *Young the commander*
> *Who created that Monday-combat.*
> *Slim blades sang there*
> *South on Oykel's bank.*[14]

The aftermath, for those living in the area, was almost worse than the battle itself. Thorfinn and his men burnt everything before them. 'Those of the men whom they found they killed, but the women and old people dragged themselves into woods and deserted places, with wailings and lamentations.' Perhaps the smiths at Portmahomack, which lies only a few miles inland from Tarbat Ness, avoided this newest calamity, or perhaps they too were forced to run for their lives. Interestingly, the victorious Orcadian was also said to have driven 'the fugitives before him through Scotland, and subdued the country wherever he went, and all the way south to Fife', a ridiculous claim which might nevertheless hint at some garbled recollection that Thorfinn held lands there, which he later gifted to his son.[15] Well might the Norse praise-poets have bent joyfully to the task of immortalising this epic battle, while those in the employ of the ruler of Moray could only hope for brighter days ahead.

Malcolm II was probably relieved that the northern alliance had amounted to so little, but still deeply concerned that the competitors for Duncan's throne had not yet been dealt with. So long as Maelbaethe lived, allied to a hostile house of Moray, his own ambitions – indeed, his own life – remained in jeopardy. As an old man well into his fifties, the king recognised that time was running out. At the same time, Gillacomgain – if he really did take on Thorfinn – already had questions to answer about his military abilities, despite his comparative youth. The advantages and weaknesses of each looked finely balanced and the future, of Scotland and Moray, lay poised between them.

Where was Macbeth while all this excitement was taking place? The response must remain as equivocal as ever for this period in his life, but common sense would dictate that he should not remain in exile for much longer if he wished to have any chance of resurrecting his fortunes in his native land. 1030 marked the tenth anniversary of his father's death. It was time to start manoeuvring himself into a position to exact revenge for a murder that would neither have diminished nor cooled in his memory in the intervening years. To do so required contacts, messages sent secretly to those Moravian families who had good reason, given Gillacomgain's apparent shortcomings, to have serious doubts about his leadership qualities. Macbeth had grown up with these men, the sons of his father's cronies. His own reputation remained intact, untried perhaps, but at least not tainted by failure. If he could persuade those 'on the inside' that the future lay with him, then the rest would follow.

The plot that Macbeth almost certainly hatched, and surely executed, was terrible indeed.[16]

Only the milky glow of a failing moon serves to guide the boat towards the men and horses waiting on land, its oars muffled in cloth to disguise its approach. Greetings are silent, but heartfelt as the newcomers spring to shore. Macbeth kneels to touch the sand, savouring its cool roughness, then turns quickly away to mount a horse. The riders head inland, across moorland and farmland, keeping away from the few rough tracks to cross the plains of Moray. Soon a warm, glowing light creeps through the darkness towards them and they can just make out a clutter of turf dwellings flanking a large timber hall. Dismounting, Macbeth and his friends move quietly towards the hall, gently pulling one horse behind them with its precious load.

The sound of raucous singing fills the air, drowning out any noise that they might inadvertently make. There are many men inside, their full bellies and befuddled heads disarming them more effectively than any invading army. Sentries have been posted, of course, but Macbeth knows that friends have been bought among them and they will have long since slipped away. Silently they heave the bulky package from the horse, laying it gently on the ground and removing the cloth cover. One by one they seize an armful of firewood covered in candlegrease and lay it in piles around the outside of the hall. Suddenly, the door is thrust open. The men outside hold their breath and dive for the shadows. Round the corner trots a large, coarse-haired dog, his fur matted and weeping with sores. He stops, surprised by the strange smells, but has no time to broadcast his discovery before a knife is expertly drawn around his throat.

Meanwhile, a trilling whistle alerts Macbeth and he watches as one of his companions comes running out of the gloom with a burning branch. Deftly he plunges it into the heart of one of the piles of wood, seizing another branch to be lit and passed on to the next. Within seconds tentative smoke has turned to flames, lighting up the night sky. The intruders move back, away from the blaze, a section of the timber frame already alight. It is difficult now to hear the noise inside the hall for the crackling and snapping of wood outside.

It has taken some time for those inside to notice the danger. Gillacomgain is slumped against the back of his high seat in the middle of the far wall, opposite the door. He knows the virtue – the necessity – of entertaining in style and this feast was meant to mark a new beginning, to draw a line over certain recent difficulties. At least fifty men have eaten and drunk their fill at his expense and are now vying with each other to sing the loudest and the longest, his own poet having vacated the floor in disgust hours ago. He thinks briefly of his wife and son, glad that he did not request their company tonight. He is in a good mood; perhaps one of the serving girls will keep him warm in an hour or so, willingly or otherwise.

Frenzied movements over on the far side of the hall catch his attention. The sight of men with panic on their faces struggling to rise from their benches brings a cold chill of fear flooding across his chest into his throat. Fire! Man's hospitable friend and uncontrollable enemy. Fortunately Gillacomgain knows that this hall has another door near to the dais where he and his most honoured guests sit. He thrusts his chair back and grabs the curtain covering the door, roughly pushing away those that seek to overtake him. Cool night air momentarily relieves the suffocating heat. He can feel his heart beating wildly and smiles with relief.

Only then does he hear the screams. Instinctively his hand leaps

*to the dagger at his waist, but it still lies, useless, on the table.
Shadowy figures weave and twist in the firelight, cutting down his
men with flashes of cold steel. Gillacomgain feels sobs of fear and
frustration rising as one of the dancing figures moves towards him,
sword bloodied and ready. He recognises the face, though it is many
years since he last saw it, a face etched with familiar lines and
curves, a vague reflection of his own. Now he understands. Macbeth
has returned and he will die, one way or the other. The timber hall
begins to collapse, broad beams birling and diving in the flames'
embrace. Gillacomgain runs forward, arms outstretched, onto his
cousin's sword.*[17]

Macbeth was back, and with a vengeance. He would have known
that this, in theory at least, was merely the inevitable next step
in the bloodfeud, but he had no quarrel with Gillacomgain's
wife and child, who were not present at the fatal feast.
Nevertheless, Gruoch must surely have been seized with a terrible
fear for her son, Lulach, when news of the slaughter was brought
to her. Her thoughts must also have turned to her brother. She
must have realised that there would be little hope of vengeance
from that quarter, given that Maelbaethe would have enough
to do to ensure his own survival. This royal princess was on
her own.

Malcolm II may have been in two minds about Gillacomgain's
comprehensive removal from the political scene. He cannot
have been sorry, but he was probably concerned to find out
what was in the new man's mind. It was to be hoped that this
Macbeth would have enough to do finding his feet, leaving the
king free to attend to one final piece of outstanding business.
Within a year of Macbeth's return to Moray, Maelbaethe was

murdered, the finger of blame pointing unequivocally at Malcolm.[18] Perhaps now the old man could rest easy.

But the north continued to trouble him in his final years. The king could not have greeted the news that Macbeth had married his cousin's widow, the newly dead Maelbaethe's sister, with any degree of equanimity. The forces that Malcolm had worked long and hard to stamp out were still there, capable of marshalling themselves against him or – perhaps more importantly – against Duncan at any time. For Macbeth, this unlikely union with Gruoch made political sense, and, given that he was now in his thirties, it was long overdue. In the first place, he must have hoped that taking on the grieving princess and, more specifically, her fatherless child, might put an end to the bloodfeud that he himself had helped to perpetuate. Lulach would surely think twice in later life about plunging a knife into the man who, on the one hand, had killed his father, but had also brought him up.

Secondly, Macbeth's marriage to Gruoch united the royal lines of descent from both Aed mac Kenneth (his own) and Constantine mac Kenneth (his wife's). There was a clear purpose to this match, one which Scotland's nobility, and its king, would have understood. No-one, least of all Duncan, could be in any doubt about the strength of the potential rights it represented, though it remained to be seen whether Macbeth would – or could – make anything of them. Claims to the throne were one thing; putting on the crown was quite a different matter.

As for the bride, who knows what she felt on the day she married her first husband's murderer. She knew that Macbeth was capable of great cruelty, that he would not shrink from any of the responsibilities expected of a warrior – Gillacomgain's death proved that. Sisters and daughters all served a useful purpose in furthering their family's interests in marriage, but we should not necessarily see Gruoch as a voiceless pawn in these negotiations. As a widow, she had her own lands, giving her much more clout in any future relationship. We might even imagine that she ignored her own family's wishes in allying herself with the new power in Moray. What Gruoch and her son, Lulach, needed was a strong protector. In the circumstances, Macbeth fitted the bill perfectly.

By 1030, Malcolm II must finally have held up his hands and declared himself satisfied that he had made his arrangements, done everything to see off the competition and secure enough support to propel his grandson onto the throne in what would probably be the very near future. He had proved a strong and effective king. Most right-minded men would want to put behind them the greatest weakness in Scotland's political life, the turmoil of an uncertain succession, the murder of king after king. Duncan was the solution and Macbeth, should he choose to activate his claim, would surely be seen only as a problem.

Not surprisingly, Macbeth had an entirely different view of the situation, having spent more than a decade pondering it. Malcolm had many enemies, even in the south, and the new ruler in the north might have considerable success in exploiting that fact. Later tradition has it that an alliance between the families of Dubh mac Malcolm and Constantine mac Culen, both later tenth-century rulers, fielded a force against the king in November 1034.[19] Dubh's family may well have been that of Maelbaethe mac Boite, forfeited as mormaers of Fife for the latter's own rebellious activities which, from his own point of view, felt remarkably like self-defence.* In that case, a senior member of the family was none other than Macbeth's wife, Gruoch.

Macbeth himself could lay claim to be heir to Constantine mac Culen's line, the descendants of Aed mac Kenneth, just like his father and his cousin. In other words, the army that set out to take on the ageing Malcolm had very close connections with the ruler of Moray. Macbeth may not have led it himself – a wise man does not necessarily perform controversial deeds when there are others eager and willing to do them for him. But this army could well have ridden out on his behalf, even if the thoughts of its leaders were with the hardships they believed they and their own families had suffered. Rather more contemporary sources describe Malcolm's opponents in this battle as the 'parricides' or, in another translation, 'kin-slayers', which has been taken to mean the family of Malcolm and Gillacomgain, but which could equally apply to Macbeth himself.

The force that made its way towards Glamis in November 1034 was no doubt a last-ditch effort to prevent the succession from passing to Duncan, given added momentum by some of the terrible things that Malcolm II had deemed necessary during his long reign. The king was soon made aware of the threat, gathering an army of his own and advancing to meet his enemies. The two sides lined up beside the village of Glamis on the broad plain of Strathmore and battle commenced.

---

* King Dubh's son was Kenneth III, who was probably Maelbaethe and Gruoch's great-great-grandfather.

Malcolm was still an impressive warrior, able to rouse and lead his men in a manner worthy of his soubriquet 'the Aggressor'.[20]

But this was to be his last battle. The king managed to see off the invading force, but was severely wounded. He was carried back to the nearby hall at Glamis where attempts would have been made to bathe the wounds and staunch the bleeding, but to no avail. There was perhaps only time to gasp out a few last-minute instructions as those around the dying man tried not to think what the future might hold. On 25 November 1034 Malcolm II – 'honour of all the west of Europe' as one Irish chronicler described him – died.[21] Long live the king!

And, for the moment at least, there really was no doubt as to which king. Defeating his enemies on the battlefield was the last, and perhaps the greatest, gift that Malcolm could give to his grandson. This was an important moment in Scotland's history, the first step on the road towards a new cult of kingship, based not so much on the sacred status of the office itself – though that was important – as on the inherent God-given rights of a particular family to hold it. By the time Shakespeare got round to writing his 'Scottish play', the family of his patron, James Stuart, had ruled Scotland for nearly two hundred and fifty years and primogeniture had long been regarded as the only system capable of 'choosing' – or should we say 'revealing' – kings.* Indeed, the entire tragedy of the play stems from the fact that Macbeth, despite being related to the king,[22] is explicitly *not* entitled to his throne. If Duncan had been the one to

---

* By the time James VI/I became king of England in 1603, the system had evolved even further to allow a woman to inherit the throne, his mother, Mary, in Scotland, and his predecessor and cousin, Elizabeth, in England.

deny Macbeth his rightful inheritance, then a Jacobean audience would have had few qualms about the dire method used to bring about his death and there would be no tragedy. The injustice was not so much in the deed, as in the legitimacy of the motivation behind it.

Nevertheless, there is no doubt that later Scottish chroniclers did become obsessed with issues of legitimacy in relation to the throne, plotting with hindsight the twists and turns of the succession in order to explain the eventual outcome as Divinely ordained, inevitable. This obsession stemmed from the troubled times of the late thirteenth century, when primogeniture finally failed and it was necessary to work back into the distant past in order to identify the rightful heir to the Scottish throne.[23] For the monks who wrote history, craving peace, the catastrophe that had befallen them after their king died in 1286 without an obvious heir was an evil that must not be repeated. Those who played fast and loose with dangerous claims threatened not just the kingdom's stability, but its very existence. It is not hard to imagine how they viewed the actions of those who sought to install primogeniture, evincing no sympathy for the perfectly legitimate claims of another age.

Three centuries earlier, the truth looked very different; so far as Macbeth and his contemporaries were concerned, the best man for the job was not necessarily the one with the strictly 'superior' claim. The new approach that brought Duncan to the throne of Scotland did away with the notion of choice (albeit from a particular gene pool) and the violence that accompanied the decision-making process. Inevitably, it also reduced the power of those who did the choosing, the senior noblemen to whom claimants might appeal, with honeyed words or thinly veiled threats, to join them in an attack on the incumbent. However, this cannot have been obvious yet, as word of Malcolm's death filtered out. Whatever promises they had made to the old king, Scotland's senior men need not necessarily stand by them once he lay, forever silent, at Glamis. But perhaps the choice was made for them, for where would they find an alternative?

Macbeth was surely right to judge that now was not the time to challenge Malcolm's plans for the succession. The decision to accept Duncan as king, such as it was, must have been made more or less immediately. Within five days, Duncan had been inaugurated as king at Scone, some twenty-four miles west of Glamis. Such a speedy transfer of power hints at an attempt to pre-empt trouble, wherever that might have come from. The event itself seems to have passed without incident, although a delegation from Ireland, which may well have visited the new king soon after his inauguration, met with the kind of wholesale tragedy that underlines the perils involved in sea travel. Maicnia ua hUchtáin, the lector of Kells, was drowned, along with thirty men, on his return to Ireland from Scotland in 1034. This was hardly an auspicious start to Duncan's reign, not least because St Columba's fan and three relics of St Patrick were also lost to the sea.[24]

The new king's grandfather had accomplished an impressive list of achievements through the force of his own effective personality and abilities, much like Cnut. With the removal of that firm grip, all sorts of political mischief might now be contemplated and apparently stable situations suddenly prove they were getting out of hand. This was not necessarily the new king's fault; Malcolm II's meddling in affairs beyond his own borders was almost bound to stir up trouble for the future. Nevertheless, Duncan would certainly be judged by how he dealt with any such challenges.

He was not a particularly young man, being already the father of at least two sons by his wife, Suthen – Malcolm and Donald Ban ('the fair'). However, that should imply that he was sufficiently experienced in the affairs of war and politics to make a reasonable job of those first tricky years in power. In one important respect, too, Duncan was lucky. Within a year of his accession, Cnut of England was also dead and his great empire descended into turmoil. For the next five years, his sons, Harold Harefoot and Harthacanute, squabbled over the English throne.

Without a strong hand at the helm of England, it was – as it always had been – tempting for the Scottish king to start nibbling away at the territory immediately to the south of his own kingdom. The situation had not changed, on the surface at least, since Carham. Another Anglo-Saxon, Ealdred, Earl Uhtred's son, controlled Bernicia. Deira, to the south, was now in the hands of the Scandinavian, Earl Siward. Both were keen on expansion, though it was Ealdred who initially made the most of his opportunities, perhaps attacking Cumbria, part of the independent kingdom of Strathclyde, in 1030. His brother and successor, Eadwulf, certainly did in 1038.[25]

Duncan was no doubt watching the situation across the border with great interest. Perhaps his own nobility were proving restless, the need to get back on horseback and act like great warriors making them sullen and edgy. He may have realised that he could not take their support for granted. He may, too, have been wondering about Moray. These years could have been difficult for Macbeth, but a wise man is a patient one and there were more fish to fry than Duncan. The Moravian may have taken up his sword and spear once more, honing his skills against a less problematic target, Earl Thorfinn.[26] The Orcadian, reconciled with his dashing nephew, Rognvald, who was given part of his earldom, now sought to make himself master of the northern and western seas, as his father had done, raiding at will. 'For eight winters [1038–46] they shared the Orkneys; and every summer they went on plundering expeditions, together or separately.'[27] Though we do not know the details (the Sagas, unsurprisingly, relate only constant tales of unqualified success about their hero), this may have been the testing ground on which Macbeth began to emerge as a man worth following.

Meanwhile, in 1040, as Harthacanute lay anchored in Flanders, poised to invade England against his half-brother, Harold, Duncan judged it to be the right time for an invasion of Northumbria, probably in the hope that his own reputation would be given the kind of boost that his grandfather had enjoyed after Carham. Once again a great army assembled just north of the border and stormed its way across it. The target was Durham, just as it had been for Malcolm in the terrible campaign of 1006. This time there was no Uhtred to stir up the good people of northern England against the invading Scots. This time the citizens of Durham were able to force the Scottish king to turn tail all by themselves, routing his army as it fled. At least in 1006 Malcolm had found himself trapped between two forces, rather than humiliated by those whom he had intended to crush. The English chronicler, Symeon of Durham, was clearly not surprised by what happened next: 'Not long afterwards, the king himself, when he had returned to Scotia, was killed by his own men.'[28]

There was a bit more to it than that. Duncan would know, as he rode dolefully back to Scotland, that his kingship, not to mention his life, was in jeopardy, just as his grandfather must have given grave thought to his own situation thirty-four years before. His leadership qualities had been tested and he had been found wanting, a cardinal sin for a medieval king. Were his instincts when he returned to Scotland after the dismal failure at Durham those of the bully? Brutality was a necessary attribute in a king, but he must not overstep the mark. Inspiring awe, even fear, in those who might prove troublesome was one thing; suggesting that you had no moral compass whatsoever was quite another and this king may not have known where to draw the line. Did he decide to risk a direct assault against the only man capable of mounting a successful challenge against him? Or was he merely getting in first, the rumours already flying that Macbeth was planning to take his throne?

Whatever Macbeth was doing or thinking over the summer of 1040, Duncan found it objectionable, or politically necessary to make it appear so. Perhaps the ruler of Moray had refused to contribute to the campaign against Durham, a clear indication that Macbeth continued to take his family's claims to the kingship seriously. Perhaps he did the minimum, sending men but finding an excuse not to go himself – Earl Thorfinn would have provided sufficient reason. However, there is no denying the fact that Macbeth did not challenge Duncan; Duncan challenged him. It was the royal army that went north, deep into Moray. Who knows how large it was, or which southern earls still supported the king. The temptation would surely have been to avoid taking sides. Medieval battles, certainly in this period, rarely consisted of huge numbers of men, despite the tendency in the chronicles to imply a cast of thousands, and this one was probably little more than a small encounter undertaken, in effect, by two private armies. It was also, so far as Macbeth was concerned, self-defence.

This was it, then. Macbeth would either die on his own soil, forever condemned to the ignominy of being branded a failed pretender to the throne, or take everything, the life of the king and his kingdom. The traditional site of the battle is Pitgaveny, situated on the marshy ground between Elgin, which is currently the administrative capital of Moray, and the Moray Firth. There can be no doubt that Duncan had travelled by boat, landing immediately to the north of the battle site on the loch of Spynie, which once gave direct access to the sea, the River Lossie hemming in the ground to the east. Macbeth, who cannot have been very far from home, came out to meet the king on 15 August 1040, the Feast of the Assumption. Both leaders entered the thick of the fray and it is quite possible that Macbeth killed Duncan himself. By the end of the day, he had won his first incontrovertible victory and Scotland was once more in need of a king.

CHAPTER 8

Macbeth the King

> Not for triumphs in the battle,
> And renown among the warriors,
> But for profit of the people,
> For advantage of the nations.

Henry Wadsworth Longfellow, *The Song of Hiawatha*

It is a well-known maxim that the winners write history. But what defines a winner, particularly in this comparatively un-documented period? A glorious victory might get you into the chronicles, but there was no guarantee that military prowess alone would persuade future generations to say nice things about you or, indeed, say anything about you at all. In truth, your place in the history books might not necessarily have all that much to do with you, unless you were truly exceptional. The real trick was to have good genes and good luck, as well as not to make a complete hash of your career.

In Scottish history, the biggest winner by far has been Kenneth mac Alpin. Here we have a Pictish king whose CV was, to be blunt, unremarkable once we scrape away the later eulogies.

However, the fact that his descendants managed to recover and keep hold of the crown of the renamed kingdom of Alba/Scotland between 889 and 1034, then again from 1058 right up until 1286, has had a profound effect on his reputation. 'From at least the late tenth century until sometime in the reign of Alexander II (1214–49) ... Scottish historians repeatedly maintained that the current political order had been founded by Cinaed mac Alpin who conquered and destroyed the Picts.'[1] For an entire millennium, then, we have believed this fiction, fundamentally distorting the history of Scotland's origins at the same time.

Not surprisingly, the flipside of the creation of the cult of Kenneth has been, at best, a disregard for other contradictory histories, particularly of those kings who did not claim to be descended from the great mac Alpin. We have already seen what happened to Giric, who may even have been the original founder of Alba/Scotland. Despite the potential significance of his reign, he has been almost entirely airbrushed out of the history books, surviving in odd snippets that can be only painstakingly and partially reconstructed. A rather different history might have been written, too, if what turned out to be a hiatus in the triumphant progress of the line of Kenneth mac Alpin – the reigns of Macbeth and his stepson, Lulach – had proved to be the first stages of a new regime. Historians at the time would surely have had to think carefully about how they could explain the transfer of power to the house of Moray within the context of what they already understood to be Scotland's history. They would no doubt have sidelined Kenneth and, in time, a founding father for the new dynasty would have emerged in his place, perhaps Macbeth's otherwise unknown grandfather, Ruari. In the end, events moved faster than the rewriting of their history, but the reign of Macbeth would still have an impact on the way historians interpreted the past.

Nevertheless, it is a testament to the strength of the grip of primogeniture on our sense of propriety that Macbeth's precise relationship to the man killed on that August day at Pitgaveny still plagues and perplexes us. It is tempting, for example, to seize on the implication of a throwaway remark in the twelfth-century *Chronicle of Huntingdon* that Macbeth's mother was another daughter of Malcolm II. Deep in our hearts, perhaps, we want him to have the 'legitimacy' of a strong relationship to Kenneth mac Alpin's line, to be able to recast the events of 1040 as a quarrel between the late king's grandsons, the senior and junior line squabbling, in effect, over the same claim to the throne.[2] Such a scenario would make a good deal of sense to a society already used to a form of primogeniture, as both twelfth-century England and Scotland were. But it will not do to explain the situation in Scotland a century earlier. Leaving aside both the lateness and the remoteness of the source, we are in real danger of throwing our own prejudices (very similar, in this respect, to Huntingdon's) at the problem. So what, then, was Macbeth's claim to the throne of Scotland?

We can, of course, take the Shakespearian line (and he was in good and long-standing company over it). Macbeth had no right, enjoying only a remote kinship with the man he murdered (a kinship no doubt shared by many of Scotland's senior nobility), so he usurped the throne and held it through fear. In the six hundred years separating Macbeth from James I, England had suffered at least four usurpations.[3] More recently, James's predecessor, Elizabeth I, had spent much of her reign worrying about the very real possibility that someone – James's mother and her cousin, the Catholic queen of Scots perhaps? – might assassinate her and take her throne. The English knew all about civil war and the terrible toll it can take on a nation; in the interests of peace and harmony, they had even managed to over-look the embarrassing fact that their king was a Scotsman. Even so, James himself suffered two attempts to remove him from his splendid new throne within a year of his arrival in London, one of which (the Main Plot) aimed at replacing him with his cousin, Arabella Stewart. Shakespeare certainly knew what he was doing when he used Macbeth to expose the perils of 'vaulting ambition' among royal relatives.[4]

But our concern is not with seventeenth-century England, nor even late-twelfth-century Scotland, when Macbeth is first accused of having 'usurped to himself the throne'.[5] Rather, we must try to enter the minds of the men who, in the early autumn of 1040, were required, yet again, to make up their minds about their next king. God had, of course, pronounced His judgement on Duncan's reign in giving victory to his oppon-ent. The bald facts of the matter strongly suggested that the experiment in primogeniture had failed, the character flaws of its very first example exposing the problem of relying on a single bloodline to provide a suitable ruler.

Yet, however they looked at it, these great men must surely have recognised the urgent need to put an end to the deadly struggles which affected almost every senior family in the kingdom. The failure of the male line of descent from Aed mac Kenneth, suspending the violent but otherwise predictable rotation between it and the line of Constantine mac Kenneth, was making dangerously disappointed men out of those used to sharing in the highest offices of state on a regular basis. To add to the misery, the murders committed among the descendants of Malcolm I, once the crown had looked set to stay within their line after 997, may well have served to isolate and, ultimately, debilitate Duncan's kingship.

Perhaps in this respect Shakespeare got it right: the horror he evokes in his Scottish play as rival after rival has to be eliminated to make the king feel safe was not too far removed from the unforgiving political environment of eleventh-century Scotland. But it was Malcolm II's family – of which Duncan was, of course, a member – which had proved the most ruthless of competitors. The feuding had to stop. Faced with these good reasons to think carefully about the man to whom they gave their support as king, the majority of Scotland's earls and senior churchmen seem to have done what they usually did: they backed the winning horse. Macbeth had defeated Duncan, so Macbeth should be king.

But in many other ways, too, the Moravian was exactly what they were looking for. Having already accepted, at Duncan's accession, that a claim to the throne could be passed on by a woman, no-one could really quibble about Macbeth's relationship to the line of Aed mac Kenneth through his grandmother or great-grandmother. In any case, both he and Duncan were in good company, following the high-profile election of Conrad II as King of Germany and, ultimately, Holy Roman Emperor, in the 1020s, despite being only the great-grandson of a previous king through the female line. 'The success of Conrad's kingship, combined with the prestige of the German kingdom, now at its height, opened the doors for uterine succession elsewhere in the Latin West.'[6] It also cannot have done Macbeth any harm that he stood with a foot in both dynastic camps, by virtue of his marriage to Gruoch, the great-great-great-granddaughter of Malcolm I. At last, Scotland might have a king who could rise above the petty regional squabbles of the various branches of the royal family, egged on by the relations, clients and hangers-on unwilling to give up the spoils of royal power.

This must certainly have been the prayer of the monks who inhabited the monasteries of Ireland and Scotland. However, praying was not their only role in life. As some of the leading intellectuals of their day, it was their research and deliberations that promoted ideas about nationhood and identity, that explained the role of kingship and its 'ancient' heritage. The origin legends that sprang up in Britain in these centuries may seem far-fetched and even downright silly to us now; but at the time they were sophisticated attempts to draw together prevailing ideas about kingship within a Christian context. In time – another few hundred years – this would lead in Scotland to an articulation of 'the concept of a sovereign realm with the authenticity of a distant and continuous past'.[7]

For the moment, though, Macbeth's accession gave these scholars something of a headache. The truth of the matter is that no contemporary or near-contemporary scholar seems to have considered that his claim to the throne was based on any relationship whatsoever to the previous line of kings. None of the king-lists or his family's genealogy suggest that the house of Moray claimed ultimately to be descended from Kenneth mac Alpin, even through a woman. This contrasts with Duncan, whose claim was also transmitted through the female line, but who is almost always portrayed straightforwardly as the grandson of Malcolm II.

Macbeth's genealogy, on the other hand, was concocted to link his immediate forefathers with former members of the Dalriadan Cenel Loarn, just as the house of Alpin was depicted as a continuation of the line of Cenel nGabrain.[8] The scholar responsible must have made the connection between Moray and the Cenel Loarn either because he understood that this was how Macbeth's family saw themselves (even if he had to make up the details by bodging together the last five generations of the House of Moray with not one but two known genealogies of the Cenel Loarn) or because he himself decided that this made the most sense. Perhaps we might read into this an understanding of the distinctiveness of Moray, an awareness that its history, over the last few generations at least, had developed rather differently from the kingdom of Scotland to which it was ostensibly attached through a shared kingship.

What both Macbeth's family and the descendants of Kenneth mac Alpin were provided with, as a result, was a lineage that stretched back into the mists of Irish history, a necessary intellectual connection developed at some point after 900 to give Scotland and its kings a contemporary legitimacy based on the past. British historians, in this period, despaired over the island's current messy disintegration into smaller kingdoms, preferring the logic of whole and discrete physical units, which God had clearly designed for a purpose. Both the Welsh and the English therefore claimed to be, respectively, the original inhabitants of, or the heirs to, Britain in its entirety. There was no point at this stage in developing a history of the antiquity of the manifestly lesser kingdoms of England and Wales.

Scottish scholars, on the other hand, were not interested in claiming Britain as a whole for their kings, though they did, from the eleventh century onwards, argue that the island had always been divided into two kingdoms. But this was clearly not good enough. To endow Scotland's kingship with the obligatory insular and ancient heritage, it was linked, via Dál Riata, to another Divinely created land mass, Ireland. In other words, the current line of Scottish kings – whether or not they came from Moray – had been provided with an ancient relationship to Ireland to justify the fact that they now ruled the northern portion of mainland Britain. This makes no sense whatsoever to those of us used to the assertive national identities of Scotland and England that emerged a few centuries later using the equally fantastical fiction that a single people inhabited each kingdom. But this was the way in which British and Irish scholars around the turn of the second millennium tried to understand and portray the workings of the Divine plan as applied to the kingdoms in which they lived.[9]

Helpful though this might have been within a contemporary context, tracing Scottish kings back to Ireland also serves to downplay one other important fact about them: their much more real and recent descent from the kings of the Picts. And here Macbeth might also have inspired some lateral thinking. He was – as the author of the *Prophecy of St Berchan* noted some seventy years later – the 'generous king of Fortriu', an unusual, and therefore carefully chosen, reference to the ancient credentials to rule that once belonged to the new king's homeland. Macbeth, then, had the potential to be no ordinary ruler. On his death, the Irish chronicles noted that he was not just Scotland's king, but – for the first time – its high king (*ard righ*), uniting Alba with Moray in a 'greater' Scotland that Malcolm II could only dream of.

But we will leave the scholars to worry about how they were going to explain the change of regime. The fact remains that Macbeth must have known within a week or so that he had the support of sufficient numbers of the senior nobility; his reign officially commenced nearly three weeks after the battle, on 8 September, the Feast of the Nativity of the Virgin Mary, at Scone, as usual, over a hundred and thirty miles away from Pitgaveny.[10] That ceremony was a vitally important one, a self-conscious moment of theatre in which the next in an 'ancient' line of kings was solemnly declared ruler and preserver of this 'enduring geographical reality' known as Alba, the northern portion of Britain.[11] Given that this was, in effect, a change of dynasty, the significance was all the greater.

A brightly decorated barge makes careful progress along the broad, glittering waters of the River Tay, the oarsmen straining against the current. The passengers on board are obviously very important, the lustre of their jewellery competing with the silver of the river. In their midst, a tall man surveys the bank, preoccupied even as his companions chatter excitedly. He is savouring the moment, knowing what it has cost to get here, and what it might still cost in the days and years to come. Soon he spies a small crowd gathered on the shore and cannot resist a broad smile of greeting. The barge is pulled skilfully to a gentle halt and the tall man leaps off first. He puts his arm briefly around the shoulders of a well-fed monk who tries to bow, grinning nervously. Macbeth turns back to his entourage, offering his hand to his wife, soon to be his queen. Gruoch nods and smiles gravely.

The weather, on this September day, is pleasant enough, the sun easily sloughing off any lingering mist, though the ladies shiver in their finery and wish for their everyday woollens. The royal entourage begins its progress through dew-sodden water meadows towards the monastery of Scone where the ceremony of inauguration will take place. In the lead is the portly monk, the ollamh ríg Alban – 'master-poet of the king of Scotland' – a very learned man indeed. This is surely the most important day of his career, presiding over the ceremony that will invest the ordinary mortal behind him in his sacred new office. Crowds of people line the route, eager to see the man who will soon rule over them, most for the first time. Macbeth does not disappoint, looking every inch a king, a strong, benevolent father for his people.

After a mile or so, the royal party can see another crowd, this one richly dressed like themselves, gathered at the bottom of a small flat mound. Everyone who is anyone in 1040 is gathered today at the Hill of Belief in Scone, with some unfortunate exceptions. As the crowd parts to let them through, most of the new arrivals take their places at the bottom of the hill. The court poet and Macbeth go on, joined by a handful of the kingdom's greatest men, up the steps to the top, stopping finally beside the Lia Fail or Stone of Destiny.[12] They turn to face the noble men and women below. Taking a deep breath, the poet begins, proclaiming Macbeth with the words 'The Blessing of God, O King of Scotland' (Beannachd Dhe, O ri Alban). Solemnly he then launches into an exposition on the royal lineage of Macbeth, son of Finlay, son of Ruari, son of Donald, and on into the depths of time, to a point – or so it perhaps felt to those listening – not long after God had brought an end to chaos and created the world as it was, and is, and always would be. At last he comes safely to the end of this eternal litany of names and stands back, relieved.

The history lesson over, Maldovine, Bishop of St Andrews, moves forward with a small coterie of churchmen to lay his hands upon the new king and say his own blessing, just as Columba was reputed to have done for Aedán mac Gabráin of Dál Riata back in 574. They are all painfully aware of the absence of the dead king's father, Crinan, abbot of Dunkeld, who should have been here to wield the portable shrine otherwise known as the Brecbennoch Choluim Chille – 'the speckled peaked one of Columba' – entrusted to his monastery by Kenneth mac Alpin. This does not discomfit the king, however, having given him the perfect excuse to make sure that his own bishop, based at Rosemarkie, stood alongside his southern brethren.[13]

The crowd begins to fidget, tired of all this talking and praying. They breathe a collective sigh of relief as Bishop Maldovine steps aside to allow the poet back onto centre stage. Macbeth's expression does not alter, but inside a flush of excitement unbecoming to a middle-aged man surges through him. His heart is beating so loudly that he can barely hear what is being said. The poet awkwardly begins to wrap the royal robes around the king, unable to prevent himself from dwelling on the pleasing thought that the royal outfit beneath them would soon come to him as a gift. The world holds its breath, has all but disappeared for the man at the centre of these proceedings as the wand of kingship is held out to him. Macbeth takes it in his hand as a noisy wave of adulation ascends the hill. Now, at last, he is king.[14]

The emphasis on historical reflection that played such an obvious role in these inaugurations was more than just a semi-fantastical attempt at giving a veneer of antiquity and cohesion to the messy business of Scottish kingship. This was one of the few arenas in which the nation's sense of self – or at least the version of it being discussed and worked upon by its scholars – could be given a public hearing and, in effect, public validation. The new relationship between Moray and Scotland must surely have given the nation's intellectuals much to ponder.

We should not forget that the bishop of Fortriu – once synonymous with the most senior ecclesiastic in Pictland – had been based at the monastery at Rosemarkie in Ross.[15] Macbeth needed the rhetoric of legitimate kingship just as much as the swords and spears of his army. Though we have nothing to prove it, the scholars of the north may well have been involved in explaining, and therefore furthering, however indirectly, the aspirations of the region's ruling family long before its current head made his mighty leap to become king of Scotland as well.

This is not meant to imply that these monks, whether they lived north or south of the Mounth, formed some sort of learned wing of government. They were independent scholars, members of a powerful transnational organisation. Nevertheless, they must have known that their deliberations might help to promote versions of events and views of the world that might suit one particular ruling group over another. How else, for example, did the genealogy that the noble crowd would have heard at Macbeth's inauguration* – quite obviously different from the one recited at Duncan's – come about if not through monastic research?

The very act of presenting the new king's credentials in such

---

* We do not know whether it was the same as the Cenel Loarn one that has survived.

a scholarly fashion, combined with the solemn Christian endorsement, the legitimacy of tried-and-tested ritual all wrapped up in a package that wasted no opportunity to allude to the past, all served to present Macbeth to the nation in a carefully planned show of unity. The reality, of course, was very different. After his death at Pitgaveny, the old king was treated with proper respect, his body no doubt washed and made presentable before being sent on its last final voyage to Iona for burial. But his family were unlikely to have approached the battle site to pay their last respects, in the well-founded belief that Duncan's young sons, Malcolm and Donald Ban, were unlikely to survive the experience.* They may even have been told to wait out the battle on one of the boats used by the invading army to approach Pitgaveny, the arrival of the blood-spattered and breathless remnants of Duncan's proud contingents prompting a hasty withdrawal.

The question of where Suthen and her sons headed as Macbeth began to make arrangements for the trip to Scone is also perplexing. The traditional story also has them going south, sailing (presumably) down the east coast to England, where Malcolm spent the next seventeen years being groomed for his eventual return to Scotland. That is the picture that Shakespeare evokes for us, though, once again, Scottish historians had been saying it for at least three hundred years before him.

---

* Malcolm died in 1093, which surely places his birth no earlier than 1030. His brother, Donald Ban, lived until 1097, having taken the throne immediately after Malcolm's death. Both men died prematurely, the first in battle and the second after being blinded.

These days considerably more credence is given to the idea that the ex-royal family headed north, to Orkney, seeking refuge with a man they already knew as someone whom Duncan had no doubt been happy to cultivate as an antidote to Moravian power in the north, his cousin, Thorfinn.* In 1040 the Orcadian earl and his nephew, Rognvald, were still ostensibly sharing power, spending the summer months campaigning the length and breadth of Britain's seaways in pursuit of ever more booty and territory. The news of Duncan's defeat cannot have pleased Thorfinn, but providing a home for the dead king's boys would at least give Macbeth something to worry about, a pleasant enough thought to be going on with.

As for the new king, Macbeth would have been well aware that getting to the throne, however difficult and traumatic the journey, was not the end of the road. From now until he breathed his last, however long God was willing to grant him, he could never rest easy in some naïve belief that his enemies had forgotten about him. Since the rules of the succession were already in a state of flux, it is likely that Macbeth always intended that his own sons by Gruoch or, failing that, his stepson, Lulach,† would follow him on the throne.

In other words, although Duncan's reign might have been viewed as an unsuccessful experiment, there was still plenty of potential in primogeniture; it was just a question of finding the right dynasty. No king could fail to see the advantages; the problem lay in persuading other claimants that it was in their

---

* Like Duncan, Thorfinn was a grandson of Malcolm II through his mother.
† Lulach was also a member of Macbeth's own family, since his father, Gillacomgain, was Macbeth's first cousin.

own best interests to put down their weapons and accept that kingship was now the prerogative of one line of a single family. Duncan had clearly been unable to make Macbeth – his main rival – feel either safe or satisfied. With Duncan's two sons out of the country, the new king would have to work on the rest of Scotland's nobility, creating bonds of loyalty strong enough to resist the challenge when it came, as it surely would. But there was no need to worry about that yet.

Macbeth took the throne of Scotland around the age of forty, a little on the late side, but giving no hint of anything other than vigour and ability. Contemporaries[16] describe him as fair-haired with a reddish complexion. Such high colouring was perhaps not surprising, given that most medieval warriors spent their days outside and their nights in gastronomic over-indulgence. Indeed, to be described as 'ruddy' may have been complimentary poetic shorthand for a popular leader's munificence. And, above all, Macbeth was renowned as generous: 'I shall be joyful in him', the poet says, seemingly nostalgic for the days when he may have enjoyed pouring forth in front of the great man himself. He deliberately contrasted the fact that 'Scotland will be brimful, in the west and in the east' under Macbeth with the implied difficulties the kingdom experienced under his predecessor, 'the Man of many diseases'.[17]

The point would not be lost on his audience. Duncan had deserved to forfeit his crown because of the danger to which he exposed the kingdom with his rashness and lack of judgement. Macbeth, by contrast, was rewarded with prosperity as a sign of God's favour, a far better verdict on the validity of his kingship than tortuous analyses of family trees, important though these were in justifying what happened after the event. Nor was this a lone eulogy from a pet poet. Even a sober Church chronicler admitted he understood that Scotland enjoyed a time of great fertility during Macbeth's reign, a traditional metaphor for peace and prosperity. These were excellent credentials for a medieval king, however partisan their source.

But what of the man beneath the crown? Medieval kings, especially of this period, will never emerge as even semi-rounded characters. Macbeth has left us no letters or diaries, no tell-all memoir or even tedious administrative documents, not a single word written by him or even by those who we might imagine to be communicating directly on his behalf, unless we count the poet mentioned above. But we do perhaps get a glimpse of the 'real' Macbeth in a chronicle, written over a century after his death, which places the king in the company of his two favourite greyhounds, evoking an off-guard, off-duty moment. The brief entry conjures up, however imperfectly, a homely image of this infamous man, perhaps stretched out before a roaring fire, fondling the ears of these handsome beasts; or riding home with them at dusk after an excellent day's hunting.

In this he was entirely in tune with the times; the Scottish court must often have entertained visitors, as well as itself, with carefully orchestrated hunts, the animals driven into a large killing area where the waiting participants could cut and slash away at close range, followed by a night's feasting of similarly gargantuan proportions. Scotland's landscape and its fauna – deer, wolf, fox, lynx, even bear, in those days – were perfectly suited to providing suitable entertainment for the idle warrior. These contemporary hints at Macbeth's character, exaggerat- edly complimentary though they no doubt are, reveal him as a paragon of traditional hospitable virtues. They could not be more different from the image of him handed down by later history. Nor do they provide anything beyond a superficial appreciation of this extraordinary man. As we will see, Macbeth was also capable of moving with the times, as well as staying in tune with them, of sensing where it might be useful to do something radically different while still conforming to what was expected of him.

Much to his surprise, no doubt, the first few years of Macbeth's reign passed quietly enough. In the south, Siward the Dane, who had taken over Deira on the death of Erik of Hladir, seized control of all Northumbria in 1041. He had no intention of stopping there, and was busy pushing away at the English border with Cumbria/Strathclyde, whose royal house may have married into Malcolm II's family, an alliance represented in practical terms by Owain the Bald's presence at Carham with the Scottish king. Fortunately for Macbeth, Siward seems to have been content to leave the eastern border with Scotland alone, for the time being at least. Certainly the Scottish king was entitled to view any encroachment on former Anglo-Saxon territory in Lothian (the region south of the Forth) as an act of aggression, Scotland having held the area formally since 975.

Trouble, when it finally came, may have had the hand of England somewhere behind it, but the main protagonist was well-known to Macbeth, an old man robbed of his son and, in effect, grandsons, as well as the satisfying position of being father to the king. Abbot Crinan waited until 1045 to march against Duncan's nemesis. Given that Edward 'the Confessor' had become king of England only in 1042, following the death of his half-brother, Harthacanute, the abbot may well have delayed seeking revenge in order to go south to negotiate English support.

There are some tantalising question marks over Crinan's own identity, which may be explored to provide us with a picture of a man from an Irish royal background, perhaps even a member of the Cenel Conall of Donegal, which traditionally provided priests for the Columban Church in Scotland but also had close ties with the Anglo-Saxon rulers of Northumbria. His marriage to Bethoc may have been his second; his first seems to have produced a son, Maldred, who went on to marry Ealdgyth, a daughter of the Earl Uhtred of Northumbria who had defeated Malcolm II in 1006. Fortunately Malcolm does not seem to have held this against him when considering him as a future son-in-law. Even more crucially, Ealdgyth's mother was King Edward's sister, Aelgifu. Even though he had ousted Crinan's Anglo-Saxon relatives-in-law from their traditional control of Bernicia when he brought all Northumbria under his own rule, Earl Siward, backed, presumably, by his king, was likely to have encouraged them to support any appeal for help against the king of Scots.[18]

If he did have the ability to take advantage of English – or at least Northumbrian – politics, then Abbot Crinan was also in touch with a disparate group of disaffected men within Scotland itself, a motley crew that may have included members of Queen Gruoch's extended family.[19] So far as we can tell, Macbeth seems to have made no move to restore them to the mormaership of Fife. We can only speculate, but one reason may have been the need, as Malcolm II had recognised, to court important political interests with gifts of land. The other may have been that family's perilously close relationship to the crown itself. It was a risky, if understandable, move to keep the house of Macduff – a surname they seem to have acquired as descendants of King Dubh – out in the political and social wilderness.[20]

Crinan advanced at the head of his small army, presumably under the protection of Columba's sacred reliquary, the Brecbennoch.[21] But he proved no match for the king. The rebel army was crushed, the abbot and nearly two hundred of his men left for dead on the field.[22] Macbeth could now claim to have both God and Columba on his side. All the same, it was fortunate for the Scottish king that Edward of England was safely embroiled in dealing with his own fractious political community, particularly his father-in-law, Earl Godwin of Mercia, who had helped him to the throne. It remained to be seen whether Edward's ambitions in the north were, like Cnut's before him, merely on hold.

At last, the anticipated threat of rebellion now made real and faced down, Macbeth could relax a little and start to plan for both the present and the future. In 1045 he had been married for at least a decade, and there was no sign, as far as we know, of any children. Given that she already had a son, the fault is unlikely to have lain with Gruoch, though the gossips at court would have been quick to point the finger at her. Lulach, her son by Gillacomgain, must have been approaching his twentieth year by 1045, a grown man by any standards. Macbeth had no doubt come to realise that this young man must be his heir, perhaps entrusting him with the ruling of Moray now that he himself was needed far more often in the south. The

bond between Macbeth and Lulach, despite the catastrophically bad start to their relationship by even the mythically
troubled standards often ascribed to stepchildren and step-
parents, may even have prompted a later king-list compiler to
presume that they were father and son.[23]

Macbeth had much for which to be grateful, and he seems
to have been determined to give the Almighty His proper due
for siding with him against his enemies. Still, there was more
to his relationship with God's representatives on earth than
mere conventional piety, the usual quid pro quo that might
serve to mitigate the inevitable violence in a ruler's career if he
paid due attention to the Church's worldly needs. This was a
king who had an interest in ecclesiastical affairs, apparently well
aware of the many and varied political benefits that might come
to those who took such things seriously. Perhaps Macbeth had
the example of Cnut in mind, a northern European monarch
who was nevertheless treated with great respect both at the
court of the Holy Roman Emperor and by the pope in Rome
himself. The Scottish king would not have put himself in the
same league as Cnut, but he certainly seems to have been aware
that Church politics, at home and abroad, was now coming to
the point where its neglect might prove risky.

Once he became king, Macbeth obviously had far greater
resources at his disposal but also more political interests determined to catch his ear and, where possible, get satisfaction. Key
among these must have been *the* bishop of Scotland, Maldovine
of St Andrews. It was no doubt Maldovine who presided over
the ecclesiastical element of his inauguration, giving the Scottish
Church's blessing to his kingship. It would surely have been
Maldovine, too, who talked the king through the implications

of Church reform, both positive and negative, to which we will return. As the 1040s progressed calmly onwards, the bishop's decision to support the house of Moray began to look wise and prudent.

It must have been apparent to everyone that Macbeth's reign was blessed with those qualities most endearing to contemporaries and tedious for historians of our own time and their readers: peace and prosperity. The king's military reputation had been unequivocally established against both Duncan and his father, and Macbeth seems to have felt neither the need nor the desire to go chasing popularity with raids into England, or even British Strathclyde, whose kings were not necessarily disposed to be friendly to him.* However, the 'productive seasons' with which God saw fit to reward His servant, Macbeth, would have kept the coffers of his nobility reasonably and regularly full too, helping to keep everyone, if not happy – warriors, like readers, get fed up with peace and quiet – then at least reasonably content with the status quo.[24]

This apparent prosperity stands in contrast to the terrible afflictions visited on England at the same time. In 1046, for example, the *Anglo-Saxon Chronicle* recorded that 'after Candlemas, came the strong winter, with frost and with snow, and with all kinds of bad weather; so that there was no man then alive who could remember so severe a winter as this was, both through loss of men and through loss of cattle; yea, fowls and fishes through much cold and hunger perished'. In Ireland

---

* As already mentioned, it is possible that the royal family of Strathclyde was related to the former royal house through marriage to a daughter of Malcolm II.

a similar story of severe snows and frosts was noted.[25] In truth, Scotland is unlikely to have avoided the impact of adverse weather conditions, famine and disease during the seventeen years of Macbeth's rule. The perception of prosperity, which occurs independently enough for it to be clear that this is, above all, what people remembered about him, was surely more to do with the absence of war. Once Crinan's rebellion was over, the country does seem to have settled down into a period of relative peace and stability. Men could go about their daily and seasonal business – a difficult enough job at the best of times – without the added worry of a call to arms. Their womenfolk could live without the fear that their men might never return from the latest grand escapade into Northumbria.

With Scotland settled, the borders quiet and the harvests good, Macbeth now began to ponder an audacious plan that had much to recommend it, should all go well. Making a pilgrimage to Rome was currently in vogue among British and Irish leaders, no doubt prompted by the edifying spectacle that Cnut had made of himself twenty years earlier. But no Scottish king had ever made the trip, probably because domestic politics had made going abroad an open invitation to anyone interested in seizing his throne. The astonishing implication is that Macbeth clearly viewed any threats to his own position as minor and remote – literally, perhaps, given that Malcolm, Duncan's son, had taken up residence in Orkney. This could have marked the beginning of a new era in Scottish politics, one which looked beyond the narrow confines of dynastic bloodfeuding to inform other leaders that, however insignificant and inaccessible Scotland might appear to be, it still intended to play a part in European politics.

Having made up his mind to leave his kingdom, Macbeth had much to do before he went. Obviously he needed to appoint someone to act in his stead and, though there is no evidence for it, Lulach was surely the obvious candidate, perhaps with the counsel of men like Bishop Maldovine. Though women certainly made pilgrimages, it was not all that common for queens or noblewomen to accompany their husbands on such perilous expeditions. However, Gruoch may have felt inclined to make her peace with God and, perhaps, with her husband too. A penitential journey to the very heart of Christendom might lay to rest the memory of all those terrible deeds – the murder of a husband and a brother – for which she may have felt, if not some responsibility, at least some unintentional involvement.

Once all the many preparations had been made for their departure, there was still one very important task for the royal couple to complete. Since neither Macbeth nor Gruoch were in the first, or even the second, flush of youth, and given the considerable dangers of travel in general, and travel through the Alps in particular, some form of insurance would be prudent. The insurance the king and queen had in mind related not to the loss of their baggage, or the contraction of some terrible Continental disease, likely though both these eventualities were. Rather, they wished to ensure that their eternal souls would be properly cared for by a gift of land to the Culdee monastic community of St Serf's, an island in Loch Leven, Fife.

At perhaps the same time, Bishop Maldovine of St Andrews also made a gift to St Serf's monastery of the church of Markinch, also in Fife, with all its lands.[26] We have no idea why St Serf – a sixth-century monk whose own monastery

seems to have been at Culross on the northern banks of the
Forth and who died at Dunning twenty miles north-west of
Loch Leven – was singled out by the royal couple and the
bishop of St Andrews.* Though the monastery on St Serf's
island was supposedly founded by Serf himself, another tradition states that the island was given to the Culdees in his
honour by the 'last' Pictish king, Bridei son of Dergard, Kenneth
mac Alpin's immediate predecessor and, presumably, the man
he killed in order to become king himself.

St Serf's is a low, flat pancake of an island, with the slightest
of inclines towards the south-eastern end, out of which the
monastery itself protruded. The distance from shore is about
a quarter of a mile and the monks are supposed to have sheltered their own boats in a bay on the north side of their island,
'which was also frequented by pike during the spawning season'.
The remains of a structure there have been described as 'a plain
building of the early Romanesque or Norman period, probably
the eleventh century, and may be one of those churches stated
to have been erected between 1040 and 1093'. Whether or not
this had anything to do with Macbeth is impossible to say, but
his interest in this particular monastery cannot be denied.[27]

The lands given by Macbeth and Gruoch were called
Kirkness and lay next to Portmoak on the east side of Loch
Leven. Macbeth also gave to St Serf's the lands of Bolgyne
(Bogie), which apparently belonged to 'the son of Thorfinn'.
How the king came to acquire these lands, which lay near
Kirkcaldy, is far from clear but, as already mentioned, it is

---

* Of course, these grants may not be the only ones made by Macbeth and
Gruoch, but merely those we happen to know about.

possible that they had been previously granted by Malcolm II to his Orcadian grandson from the lands forfeited from Maelbaethe, and Macbeth then, in turn, forfeited them from Thorfinn's son.[28] All three grants – Kirkness, Bogie and Markinch – were situated in a region known in the Middle Ages as Forthrif, a sub-province lying to the west of Fife.[29] The parish of Ballingry, to the south of Loch Leven, means 'the king's town', implying that there were royal lands in the vicinity.[30] It is more likely, however, that Kirkness belonged to Gruoch, or at least formed part of her dowry.

Both these grants exempted the monks from any secular dues that might be demanded by the king, his sheriffs, or his son. This last intriguing reference might indicate that Lulach was indeed viewed as Macbeth's 'son' and heir, and would have to play a leading role in government while the king was away. In return, Macbeth and Gruoch would presumably expect the rents of these lands to pay for a priest to say Masses and pray for their souls 'at a specially dedicated altar in either the church at Kirkness or St Serf's Monastery'.[31]

Though all we have left is an echo of the original document, translated from Gaelic into Latin centuries later as part of a property dispute between St Andrews (which eventually appropriated St Serf's) and a later owner of the lands of Bogie,[32] it is the nearest we have to a direct link with this very real king, Macbeth. It is also remarkable for being the first mention, by name, of a queen of Scots, albeit alongside her husband. It is, unfortunately, the only direct evidence for the actions of a woman who has perhaps been wronged by history even more terribly than Macbeth himself.

It would be tempting to interpret Gruoch's absence from the sources as indicative of a meek and submissive personality. But to do so would be to presume that all medieval women were similarly reticent. They may be more or less silent to us, but their actions occasionally speak far louder than words and, though they usually had to subvert the system to achieve their own ends, they should not be underestimated. Indeed, the very uniqueness of Gruoch's only surviving foray into public life gives it enormous significance, an undeniable hint that this doubly royal woman played an active role both in her marriage and in public life more generally.

The clouds scud across the hill on their way south, bringing a chill to the air as a small group of travellers pick their way through the tussocky grass alongside the Lochty Burn. At the front strides a ruddy-faced man, each of his long steps shadowed by two large deerhounds. A cry from further back catches his attention and he turns to look down on his companions. His wife is waving to him, smiling, wanting him to come to her. He smiles too and goes back down to kneel with her and take a handful of cool, fresh water from the well. Gruoch's well.* He should have known that he would not be allowed to pass by, having heard countless times of its virtues, and the place it holds in his wife's affections, a symbol of a care-free childhood long gone. He pulls her up and they climb the rest of the hill together, a middle-aged couple out for a breath of very fresh air.

* Gruoch's well is probably the only place in Scotland still named after Macbeth's queen. It lies on the southern flank of Benarty Hill, at the source of the Lochty Burn.

But there is more to this jaunt than nostalgia. At the top they catch their breath and walk on, the grey waters of Loch Leven emerging ever more expansively with every step. Gruoch spots the island of St Serf first, lying immediately below and to their right, a faint glimmer of smoke rising from the monastery before being jostled away by the wind. In the far distance they can just see the lands of Kirkness. They take comfort from imagining that the cattle and sheep grazing invisibly on the Lomond hills, the oats and barley slowly ripening in the ploughed soil, the eternal toil of the peasants of Kirkness will be transformed into the prayers of a diligent priest, hastening on towards Paradise the souls that will one day leave behind the warm, vital flesh that lies in each other's hand. Macbeth nods, his curiosity satisfied, and turns his gaze north, across the hills that hide Perth and the River Tay. This is the heart of Scotland, the place where he was made king, where he pours forth so much of his hospitality to keep his restless nobles sure of their worth to him, and his to them, but which will never truly feel like home.

Gruoch and Macbeth, poised on the brink of an adventure from which one or both of them might never return, wished to leave Scotland with their sins absolved, their consciences clear and their immortal souls in good hands.[33] Now they were ready to set off for the Eternal City, a journey that they would share with a multitude of other pilgrims. The royal pair would be suitably penitent, of course. But Macbeth was perhaps already planning how the king of Scots would let the world know of his arrival in Rome.

CHAPTER 9

The Testing Time

Out, out, brief candle!

Macbeth, Act V, Scene v

The poor of the Eternal City in the mid-eleventh century looked forward to the visits of foreign kings and princes. For a start, the arrival of far-flung rulers usually meant that Pope Leo IX was in residence in the Lateran Palace, an unusual occurrence in itself, but one which brought with it the welcome prospect of picking over the remains of his hospitality. Then there was always the chance that visiting dignitaries would wish to make a good impression in this proud, touchy city. Doubtless Rome's older beggars were still telling stories about the visit of the mighty Cnut, ruler of Denmark, Norway, England and parts of Sweden, some twenty years before. On his arrival *and* his departure, the great Dane had distributed unprecedented amounts of alms, as well as making generous offerings to the church of St Peter and holding lavish banquets during his stay.[1] No resident of Rome could have been left in any doubt about

Cnut's piety, nor his wealth and power, however much their instincts were to ridicule this second-generation Christian from a distant northern empire.

In April 1050, a throng of beggars would once more have gathered hopefully around the Pilgrims' Gate, the northern entrance to the Leonine city whose two-hundred-year-old walls protected St Peter's Basilica and the Lateran Palace, as well as the foreign schools that lodged the dignitaries and pilgrims of various nations. Pope Leo was currently preparing for the Easter synod to be held at the end of the month. However, the crowd was perhaps unsure whom to expect at this gathering since so many of western Europe's senior figures had attended Leo's big event of the previous year, the consecration of Rheims Cathedral in the presence of his cousin, the Holy Roman Emperor, Henry III.

Fortunately, at least one king was making his way to Rome in 1050. Though we have no evidence for his itinerary, presumably, since he was coming from the north, he and his entourage followed a pilgrim's trail that was already well-established. The straight lines and steep gradients of the imperial roads that once fanned out from Rome to maintain contact with even the furthest-flung outposts of empire had long ago succumbed quietly to nature. The northern European pilgrims who picked their way through France or down the Rhine into Switzerland before crossing the Alps into northern Italy did not therefore make this trip lightly.

This was certainly no holiday jaunt, but a long and arduous journey of several months on horseback. It had to be timed right, too, to avoid treacherous winter conditions crossing the Alps in either direction. The traveller also had to take care that he or she did not end up in Rome during the sickening heat of summer.[2] A century before Macbeth ventured towards Rome, Archbishop Aelfsige of Canterbury had frozen to death en route to his investiture by the pope. In 1051 the Irishman Laidhcenn of Gaileanga and his wife both died 'in the east' on their way back from Rome.[3] They would all have known – and made provision for it before they left – that their chances of returning were far from certain.

As an important traveller, King Macbeth would have been made welcome in abbeys and monasteries along the way, and might also have taken advantage of the many inns that catered for those with wealth to spend. Such establishments supplied a bed and meal for the night and accommodation for retainers and horses, but could also provide medicines and laundry facilities to ease, a little at least, the rigours of the road. The experience of travelling was certainly not dull: the routes were thronged with vendors, dancing girls and singers, eager to tempt passersby to part with their money. The popularity of these pilgrimage trails also provided good business for those equally intent on relieving solitary or unwary travellers of their belongings by force.[4]

The final stretch of one of the most popular routes – known simply as the Via Romea on the way south and the Via Francigena on the way back north – picked up what remained of the Via Cassia, a former imperial road, at Sienna in northwest Italy. About ten miles from Rome the road split in two, the pilgrimage route then abandoning Via Cassia for the Via Trionfale. A few miles from his final destination, Macbeth would have reached the top of the Mountain of Joy (now the Roman suburb of Monte Mario), so called because here, at last, after a long and perilous journey, the traveller could bask in the heady emotion of his first sight of the Eternal City.

St Peter's Basilica and the Leonine city lay immediately below him, Rome itself, both the ancient remains and its degenerate successor, sprawling along the far bank of the Tiber. Perhaps the king paused to pray in the little chapel of St Lazarus in gratitude for his safe arrival. Here, too, he might have found an emissary waiting to conduct him into the city. In any event, he and his entourage would soon have covered the last downhill stretch to reach the Pilgrims' Gate.

The beggars lurking hopefully there were unlikely to have known who this king was. They could see that he was tall and fair, like Cnut had been, but even if they found out his name, it would have been difficult to pronounce. *Mac-beth-ad.* Outlandish, they probably thought, definitely a northerner. But, despite being the first ruler of his kingdom to come to Rome, this king knew what was expected of him. As the small procession advanced towards the gate, handfuls of silver flew into the crowd.

Any doubts about the newcomer would be cast aside as the crowd fell swiftly to the ground to retrieve the coins. While this largesse was certainly not on the scale proffered by Cnut, it was no paltry gesture either. News of it even reached an Irish monk, Marianus, who, later in life, compiled a chronicle in which he recalled that, in 1050, 'The king of Scots, Macbethad, scattered silver like seeds to the poor of Rome',[5] the only reference we have to this extraordinary journey. That this king was able to make such a show of alms-giving – despite the fact that his kingdom did not even mint its own coins – and that word of it reverberated back through northern Europe, speaks volumes about the impression he was out to make on the Continent. Such gestures were calculated for their political, as well as their penitential, value.

But what, we might wonder, would Macbeth have made of Rome? There was certainly nothing like it in Scotland, where urban centres were still in their infancy and whose Roman remains largely consisted of the odd fort, probably already plundered for its stone, and the remains of the Antonine Wall, designed to keep the early Scottish tribes out of the empire.

Entering the Pilgrims' Gate, Macbeth would have been immediately confronted by the impressive walls of St Peter's Basilica, built on the instructions of the Emperor Constantine some seven hundred years before, allegedly on the very spot where the first apostle was martyred during the reign of the Emperor Nero around AD 64. As one of Christianity's greatest sites for veneration, St Peter's already boasted a veritable cornucopia of riches in gifts and decoration, inside and out.

It was built, literally, around what is known as the 'Trophy', though even recent excavation has not been able to reveal whether this really contained the relics of St Peter himself. It does not greatly matter; the important point is that, within a century of his martyrdom, people believed that it did. The tomb containing the Trophy lay, since the beginning of the seventh century, beneath the altar. To get there, Macbeth would have descended stairs into the crypt and then walked along a passageway that brought him level with the corridor that held the Trophy itself. No doubt he would, like all pilgrims, have paused for a moment to offer his prayers to Peter, the brother of St Andrew, whose remains now lay in Scotland.* Perhaps, as an important royal visitor, he might even have been allowed to venture closer to the holy relic. Once he had completed his devotions, he would have continued along the corridor and up the stairs at the far end.[6] Who knows what emotions played across his mind at that moment, what necessary misdeeds might have been lifted from his shoulders as he emerged from the cool, damp earth into the splendour of the church above?

Beside St Peter's lay the papal residence, the Lateran Palace, with its own church of St John, rebuilt at the beginning of the tenth century after a terrible fire. The rest of the Vatican hill was cluttered with yet more churches, as well as monasteries, hostels and cemeteries dedicated to the service of St Peter and his successors, the bishops of Rome, and the many visitors drawn to this sacred site. If the pilgrim was so minded, there were more than twenty churches, both inside and outside the city walls, to be visited. Thankfully, specially commissioned public conveniences, fountains and baths supplied from the city's aqueducts helped to ease the pressure of the pilgrims on the local infrastructure, though it is unlikely that such measures did much to hinder the rapid spread of disease.[7]

All this hustle and bustle may already have proved quite overwhelming for a Scottish king used to the less invasive sounds of forest and glen. But surely no visitor who had spent so much time and trouble getting to Rome would fail to cross the Tiber and explore the city proper? Of course, Rome was

---

* The relics of St Andrew were supposedly brought from Constantinople to Kinrighmont (later St Andrews) in east Fife by St Rule in the ninth century.

not what it had once been, the unrivalled capital of the world. For a start, its population had collapsed, from a peak of more than a million around AD 250 to less than fifty thousand over the course of the next millennium. It is worth noting that, in AD 1000, a reliable contemporary writer estimated that the population of York was as much as thirty thousand.[8] Rome was not, then, the city it had once been, reduced now to squatting over only a single bend in the river and overshadowed by the remnants of its ancient predecessor.

Macbeth would also have noticed that most of the ordinary dwelling houses in the modern city were made of timber, while the great stone monuments of the past, if they had not been incorporated into the walls of more recent buildings, had been left gently to disintegrate under a layer of vegetation on which the citizenry grazed their flocks. Even the Roman Forum – the very hub of the ancient city – would have been described to Macbeth as the *Campo Vaccinio*, the cow pasture. Once he had taken a closer look, the Scottish king may well have felt slightly more at home.

Even in its decline, though, Rome was full of wonders to enthral and appal the medieval visitor, brought up to abhor the non-Christian world. These included obviously eye-catching attractions, like the Colosseum and the Pantheon, as well as the remains of triumphal arches, palaces and baths, bronze and marble statues. The papal authorities were eager to put forward their own 'official' view of the relationship between the classical past and the Christian present. As early as the 1140s, they circulated a written guidebook, the *Mirabilia Urbis Romae* (Wonders of the City of Rome), explicitly linking buildings and places of pagan origins with particular saints.[9]

No doubt guided tours were also available for the edification of the less literate faithful, not to mention kings and princes with no desire (or ability) to be seen with their noses stuck in a book. However, ignorance, or perhaps the haste to place such an obviously glorious non-Christian past within a Christian framework, produced some equally glorious errors in the descriptions of what was left of the ancient city. As one modern writer tersely remarks, it was entirely possible that 'travellers who used this text as their Baedeker would leave Rome not knowing where Caesar died or Nero fiddled'.[10] For the ruler of a country that could proudly claim never to have succumbed to the might of the empire, this was probably immaterial. Macbeth had business in Rome, very practical and pertinent business concerned with the here and now, not some distant, near-mythical past, however marvellous it was to look at.

But to experience a world so far removed from home was surely exciting too. Though medieval rulers spent most of their lives on the move – seeing and being seen, attending to business and escaping the swift descent of squalor upon their communal living conditions – the blatant exoticism of the Continent must have thrilled the senses, even as it might have frightened and confused those of a timorous nature. As we will see, it seems to have had a profound effect on Macbeth, meeting men with new ideas, different ways of doing things to those in which he had been educated since birth. To be fair, Scotland was far from homogeneous – different languages, cultural norms and preferences, legal and administrative practices all testified to the kingdom's inherent diversity. But these were known incongruities. Rome was a world of the unknown, an unsettling profusion of differences that might challenge and inspire a man of intelligence.

Like most high-born pilgrims, Macbeth would have been moved to go to Rome for more than one reason. However, we must try not to be too cynical about the religious or spiritual appeal of these arduous journeys. Pilgrimages were genuine attempts, by one's own efforts, to bridge some of the gap between here and eternity. There was nothing unusual about the undeniably violent course of Macbeth's career, so we should not read too much into any desire on his part to seek absolution for past misdeeds. But it surely felt good, nonetheless, to have left Scotland as a friend to its Church and now travel to the very heart of western Christendom.

Macbeth's relationship with his own Church surely extended far beyond his grant to the monastery at Loch Leven, which was essentially an act of conventional piety on his own behalf, rather than a gesture signifying much in the way of political advantage to either side. It is true that Bishop Maldovine had seen fit to make his own gift in honour of St Serf, and this might be interpreted as confirmation that the king and queen were acting with his advice and support.[11] But Macbeth could do far more for Scotland's premier bishop than merely endow a tiny Culdean monastery. If he managed – as he no doubt would – to secure an audience with Pope Leo in Rome, then there was one particularly delicate issue that the king might bring to the pontiff's attention, an issue that struck at the very heart of Scotland's formal identity and its place in western Christendom.

Bishop Maldovine was regarded very highly within the Columban Church, the Irish annals describing him on his death – unusually for a Scottish bishop – as 'the glory of the clergy of the Gaels'.[12] He, together with other important members of the Scottish Church, must have played a key role in preparing Macbeth for his pilgrimage. Indeed, it is quite possible that Maldovine in particular was responsible for persuading Macbeth of the wisdom of such a journey in the first place, since he, like the rest of Christendom, would have wanted to find out exactly what the pope was planning in his programme of reform. Given the interest that both king and bishops had in papal pronouncements, Macbeth may even have been present at Leo's second synod, held in October 1049 in Mainz, which lies 'on the main route travelled by Scandinavians and Gaels on their way to Italy'.[13]

As (mostly) members of the Culdean Church, with its principles of asceticism and withdrawal from the world, Scotland's regular clergy would no doubt have been pleased to see the papacy start to clean up its act after the embarrassing lows of the 1030s, when the highest ecclesiastical office became the preserve of aristocratic Roman playboys.[14] Bishop Maldovine and his colleagues would also have had sympathy with the ideas that the current pope, Leo IX, was keen to promote.* However, the desire to rationalise the current rather vague and regionally idiosyncratic system of Church government posed a particular, and potentially hazardous, problem for Scotland, however sensible its motivation.

What caused the problem, from a Scottish perspective, were the eighth-century writings of the great Northumbrian

---

* Scotland's lay clergy, those not bound by monastic rules, on the other hand, were exactly the kind of morally questionable churchmen – often married, able to purchase their offices, or holding them heritably – that the reform movement wanted to stamp out.

historian, Bede. In his *Historia Ecclesiastica Gentis Anglorum* (Ecclesiastical History of the English People), Bede asserted that Pope Gregory the Great had intended 'that Britain should be divided between two archbishops, with northern bishops falling under the obedience of the archbishop of York'. What this statement does not disclose is the fact that, at the time, the Celtic Church had its own system of government independent of the Roman one to which the rest of Britain adhered. Three centuries later, with St Peter's throne occupied by men like Leo IX, intent upon working out 'a clearly defined hierarchy of obedience embracing all the faithful', Bishop Maldovine may already have realised that Scotland needed an archbishop of its own to combat the inevitable absorption within the English Church system that Bede's statement implied.[15] As Scotland's premier bishop, he was also no doubt well aware that this would bring about his own promotion.

Over the next few centuries, the relationship between the Churches of England and Scotland would become a jurisdictional battlefield echoing – even helping to fuel – the tensions between the Scottish and English kings over the independence or otherwise of the northern kingdom. Though it would take until 1072 before the heated arguments began to grumble their way in earnest between Rome, England and Scotland, these debates did not emerge out of nowhere. Indeed, the spirit of reform that Pope Leo IX began energetically to extol from almost the first minute of his pontificate in February 1049 must already have given Scottish churchmen good reason to be concerned over their anomalous position. A royal visit to St Peter's successor would do no harm to the state of Macbeth's eternal soul. It was also the ideal opportunity to make the pope aware of the fact that the Church in Scotland languished – so far as the Scots were concerned – under the authority of the Church of another kingdom.

If the Scottish king did manage to raise the issue with the pope, then Leo had neither the time nor, probably, the inclination to pay much attention. We can hazard a guess, though, that this may have been something that he brought up with the new archbishop of Canterbury, Robert of Jumièges, when he arrived in Rome in 1051 to receive his pallium. If so, Robert's response was likely to have been robust in defence of Pope Gregory's bipartite division of Britain. If so, it would not have taken long before King Edward heard about Scottish ambitions. He was unlikely to have taken the news well.

Even if he did not get an archbishop for Scotland – a very tall order in any case* – Macbeth had at least made use of an ideal opportunity for a Scottish monarch to involve himself personally in European politics at the highest level. He was both the first, and the last, Scottish king to make the trip to Rome and in doing so he lent a new dignity to his own kingship, whatever the European hoi polloi, or even their superiors, might have thought of it.[16] Above all, this remarkable journey was an expression of the king's belief that Scotland had a place in the world far beyond the islands of Britain and Ireland. Here, surely, was proof that Scotland's leaders had much to gain from setting their sights well above the debilitating feuds that had

---

* Scotland did not achieve metropolitan status until 1472, and even then only because there was a schism that provoked the unseemly spectacle of competing popes giving away political advantage to gain the support of particular national interests.

so preoccupied them over recent generations. Scotland, under Macbeth, was finally growing up.

While in Rome, the king may have been intrigued to hear of the arrival of yet another visitor from the far north: Earl Thorfinn of Orkney. The Norseman had also succumbed to the fashionable appeal of a pilgrimage, though his motivation was apparently entirely serious. Ruing, or at least politically sorry for, the murder in 1046 of his popular nephew, Rognvald, with whom he had previously found it expedient to share his earldóm, Thorfinn now apparently intended to take a vow to give up fighting beyond his lands as a penance.[17] He too may have been feeling his age, and the desire to acknowledge and purge himself of the inevitable misdeeds of his political life before he met with his Maker in the next world. This was good news for the Scottish king, who must have felt truly blessed if the Orcadian really did mean to keep his raiding parties to himself. 1050 was, without a doubt, the high point in the reign of Macbeth, and a glorious moment for Scotland itself.

Leo IX held his synod on 29 April 1050. There the delegates heard evidence relating to the potentially heretical writings of Berengar of Tours, who was currently trying to debate the nature of the Eucharist. In particular, Berengar referred back to the teachings of the ninth-century Frankish theologian Ratramnus, who asserted that the bread and water consumed during Holy Communion did not miraculously become the body and blood of Christ, but was instead intended to be symbolic of Christ's presence in the act. By the end of the year, Berengar had been declared a heretic and Ratramnus's book, *De corpore et sanguine Domini liber* (On the body and blood of Our Lord), had also been condemned as heresy.

Macbeth probably had little interest in such esoteric debates and was perhaps more fascinated by stories of a miracle – the restoration of a smashed wooden goblet given to Leo by Herimar, bishop of Rheims – that had probably taken place in the Lateran Palace even as the Scottish king was visiting the Holy City.[18] However, Berengar, in trying to defend his position over the next few years, made an important point that should have given even the Scottish king pause for thought. A profound believer in Scripture and with no real quarrel with the Church's teachings generally, Berengar objected to being made to agree with something that he found irrational, pointing out that the authorities condemning his argument were only human and therefore capable of being wrong. As the pace of reform began to quicken, especially during the pontificate of Gregory VII (1073–85), the Church's desire to keep its own house firmly in order had serious repercussions that spread far beyond the purely ecclesiastical.

The issue of its lack of archbishop was one that impacted profoundly on Scotland, most particularly in terms of the kingdom's relationship with its larger, more powerful neighbour, England. What made sense on some papal drawing board might find itself entirely at odds with the needs of particular national Churches and the secular rulers with whom they inevitably had close dealings. A rational decision taken in the Lateran Palace might seem entirely irrational – indeed, downright wrong – once it had been communicated across Christendom.

Not that the thinking behind these reforms was either unreasonable or devious. The need for change stemmed from a desire to build the Church on sure foundations, something that could only be achieved through rational organisation to provide a clear hierarchy that would settle everyone in their place below the pope himself. The reformers were no longer satisfied with the veneer of ultimate authority, not least because some senior churchmen in the east – such as the Patriarch of Constantinople – were inclined to doubt the validity of that claim and, as it was no doubt suspected, had a tendency to look down on the turbulent and fragmented condition of western Europe.*

However, the drive for reform had unforeseen consequences; frowning on anomaly or difference in organisational or doctrinal terms was bound to provoke tensions. Even worse, the resolution of difficult issues might seem to favour those with the most clout, drawing the papacy ever further into secular politics driven by concerns that were all too human. Such a suspicion certainly lingered over attempts to secure an archbishopric for Scotland, though the Scots also proved adept at manipulating the papacy's antagonism to the growing strength of medieval England.

Who knows what the Europeans whom Macbeth met on his momentous journey made of him; they have left us nothing from which to judge their opinion. We can speculate that his show of wealth was more about style than substance, but that

---

* Only four years after Macbeth's visit to Rome, the see of St Peter finally acted on its claims to supremacy, excommunicating Patriarch Michael of Constantinople and thereby severing the formal links between the Roman Catholicism of western Europe and the Greek Orthodoxy of the east (Barber, *The Two Cities*, pp. 490–1). This did not mark the end of the relationship between the two halves of the former Roman empire, but it drove a wedge between them that ultimately paved the way for the appalling Fourth Crusade, which sacked Constantinople in 1204.

would only be conjecture. What we do know suggests that he, like Cnut, went to great lengths to display the affluence of northern kingship. It should be remembered that even the French had paused to mark, with respect, the passing of the Scottish king, Malcolm II.

It is worth recalling, too, that Macbeth of Scotland was lauded by his contemporaries for bringing peace and prosperity at a time when Italy and France, even England, struggled with internal discord. Though such eulogies must be taken with a pinch of salt, they were meant to make clear that God was well pleased with this man.

Macbeth's own relationship with England is harder to characterise, at least until he returned from his trip to Rome. He would not, unlike later kings of Scots, have worried unduly about the idea that he was equal in status to the English king. In a time when gradations of kingship were still not just possible but entirely normal, the Scottish king would have had no wish to denigrate the kind of royal authority claimed by his father in the north, any more than he would have failed to acknowledge all number of Irish rulers, but particularly his ally, Diarmait mac Maíl na mBó, who hoped to become high king of the whole of Ireland. The concept of sovereignty – the discrete and unassailable jurisdiction of the royal office over a particular geographical unit – had not yet surfaced above the horizon of the mental landscape of eleventh-century Scotland.

However, that is not to say that Macbeth would have found it acceptable to see his own authority either flouted or denigrated. Nor could he countenance encroachment on the current borders of his kingdom from anyone – Norse, British (i.e.

Strathclyde) or English – not least because doing so was tanta-
mount to political suicide. Fortunately – and it is a testament
to the success of his own kingship – Macbeth returned from
Rome, presumably some time in the late summer or autumn
of 1050, to find Scotland just as he had left it. He had proved
that a Scottish king could undertake the journey and go home
with no harm done, something that would have been unthinkable even ten years before.

Macbeth was now entering his sixth decade and his second
as Scotland's ruler. Though he does not seem to have shown
any outward signs of a lack of vigour, he was still an old man.
And old men were vulnerable if they held a position that others
might wish to take for themselves. Presumably Lulach, who
may well have performed admirably as his stepfather's lieutenant while the latter was away, was no threat, though both
men may have found it awkward to adjust to the king's safe
return. On the other hand, the news from the north that
Macbeth must have brought back with him was surely reas-
suring. If Earl Thorfinn now preferred to stay at home, that
presumably meant there was little likelihood of an army setting
sail from Orkney with young Malcolm, Duncan's son, on board.
All in all, the Scottish king could continue to feel that he
exerted a firm grip over his kingdom, hopeful that any potential threats were, if not extinguished, then at least kept at bay.

In contrast to the composure of Macbeth of Scotland, the
English king was almost at the end of his tether. Another
remarkably tall man with, apparently, the wrath of a lion, Edward
(known only from the twelfth century as 'the Confessor') had
married Earl Godwin of Wessex's daughter, Edith, in 1045, the

price of the earl's support in securing his accession to the English throne two years earlier. But there was a limit to Edward's gratitude towards his father-in-law and that limit had been well and truly reached by 1051. It did not help that the king blamed Godwin for handing over his brother, Alfred, to Harold Harefoot during a previous attempt to restore the Anglo-Saxon royal line to the English throne. Alfred died after being blinded to prevent him from ever being able to rule, a terrible outcome that Edward never forgot or ever forgave.

The immediate cause of what almost became a bitter civil war was the king's closeness to the Norman friends of his youth (he lived in exile at the court of his mother's brother, Duke Richard of Normandy, from 1013). These friends accompanied him back to England when Edward returned there at the invitation of Harthacanute in 1041, a comforting presence that Earl Godwin soon came to interpret as a conspiracy to exclude him from the royal ear and destroy him and his family. Tempers began to rise, as the other two great earls of England – Leofric of Mercia and Siward of Northumbria – took the field against Godwin. In the end, the royal father-in-law decided not to challenge the king in open battle, escaping to Flanders.

However, Godwin returned to England with an army in the autumn of 1052 and this time it was Edward who lost his nerve. His Norman favourites, including Archbishop Robert of Jumièges, fled from London and on 15 September king and earl were reconciled. Both sides had learned a lesson and, in any event, Godwin died of a stroke seven months later. The fact that much of England ended up in the hands of his four sons (Harold, Tostig, Gyrth and Leofwine) also proved useful to Edward, who found that he could rely on them to deal with any military business while he himself concentrated on devising grand imperial strategies.[19]

The Scottish king had no doubt watched with interest, and continuing relief, as Edward and Earl Godwin squared up to each other over the course of 1051–2. His curiosity was more than merely a natural Scottish instinct. His recent trip to the heart of Europe seems to have opened up Macbeth's eyes to all sorts of possibilities that might serve to modernise certain aspects of Scotland's government. He was particularly interested in the notion that the crown's military strength could be shifted away from an overwhelming reliance on the king's own personal connections, mostly among the kingdom's senior nobles, and onto a more professional basis, as was the case in Normandy and, to some extent, England. Macbeth knew as well as anyone in Britain at the time that relying on the loyalty of great men was a delicate and dangerous business. Though he did not get very far with the project, he seems to have appreciated the wisdom of creating a warrior class independent, to a degree, of the existing social structure. Its members would thus owe their positions directly to the crown, rather than the individual who currently wore it, burdened as he was with the inevitable regional politics that had got him the throne in the first place.

King Edward had his own housecarls, a retinue of professional household troops that was a welcome innovation – so far as the crown was concerned – introduced to England by his stepfather, Cnut.* So too did Earl Siward of Northumbria,

---

* Cnut had taken, as his second wife, Edward's mother, Emma of Normandy, who had previously been married to King Aethelred II of England, Edward's father.

whose own large retinue was 'paid out of the income from his extensive estates in Northamptonshire and Huntingdonshire'.[20] However, Macbeth, who would certainly have had his own small group of bodyguards, was unlikely to do likewise for fear that his own people would rebel against taxation raised for such a purpose. What interested the Scottish king most was the example of some of Edward's Norman friends, who had been given land in England, often strategically placed in 'problem' areas, which they were supposed to sort out, satisfying both their own immediate interests and the longer-term security of king and kingdom. How helpful it would be to have men in Scotland who owed the kind of loyalty to the crown that would persuade them to carry out royal policy without argument, petulance or the continual need for some new sign of royal favour.

So Macbeth was very interested to learn of the plight of these same Norman friends of King Edward once Earl Godwin had returned to purge them from the kingdom. Most of those at court returned to their native land, but some fled west, to seek shelter with Osbern Pentecost, who had built a castle at Mulstonestone in Herefordshire on the Anglo-Welsh border;[21] castle-building was a favourite occupation of the Normans, as England would soon find out, and this was one of the earliest ever built there. The Normans were pursued and forced to submit, fortunately not to Earl Godwin but the rather more sympathetic Earl Leofric of Mercia. Most intriguingly, Osbern Pentecost then requested – and got – the earl's permission for himself, his esquire (*socius*), Hugh, and presumably the rest of the garrison, to go north and enter the service of the king of Scots.[22]

The brief chronicle references to this remarkable development, which 'marks the earliest recorded Norman presence in Scotland',[23] unfortunately beg more questions than they answer. For a start, such a request strongly suggests that Osbern knew the Scottish king, or at least had reason to suppose that Macbeth would be sympathetic to the arrival of a boatload of Norman refugees. In any case, Scotland was not the kind of place that most Continental Europeans would have made for without some kind of prior knowledge. Given the improbability of Macbeth ever going anywhere near the Herefordshire border with Wales, we might be forgiven for imagining that the most likely place that the two could have become acquainted was Normandy itself.

The duchy lay on the southern side of the shortest crossing over the English Channel. It also possibly marked a point of Continental landfall – or departure – for a Scottish king travelling the length of Britain by boat. 'On the eve of the long expedition of 1066 ... the duchy of Normandy had already experienced a good half-century of demographic and economic growth.'[24] This would have been an interesting place for Macbeth to spend some time and the Scottish king may have come across Osbern on his travels to or from Rome and listened, enthralled, to stories of his adventures in England, paying particular attention, perhaps, to the knight's vehement support of the new fashion for fighting on horseback. With nowhere to go in the autumn of 1052, the Norman may have remembered the interest shown by the Scottish king and resolved to take his chances in the north.

The stone walls of the castle do their best to absorb the sound of the many voices chasing frantic conversations across the hall. The scattered remains of a most satisfying feast lie strewn above and below the long tables, where a number of less hardy souls will soon be joining them under the footrail. On the dais, the Norman lord and his honoured guest, the king of Scots, discuss the merits of stone versus timber for domestic construction, so far as they are able with no common language and, therefore, a monastic translator, between them. Macbeth no longer finds this exasperating, having spent most of the year engaged in similarly disjointed conversations. But he is getting tired, as he so often does these days with his belly full and his eyes stinging with the smoke. He looks down fondly at his cup of blood-red wine, wondering if he might be able to encourage French traders to come as far north as the River Tay. He is glad to be going home, glad that they have all survived the rigours of the journey, and the astonishing experience of Rome itself.

The Norman gets up to relieve himself and the king considers whether this might be an opportune moment to take a polite leave of his host. As his eye drifts around the room, taking in and still able to marvel at the collection of races and languages sitting easily with one another, his attention is caught by a cluster gathered around a young man whom the others are clearly finding amusing. When his host resumes his seat, Macbeth turns to the monk hovering between them to ask who they are, adding, 'They are talking about England, are they not?'

The Norman looks and listens too. 'Indeed', he replies. 'You honour us with your knowledge of our language, my lord.' He smiles. 'But perhaps you know only the words that matter.'

Macbeth smiles too. 'I would like to speak with that one there, the one with the dark hair and the red tunic. What is his name?'

The Norman consults his steward. 'Osbern Pentecost, my lord. He is just passing through, on his way from England to the Vexin for Duke Ralph, his master.'

The young man approaches the dais; he has a pleasant face, and a quick, eager manner about him. He looks inquiringly at this king, whose name he has never heard before today. A stool is brought for him to sit at Macbeth's right. 'My French is not good,' the Scot admits, 'but shall we try?' Osbern nods and the monk is dismissed. 'What are you doing in England?' the king asks. Osbern slowly explains that he is in the middle of building a castle in wild country near Wales. He stops himself in time from making a witty, but potentially costly, comment about Celts and their barbarous ways.

'And if you met one of these Britons,' Macbeth inquires, 'would you fight him on foot or from your horse?'

'Oh, but my lord, why would I get off my horse?'

Macbeth shakes his head and harrumphs sceptically.

'You do not care to ride, my lord?'

'Of course! My wife will tell you that I spend more time with my horses than I do with her, though I swear she is glad of it. But even in the hunt we kill on foot, a fair fight, my skill against the beast's strength and cunning. I could do no less against a man.'

'Oh well, that is very honourable, I'm sure. But I call it fair only when I win.'

The king thoughtfully chews his moustache. 'It is not just about honour,' he finally responds. 'On foot, we have a choice of weapons and can wield them with perfect control. But to ride on horseback with sword or spear, that would be madness. I dare not think about the damage my own army would do, on itself.'

'Then you must practise, my lord. And get yourself a saddle that's high at the front and the back.' Osbern pauses, thinking how best

to couch his next question diplomatically. 'You have perhaps never considered the need for stirrups?' Macbeth shrugs and shakes his head. 'Perhaps you might care to try mine tomorrow, before we leave? They will help you to keep your balance even when you use your sword.'

'I will do that, Sir Osbern. And now you must excuse me. I have kept you from your friends for too long and an old man needs his sleep. But I will think on what you have said.'

Osbern rises and the two men smile. 'I wish you well, my lord. I am glad to be of service to you.'

'You have indeed, Sir Osbern. I am tempted to wish we had men like you in Scotland.'

The arrival of Osbern Pentecost and his companions in Macbeth's service underlines, along with the journey to Rome, just how much of a break with the past this king represented. This was not revolution, of course; far from it. But there is a sense of moving on, away from the difficulties of previous reigns, which, despite glorious episodes like Carham, seem insular and conservative in comparison.

On the other hand, the connection between Macbeth and the increasingly powerful Irish king of Leinster (from 1042), Diarmait mac Maíl na mBó, suggests that the Scottish king was also capable of involving himself in the convoluted – but strategically important – politics of the Irish Sea world. Perhaps Macbeth's messengers brought the Leinsterman the news that Earl Thorfinn was now planning to stay at home, a welcome reduction in the number of players interested in the region. In 1052, Diarmait managed to seize control of Dublin from no less a king 'of the Foreigners' than Echmarchach, former ally of the Scottish king's cousin, Malcolm of Moray.[25] Given that Echmarchach fled Dublin for the Isle of Man and was, by the time of his death in 1065, exerting some control over the south-westernmost tip of Scotland, both Diarmait and Macbeth were likely to have shown an interest in his maritime empire that straddled the kingdoms on either side of the Irish Sea.[26]

The *Lebor Bretnach*, the poem which provides the evidence for the relationship between Diarmait and Macbeth,[27] was perhaps written around this time, both men having been king for the best part of a decade. Both had also dealt successfully with challenges in their early years. Though focused on the voyage of the Picts, via Ireland, to Scotland, the *Lebor Bretnach* provides a version of Scotland's history that passes without comment over Kenneth mac Alpin, who thus becomes the unremarkable successor to the kings who came after the Pictish king, Eoganan of Fortriu, after a decade of turmoil following the latter's death in 839. Macbeth comes at the end of that list (though it was later updated to include both Lulach and Malcolm III), placing him 'straightforwardly as the heir' to the ancient Pictish kingdom and, in effect, the unequivocal supplanter of the currently defunct house of Alpin.[28]

In the reign of Macbeth, then, scholars were exploring another version of the past that did not have the kings of Dál Riata destroying the Picts. As well as recognising that the stories associated with Kenneth mac Alpin were no longer appropriate, they may also have been aware that the current Scottish king hailed from Fortriu, with its illustrious history as the power-house of the former Pictish kingdom. To add to the mix, another poem that came into circulation in the reign of Malcolm III, Macbeth's successor, betrays one crucial element that suggests the extent to which Scottish history had been tweaked thanks to the house of Moray. Focusing once more on the Irish foundation legends, this version names the first king of Dál Riata after the legendary Erc as Loarn, followed by his brothers, Fergus and Angus.[29] Loarn was, of course, supposedly the father of the dynasty that ultimately wound up in Moray and produced Macbeth; Fergus, on the other hand, was considered to be the progenitor of the Cenel nGabrain, Kenneth mac Alpin's family. What other accommodations would have been required of the historians of Scotland to bring the kingdom's past up to date with Macbeth's ancestry if he had not proved, in effect, to be the first and (with the brief exception of Lulach) last of his line?

Meanwhile, Macbeth's alliance with Leinster may have prompted a more aggressive foreign policy much closer to home. The kingdom of Strathclyde, lying to the south-west of Scotland, was an obvious area for the kings of Scots to consider expanding into. Malcolm II seems to have arranged for one of his daughters to marry either its king, Owain the Bald, or one of Owain's sons. As we have seen, he had also, perhaps, insinuated his brother, Suibhne, into a maritime kingdom on Strathclyde's western margins. Though Strathclyde seems to have kept its head down once Macbeth came to the throne of Scotland, the Scottish king may have been tempted to intervene further, especially after Echmarchach's expulsion from Dublin which could easily have led to the promise of an Irish contingent sent from Macbeth's ally Diarmait mac Maíl na mBó attacking from the west.

However, in intervening in Strathclyde, the Scottish king jumped the gun if he thought that Edward of England was too caught up in his own domestic problems to pay attention to his north-western border. For a start, it was not Edward who was keeping an eye on Cumbria (the southern part of Strathclyde), but Siward of Northumbria, who had his own designs on that part of the world. Secondly, after 1052 when England's internal difficulties were effectively resolved, King Edward did indeed have time to attend to other matters. He was particularly taken with Siward's plans to extend his domains further north-west. So far as Scotland was concerned, this almost certainly meant making sure that the Scottish king did not get far with his own plans to encroach on Strathclyde.

From Edward's point of view, it would perhaps have been churlish not to give support to Earl Siward, who had proved so loyal during the king's stand-off with Earl Godwin, and it did sound like a very good plan in which the king played the satisfying role of commander-in-chief from a distance. It was precisely at this point that an English chronicler described Macbeth as 'a Scottish king with a barbarous name', an insulting description that underlines the renewed hostility in the southern kingdom's attitude towards Scotland. This display of racial superiority was replicated in similarly undiplomatic language towards Wales.[30] Edward, the lion[31] of England was rousing himself to assert his predecessors' claims to be Britain's ultimate lord.

But the prime mover behind England's aggression on this occasion was Siward of Northumbria. Despite marrying Aelfled, granddaughter of Earl Uhtred, the earl had shown no compunction about getting rid of his wife's uncle, Eadwulf of Bernicia, in his ambition to become ruler of both parts of Northumbria. 'Earl Siward, like the men of the house of Godwine, was regarded by his contemporaries as a figure larger than life, around whom legendary stories quickly gathered'.[32] A regular at court, he was left to his own devices in the north. However, King Edward was happy to lend his overt support – and some of his house-carls – to the earl's plans for an invasion of Scotland.

Even from an English point of view, there had to be some reason, however contrived, for casting asunder a relationship that seems to have remained distinctly civil ever since Macbeth took the throne in 1040. The chronicler who could not get his pen round the Scottish king's Gaelic name states that he was also guilty of having 'rebelled against Edward'.[33] Given that no source, English or Scottish, asserts that Macbeth ever went anywhere near Edward, never mind acknowledged his superior kingship, a likely cause for England's pique may have been an attempt to secure independent metropolitan status for the Scottish Church, as reported back to Edward from Rome by Robert of Jumièges or another visiting English churchman. There is certainly 'some evidence that Siward attempted to exert ecclesiastical pressure by having two Scottish bishops ordained by the Archbishop of York',[34] perhaps as a reaction to this unwelcome news. Another potential flashpoint was any effort on Macbeth's behalf to secure Scotland's influence over Cumbria. It is even possible that the king of the Cumbrians had gone to Siward (who was not averse to attacking the region himself) and placed his kingdom under England's protection, on the basis that the latter was likely to prove a more effective rock against attack from the king of Scots.

This was the first such incursion into Scottish territory for more than a century, since Athelstan's highly successful inva-sion by land and sea in 934.[35] As Macbeth learned of the presence of an English force marching through Lothian, backed by a fleet advancing up the east coast, he faced a stark choice. He could take the glorious route, moving his own army south to meet Siward, but he would have been under no illusions as to the chances of success. Having witnessed the fall-out from the disastrous siege of Durham that led to the fatal collapse of King Duncan's regime fourteen years before, he was surely not minded to see his own reign go the same way.

So Macbeth took the difficult decision to go to ground, reckoning that Siward would tire of not being able to find him and be forced to retreat. He knew that this might upset his own nobility, but at least they would all survive to fight again, if absolutely necessary. In the summer of 1054 the king and his men passed through Scone and headed into the long chain of hills that shadows the River Tay between Perth and Dundee. Later tradition has it that they were making for an ancient hill-fort long abandoned for regular use but still capable of housing the king and his men. Its name was Dunsinane.

This is, of course, exactly where Shakespeare placed Macbeth's last battle and demise. We might speculate that the story of Birnam wood coming to Dunsinane is actually a garbled echo of the more historically likely backing given to Siward's army by those at Dunkeld who still supported the family of their former abbot, Crinan, father of Duncan.[36] This was a serious challenge to Macbeth and, ultimately, he miscalculated. Earl Siward was made of stern stuff, directing his men into the mountainous terrain where the Scots had disappeared. Tracked down, the Scottish king was forced into battle on 27 July 1054 – the day of the Seven Sleepers.

It was a fierce engagement, resulting in heavy losses on both sides: three thousand of the Scottish army, fifteen hundred of

Siward's men, according to one chronicle. These included the Northumbrian earl's eldest son,* many of his housecarls and some of King Edward's, as well as the unfortunate Osbern Pentecost and his fellow Normans. They fought valiantly for their new master, proving their worth in loyalty if not, ultimately, in success in battle. Siward's victory left him free – supposedly on Edward's orders – to appoint Malcolm, son of the king of the Cumbrians, as puppet king, presumably over Strathclyde. Siward himself may have annexed certain parts of Cumbria to his own earldom.37

There was only one problem. Macbeth had escaped, his kingship intact, if severely compromised. It speaks volumes about the respect in which he was held that the house of Moray faced no challenge to its position from the far-flung remnants of the many branches of the royal family in the wake of such a catastrophic loss of face. But even a king as well-loved as Macbeth could not expect to walk away unscathed from such a humiliating defeat. There must have been discussions, both in his presence and in quiet corners elsewhere, over what should be done. He had delegated responsibility once before. Now was perhaps the time to consider a form of retirement. However, within little more than six months of the battle, fate had stepped in to alter the political situation in Macbeth's favour. Perhaps this wise old king could weather the current unfortunate storm, like Constantine after Brunanburh a century before?

---

* Shakespeare, in his play, has Siward ask for proof that his son Osbern met his death bravely. This story was already in circulation a century or so after the battle.

It was Earl Siward who proved the loser in the end, enjoying his triumph for little more than half a year – much like his former antagonist, Earl Godwin. His end was perhaps the worst imaginable for such a hardened warrior. At the beginning of 1055, he was seized by a bad attack of dysentery. Realising that fate really did have 'the death of a cow' in store for him, he rose from his sick-bed, strapped on his armour and went off to meet his Maker on duty on the walls of York. Thus he died, larger than life and a fighter to the end.[38] But his victory over the king of Scots had brought Northumbria only temporary hegemony over Strathclyde.

Macbeth was proving resilient even in defeat. He outlived Earl Siward and soon heard of the death of yet another former enemy, Earl Thorfinn of Orkney. All around him a new generation of leaders was coming to the fore, with their own ideas and goals. However, in the years immediately following the battle against the Northumbrians, Scotland remained at peace, its king perhaps daring to sleep soundly again.

But this was merely the calm before the storm. England proved only a temporary threat; the real danger resided in the north where Duncan's son, Malcolm, had taken himself a bride: Ingebjorg, Earl Thorfinn's (presumably much younger) widow. This lady was cousin to the king of Norway's son, Harold, who was currently on the lookout for an interesting and lucrative project to keep his men happily involved in the right kind of mischief. As part of an ambitious – but largely spur-of-the-moment – plan that also involved an invasion of England, Harold was persuaded by Malcolm and his new wife to help them launch an attack on Scotland first.[39] Given the strength of later traditions, it is likely that a representative of the Fife family, forfeited by Malcolm's great-grandfather and kept in obscurity by Macbeth, sailed with him. He is known to legend as Macduff.[40]

Towards the end of 1057, Lulach seems to have persuaded his stepfather to retire from the kingship and he was inaugurated at Scone before the end of the year. Who knows how Macbeth felt about giving up the power that he had so painfully won and so carefully used. It is true that he had already contemplated his own death prior to his departure for the Continent over seven years previously; surely relief must have been at least one of the emotions that came to him now? He would just have to trust Lulach to do a good job and keep his mind on other things. Perhaps he even entered a monastery, as his predecessor, Constantine, had done.

And so it was Lulach who had to deal with the news of a fleet advancing out of Orkney and down the far north-eastern coast of Scotland. He took his army into the forests of Strathbogie (currently in Aberdeenshire, but then in Mar), presumably having heard that Malcolm's force had landed somewhere on the coast immediately to the east of the River Spey, which separates Buchan/Mar from Moray. The two sides met in the uplands of Aberdeenshire at Essie on 17 March 1058. Perhaps Malcolm and Lulach agreed to talk – there is a suggestion of treachery, presumably under truce. In any event, Lulach was killed.

But this was not enough. The house of Moray was still immensely powerful and there does not seem to have been any immediate rush to embrace this latest scion of the line of Kenneth mac Alpin. Who knows what Malcolm and his army did in the following months, but if his grandfather's family held lands in Mar – and more specifically, Garioch – then we can understand why the young man chose to land in the north-east and can imagine that he spent time cultivating family and friends who were already predisposed to welcome his return. However, he must have known that he was only part of the way towards securing the throne.

The news of his stepson's death must have been devastating to Macbeth, for Lulach's son, Maelsnechta, cannot have been old enough to be a credible heir in 1058. If the old king chose to fight, then he was putting a lot of faith in his nobility's willingness to accept a child as their future king, given that he himself was unlikely to live to see him to full manhood and there was another adult male, already victor of one battle, waiting impatiently nearby.

But fight is exactly what Macbeth did, casting aside the peaceful pastimes of his retirement to put on his helmet, strap on his armour and sally forth with axe and sword, just as Earl Siward had done. This was no vainglorious determination to die in combat. There was no-one else left to lead all those still loyal to the house of Moray against the invaders.

Macbeth, like his stepson, headed into Mar to meet Malcolm, perhaps having rallied the remnants of Lulach's army, probably in August 1058. They met at Lumphanan, some forty miles south-east of Essie, but which, more significantly, lies immediately south-west of the Garioch. We might assume that Macbeth was coming south-east out of Moray, but he could also have been coming north over the Cairn o' Mount pass. There was no hint of treachery this time, but perhaps such a battle was always bound to be less than a fair fight. For the second time in a matter of months, Malcolm and the Norwegians destroyed the Scots. This time, too, a king lay dead on the battlefield, the man who had killed his father. Finally, faced with no real alternative, Scotland was ready to welcome back this great-great-great-great-great-great-grandson of Kenneth mac Alpin. And it was Malcolm, blessed with a long reign and a clutch of highly effective sons, who finally provided Scotland with its first royal dynasty, one which lasted until 1286.

Legend has it that, in the heated moments immediately after defeating his enemy, Malcolm placed Macbeth's weapon on the ground. He then put his own weapon on top of it at right-angles and jigged victoriously around them. This supposedly accounts for the origins of a tradition that Scotland has since exported around the world – the Sword Dance. It is no taller a tale than any of the others told about Macbeth.

As usual, the facts are more prosaic. In a public show of respect and continuity, the victor at Lumphanan allowed the dead king to be removed to the ancient royal burial ground on Iona, the island's Norse rulers still apparently willing to acquiesce in this important Scottish ritual. This final act is testament to the place Macbeth occupied in Scotland at the time. Here was no tyrant, but a ruler of great skill and fortitude, a man willing and able to give his people peace and prosperity without losing either popularity or support. 'I shall be joyful in him', says his poet.[41] There is no better epitaph.

CHAPTER 10

From Death to Demonisation

> I have bought
> Golden opinions from all sorts of people,
> Which would be worn now in their newest gloss,
> Not cast aside so soon.
>
> *Macbeth*, Act I, Scene vii

It was Mary, Queen of Scots who said, presciently: 'In my end is my beginning'. She stitched it repeatedly into her cloth of estate to while away the tedious hours in an English prison from which she was to escape only in death.[1] Though anticipating her arrival in the afterlife, she was perhaps also hoping for a kinder press from future generations than she had received from her own. For Macbeth, her far distant predecessor, his demise heralded the opposite: his contemporaries, waxing excessively lyrical, could find nothing bad to say about him, whereas subsequent writers found it necessary to blacken his name. So how was such an apparently admirable and well-loved man's reputation completely transformed by succeeding generations? More importantly, *why* was it deemed necessary to turn him into a bloodthirsty tyrant, a reputation almost diametrically opposed to that which he enjoyed in his own lifetime?

To be fair, this character assassination was not necessarily intentional – once a myth gets going, repetition and elaboration serve just as well and the results amount to much the same thing. Once Macbeth's reputation had been demolished, the mainstream view was resistant to portraying him in a positive light until very recently. However, the existence of these two traditions – one complimentary, the other antagonistic – has led to some interesting confusions. Some writers conditioned to be hostile to him in the centuries following his death were well aware of material singing his praises, which they sometimes included but without attempting to explain how such eulogies fitted into the more general picture of cruelty and tyranny.

Refashioning a reputation is most immediately necessary for political reasons, even if the results become part of a nation's cultural identity once the facts of the matter have fallen by the wayside. Within three centuries of his death, two powerful circumstances combined to make Macbeth a particularly potent example of the evils of illegitimate kingship. The first was the reputation of Moray as a hotbed of rebellion and lawlessness, a reputation which the region began to acquire in the twelfth century but which stuck to it for at least three hundred years. The second was the obsessive concern among later Scottish historians, particularly of the fourteenth century, to portray Scottish kingship as both overtly legitimate and demonstrably ancient within the confines of Scotland's own history, a radical departure from the earlier need to exploit a very tenuous link to Ireland. This apprehension stemmed from England's perilously close-run attempt to destroy Scotland as an independent kingdom after 1296, a war that was prosecuted just as keenly by lawyers and historians on both sides as by soldiers in the field. As a result, any Scottish ruler who 'challenged' the current line of descendants of Kenneth mac Alpin was, by definition, placing his own ambitions before Scotland's best interests and was neither a bona fide king nor a decent human being.

By the fifteenth century, there was a list of those who had supposedly transgressed this code of royal conduct: Lulach; Donald Bane, brother of Malcolm III;* Duncan, Malcolm III's first-born son.[2] With Macbeth, however, something more needed to be done, perhaps in order to combat the stronger, more affectionate memories of this successful king. As a result Macbeth the Monster began to emerge from the pens of historians from John of Fordun in the later fourteenth century onwards as the antithesis of the rightful king, who alone was worthy of the Divine approval needed to keep the kingdom safe and sound. It did not matter that anachronistic standards were being applied, that the equally, if not more excessively, brutal behaviour of kings like Malcolm II was ignored, or the perfectly legitimate rights of others reinterpreted as 'corrupt'.

Above all, these writers faithfully polished the illusion that ultimate power in Scotland was, *and always had been*, the perquisite of the family in whose hands it now lay. Historians even in Macbeth's time had long been in the habit of using the twenty-twenty vision of hindsight in order to deduce God's plan for Scotland. They might even use insulting language, as Macbeth's own poet did, to cast aspersions on a predecessor,

* Malcolm III was Macbeth and Lulach's killer and successor.

all the better to heap praise on the current regime.[3] But what they did not do was question any king's right to rule, to equate the baleful experience of tyranny with an illegitimate blood-line. How are the mighty fallen, once their reputations come into the hands of the saintly scholars of later medieval Scotland!

When Macbeth died at the hands of Duncan's son, Malcolm, the nation did not breathe an inordinate sigh of relief, over-joyed at the prospect of the return of the rightful king. Eighteen years on, knowing that Scotland had experienced the rule of not just one but two kings from the house of Moray, it was perhaps the house of mac Alpin that was no longer entirely sure of its credentials. Even the scholars and poets working within the new king's regime seem to have had little desire to denigrate the man Malcolm had killed. The *Duan Albanach*, composed in the later eleventh century, possibly at Abernethy, refers fleetingly to Malcolm's predecessor, describing him as 'Macbeth of renown'.[4] In that respect, this poet was more generous than Macbeth's had been about Duncan. Lulach was not so fortunate, the prevailing fashion being to call him 'stupid' (*fatuus*). Perhaps this insult originally appeared in a praise-poem for Malcolm, the slur on the former king no doubt accom-panied by loud cheers and banging of crockery.[5]

That Lulach should be singled out for such treatment is no great surprise, given that his son, Mael Snechta, was now growing up to be the house of Moray's alternative to Malcolm. Indeed, Mael Snechta's own pretensions are amply demonstrated by the family tree, constructed in Ireland, which describes his lineage explicitly as that of the 'kings of Alba'. However, in 1078 Malcolm comprehensively defeated the Moravian, capturing his mother, 'all his best men, and all his treasures, and his live-stock'. Mael Snechta himself only just escaped and when he died, seven years later in 1085, he was described in the Irish annals as '*ri Mureb*' – king of Moray – the first time that this lesser term was used to describe a northern competitor for the Scottish throne.[6] He had been put in his place, his royal status still acknowledged within the Celtic world, but as subordinate to that of the king of Scots. Interestingly, too, Malcolm III was accorded the title of 'high king' by the Irish annalists at his death in 1093, as both Macbeth and Lulach had been, implying that Moray was slowly being absorbed into Scotland.[7]

After 1078 Malcolm (III) mac Duncan did not have to deal with any other challengers to his throne, but this was not the end of the story. Two generations later, in 1130, the government of Malcolm's youngest son, David, had to put down a rebellion led by Angus, Lulach's grandson by his daughter. Angus was joined in that rebellion – which had probably originally broken out six years earlier, when David became king – by Malcolm, a son of the previous king, Alexander I, David's elder brother.* In retrospect, we could see this as the death throes of the old system, alternative claimants continuing to take the field only to face the might – and, as later chroniclers saw it – the right of the family descended from Malcolm III and his second wife, Margaret (an Anglo-Saxon princess forced to become a refugee after William of Normandy's conquest of England in 1066).

---

* There has been considerable debate as to whether Malcolm was legiti-mate (see Ross, *The Province of Moray*, pp. 197–8), a very effective way of casting doubt on the claims of a rival.

However, it was not quite so simple, since the adoption of strict primogeniture was not achieved until the reign of Alexander II (1214–49). It happened in effect on David I's death in 1153, but his sons had predeceased him and it was his grandson, Malcolm, who became king. Before that, the fact that brother followed brother between 1097 and 1153 was a kind of halfway house that suited neither sons, nephews nor cousins of previous kings, never mind the house of Moray. This unusual succession arrangement also ignored the rights of the descendants of Malcolm III's first marriage to Ingebjorg. But these claimants were surely not fighting to have the old system put back in place. Rather, they were intent on establishing and maintaining their own segment of the royal family as the dynasty that controlled the throne.

It is not surprising that the succession continued to be a cause of instability and violence, although reign lengths were at least increasing as kings no longer died at the hands of their successors. In terms of Macbeth's reputation, though, it was the fact that these claimants were associated, to a greater or lesser degree, with Moray that proved important in the long run. As we have seen, Alexander I's son, Malcolm, joined with Lulach's grandson, Angus, to put forward their respective claims in the in the years leading to 1130. As late as 1212, King William I was forced to flee to England, where he 'obtained the services of Brabantine mercenaries to help to defeat Guthred MacWilliam'. Guthred's family was descended from William fitz Duncan, son of King Duncan II (1094), Malcolm III's eldest son by Ingebjorg 'and for over eighty years members of the kin group pressed their claim for inauguration as kings of Scotia'. William fitz Duncan had been earl of Moray and, while 'there is no indication in any source that either Moray or Moravians were directly involved in anti-crown activities after the death of Oengus [Angus] of Moray in 1130', the reputation for insubordination stuck.[8]

Moray was, then – somewhat inadvertently – caught up in the increasingly bitter prosecution of this royal infighting that quickly spread from the battlefield onto parchment. One impetus behind this was a new trend in the writing of Scottish history that became attractive to scholars describing Scotland once Malcolm III had married, as his second wife, Margaret.* On the one hand Malcolm was presented – as Macbeth had been – as the latest in a long line of kings who could trace their lineage back into the Pictish and, more importantly, Irish past to give Scottish kingship its 'authenticating antiquity'. On the other hand, Malcolm's marriage to Margaret gave their sons a claim to far more impressive royal credentials: 'the lineage of the pre-Conquest kings of England'. This was not about claiming the throne of England itself, but everything to do with exalting the crown of Scotland by asserting 'an intimate connection' with 'the British realm of Athelstan and Edgar', the most 'impressive island kingship' of them all.[9]

At the same time, English scholars were very happy to discredit, in ink, the claims of other branches of the Scottish royal family, some of which had perfectly good reason to feel aggrieved that they had been passed over in favour of David I and his descendants. These English writers did so presumably out of good old-fashioned respect for the fact that David's sister, Edith (renamed Matilda), was married to King Henry I

---

* Margaret was a niece of Edward 'the Confessor'.

of England. In *c.*1126, William of Malmesbury, in his *Gesta Regum Anglorum* (Tales of the Kingdom of England) first described King Duncan II* as '*nothus*' – a bastard.[10] As well as helping to damn in the eyes of posterity Duncan's son, William, earl of Moray, and his descendants as impostors with no good reason to pursue the crown, this propaganda has also helped to persuade historians until very recently that the Macwilliams (as this branch of the royal family descended from William are called) had very little support for their actions. In fact, there were occasions – particularly in 1211/12 – when the outcome was a close-run thing. 'The failure of various kings of Scotia, particularly William [King William I], to decisively defeat their dynastic rivals was not helped by the fact that there was clearly some doubt among the upper echelons of Scottish society concerning the ability of the reigning king.'[11]

The struggles between the descendants of David I and their distant relatives only came to an end in 1230 with the appalling murder of the last of the line. A three-year-old Macwilliam girl 'who had not long left her mother's womb, innocent as she was, was put to death, in the burgh of Forfar in view of the market place after a proclamation by the public crier. Her head was struck against the column of the market cross, and her brains dashed out'.[12] No-one should be in any doubt about the ruthlessness of those who wore the crown in this long-lasting struggle, however dreadful the activities of their enemies might have been (and were certainly portrayed as being).

Meanwhile, historians were still working on their stories on behalf of the royal dynasty. The results included a startling

---

* Malcolm III's eldest son and David's stepbrother, who died in 1094.

refinement of the origin legends constructed, originally, to authenticate Scotland's kingship. Now, a new myth was developed especially for the people of Moray, depicting them as a separate tribe from the Picts and Scots before they all came to live in north Britain. Naturally disposed to be rebellious, the Moravians were characterised as a nation of pirates who liked nothing better than to plunder the coasts of Britain. Such a comprehensive damnation of the people of an entire province – wholly made up and largely unjustified – does indeed stand as 'a measure of the seriousness of the threat posed by the MacWilliams to kings of Scotia'.[13]

This battle of the quills was by no means one-sided, however. While some scholars, presumably of southern Scotland, boosted by the efforts of their colleagues in England, sought to explain or justify the fact that the crown now lay exclusively in the hands of the sons of Malcolm III's second marriage and, more particularly (after 1153), the descendants of his youngest son, David I, those sympathetic to claimants based in the north put a rather different slant on their own histories. 'That some kind of a flyting [a poetic trading of insults] did indeed develop is suggested by the account of Malcolm Canmore's* lowly mother; clearly the Moray bards reciprocated.'[14] Though this material does not survive in its original form, enough of it has found its way into other, ostensibly unsympathetic, chronicles where it can still be retrieved. The chroniclers were not necessarily conscious propagandists; they just liked the idea of the peace

---

* This was Malcolm III, though the epithet of 'Canmore' – 'Big head' – was applied erroneously to him from the 1290s onwards (Duncan, *The Kingship of the Scots*, pp. 36–7, 51–2).

and quiet that an uncontested kingship was bound to bring with it. Perhaps, too, they often maintained a more cynical attitude towards the current regime than we sometimes give them credit for, or at least were prepared to present alternative versions of the myth for readers to make up their own minds.

The most striking example of this is the *Verse Chronicle* inserted into the *Chronicle of Melrose* and written in the first half of the thirteenth century. Here we have the first reference to an aspect of Macbeth's kingship that subsequently became standard: its illegitimacy. At the same time, the poem contradicted itself by emphasising his 'righteous' kingship, given that God had rewarded him with 'fruitful seasons'. Lulach is also described as 'unlucky' rather than 'stupid'.[15] These writers were not the first, nor the last, to end up confused by the prevailing political correctness which seemed to fly in the face of evidence that, if not entirely truthful in its unmitigated praise, at least had the virtue of antiquity behind it.

The ante in this literary contest was upped towards the end of the thirteenth century when a romance – or, perhaps, romances – was written, as was the fashion, about both Macbeth and Lulach's successor, Malcolm III. Again, we only have snippets and echoes of it/them, written, entirely soberly, into John of Fordun's *Chronica Gentis Scotorum* (History of the People of Scotland) (*c.*1384–7) and, in a much more recognisable and flamboyant style, in Andrew of Wyntoun's *Orygynale Cronykil* (*c.*1420). Fordun had no time for the more outlandish elements of the romance, but with Wyntoun the supernatural makes a spine-tingling appearance for the first time in Macbeth's story. Now he becomes no less than the spawn of the devil, who appeared to his mother in an irresistibly handsome guise during an ill-advised walk in the woods. To add to the dramatic tension, three women appear to Macbeth in a dream, foretelling his dramatic rise to become king of Scotland in three stages.

This account used well-known literary motifs to portray Macbeth in a damnable light. However, Wyntoun also had access to the counter-fiction, a story of the origins of Malcolm III. His birth is given a less garish makeover so that he becomes Duncan's illegitimate son by the rather less scary daughter of the miller of Forteviot, who was chanced upon by the king while 'separated from his companions'.[16] Despite these obviously dubious credentials for the throne, Malcolm was in good company given that William of Normandy, who was certainly illegitimate and supposedly the son of a tanner's daughter, had risen to become not only duke of Normandy, but king of England too.

Perhaps this was no less than an attempt to cast aspersions on the royal families currently occupying both thrones, since every king of England after Henry II was also related to the family of Scotland's Malcolm III.* At the very least, this story would have aroused ribald commentary among those who had no reason to feel particularly loyal to either royal house.[17]

Time and changing political circumstances also have a role to play in giving fresh impetus and substance to well-known myths. Some fifty years after the murder of the last little Macwilliam, the royal line descended from Malcolm III faced its most severe

---

* As already mentioned, King Henry I of England married Edith (Matilda), Malcolm III's daughter, by whom he had a daughter (Matilda), the mother of Henry II of England.

crisis yet, a threat that ultimately proved fatal. In 1284, Alexander III's last surviving son, David, died. Two years later, the forty-four-year-old king was dead too, after plunging from his horse at Kinghorn en route to see his new young wife. The fate of the dynasty hung on the slender hope that the queen's pregnancy would produce a boy and that the child would survive into adulthood.

By the end of 1286 that hope, too, had died. Scotland was pitched into a succession crisis that alerted the interest of Edward I of England, Alexander's former brother-in-law, the careful protector of the southern kingdom's long-standing claims of superiority over Scotland. Though Edward did set about judging the genealogical merits of the various competitors for the Scottish throne, choosing John Balliol as king, ten years later an English army invaded Scotland and its independent government was dismantled. When the Scottish throne was forcefully reoccupied in 1307 by the grandson of an unsuccessful competitor, Robert Bruce, Scotland began the long, painful and not always likely process of restoring its independence.

So far as the monastic writers of history – and no doubt many other Scots – were concerned, it was essential that the succession should remain clear-cut and incontrovertible, as well as demonstrably legitimate and independent, to avoid any possibility of the resumption of this evil war. Centuries of debate, beginning with the position of Scotland's bishops in relation to England's archbishops within the overall ecclesiastical hierarchy of western Europe, had given way to far more explicit and legalistic expressions of England's superiority over Scotland. From 1174, the debate centred not around whether the English kings were chief among all the rulers of Britain – a superiority that the rest of the island's kings usually acknowledged – but whether they should be able to exercise actual lordship over the surviving kingdoms of Wales and Scotland.

The result, so far as the Scots were concerned, was an unequivocal declaration of the equality of Scotland's king with that of England, since, by now, 'it was inevitable that the authority of a kingship over its people would be seen more in terms of jurisdiction rather than simply power and prestige'. To maintain this powerful mystique of kingship, to sustain the nation against the alternative claims of jurisdiction by England, Scotland no longer needed to look to anyone else's illustrious past, but began to create 'a deep continuous history that was exclusively its own'.[18]

This – both the pre-Wars of Independence struggles between the crown and its competitors, focused, by chance, on Moray, and the Wars themselves – is the context out of which a more elaborate and imaginative set of stories about Macbeth emerged. Fordun and Wyntoun were the main protagonists in the fourteenth and fifteenth centuries, creating a narrative that is recognisable as the basis for the later Shakespearian tragedy in their quest to stress the ancient authority that was vested in the Scottish crown and its wearers. Fordun, whose *Chronica* is the earliest surviving 'complete account of the kingdom's past' (though based on an earlier work),[19] makes no bones about Macbeth's usurpation of the throne, alleging that Malcolm II had changed the succession laws (which obviously made it all right) and that Duncan's death was carried out in secret through the 'wickedness of a race' which had also killed his grandfather and his great-grandfather. Macbeth was, of course, 'chief among' them, and his murder of Duncan, heinous though that crime was, should therefore come as no surprise.[20]

That Fordun should think like that is no surprise either. He was writing towards the beginning of the reign of Robert Stewart (Robert II), grandson of Robert Bruce and heir to the latter's son, the childless David Bruce, for most of his life. Fordun was not to know that the brand new, and therefore vulnerable, Stewart dynasty would survive until 1714. So far as the chronicler was concerned, too, Moray was still effectively a 'problem area' for the Scottish government, thanks to the shenanigans of Robert II's youngest son, Alexander, the 'Wolf' of Badenoch and earl of Buchan, Moray's neighbour. In the eyes of Fordun and most Lowland Scots, Alexander was running a protection racket in the north, along with his brother-in-law, John Macdonald of the Isles, and was little better than a Highland brigand for all his royal blood. Indeed, the chronicler was the first to explore in ink the distinction between civilised Lowland folk, who spoke Scots English, and Highlanders, with their own language and barbaric ways (though it was admitted that they were rather good-looking).

Since Macbeth came from Moray, in the Highlands, and was obviously a Gaelic-speaking king, Fordun's view of him was no doubt also coloured by the growing gulf between the two 'races' of Scotland. Not surprisingly, this had a rather more positive effect on his reputation north of the Highland line, where 'the fifteenth-century clans associated with the Lordship of the Isles knew perfectly well what MacBeth represented. To them he was the last great Celtic king of Scots, a challenge to the encroachment of centralising authority and a mirror of their own aspirations.'[21]

Both of these points of view – essentially two sides of the same coin – would have mystified Macbeth himself, since his own kingdom had been overwhelmingly Celtic and Gaelic-speaking, apart from the Lothians south of the Forth. But such attitudes do serve to show both the range and extent of the historical circumstances that led to the continued updating of the Macbeth legend, and the fact that the mainstream negative elements were often shadowed by other, more flattering, opinions. They also highlight the profound social and cultural changes that Scotland had undergone in the centuries following Macbeth's death, not least in the growing marginalisation of Celtic Scotland.

This pattern continued throughout the fifteenth and sixteenth centuries, writers taking an essentially pro-Stewart, and therefore anti-Macbeth, line, interspersed with incongruous bits of material showing his good side. By the sixteenth century, and especially with John Major's *Historia Majoris Britanniae* (which can be translated as either A History of Greater Britain or Major's History of Britain), Scotland's story was placed within a British context, as relations between England and Scotland began, slowly and grudgingly, to thaw out. Not only were the royal houses closely related after King James IV of Scotland married Margaret Tudor, sister to Henry VIII of England, in 1503, but, after 1560, both kingdoms had turned Protestant.

At last, now that Scotland was no longer in thrall to its alliance with Catholic France, there was an opportunity for friendly relations to supersede centuries of warfare and antagonism as both countries looked to each other for support. Admittedly this relationship was complicated in the early decades of the reign of Elizabeth I (1558–1603) by the fact that her cousin and potential heir, Mary, Queen of Scots, was Catholic and ready to be used against her by France and Spain. Mary's forced abdication and eventual flight to England in 1568 at least put the troublesome ball in Elizabeth's court. As for the new Scottish king, Mary's infant son, James, he was given no choice but to be brought up a Protestant.

In the meantime, Macbeth's tyrannical life was becoming ever more detailed and debauched in the telling. However, the ancient inconsistencies in his story had now been resolved into his characterisation as 'a man of mixed qualities'.[22] With Hector Boece's flamboyant *Scotorum Historiae* (History of the Scots, 1527), translated into Scots by John Bellenden and William Stewart, Macbeth is introduced to us as one of Duncan's generals and his wife becomes recognisable as the harridan who goads him into that first despicable murder. Banquo also enters literary history as the thane of Lochaber and 'the beginner of the Stewarts in this realm, from whom our King now present [James V, 1513–42)] by long and ancient lineage is descended'.[23]

Fifty years later, it was this account, or at least Bellenden's version in Scots, along with Major's *Historia*, that attracted the attention of a London translator called Ralph Holinshed, who was engaged in compiling *Chronicles of England, Scotland and Ireland*. Now Macbeth's story could reach a far bigger audience, one that was very curious about the origins of the most likely heir to childless Elizabeth's throne, James VI of Scotland. Indeed, Holinshed went so far as to provide some extra material tracing the line of Banquo – believed as late as the nine-

teenth century to be the progenitor of the Stuarts* – right up
to the sixteenth-century present.

Holinshed must take some of the credit for being the first
to propel Macbeth out of the febrile arena of domestic myth-
making into the wider world. Without his *Chronicles*,
Shakespeare might never have picked up on the story, and the
playwright would have looked for something different to form
the basis of his 'Scottish play', presuming he would have written
one at all. It is also important to see Holinshed as the latest
in a long line of Chinese whisperers who had forged and
remoulded the myth of Macbeth for over five hundred years
before finally handing the distorted ghost of the Scottish king
over to one of the greatest story-tellers of them all. Boece,
Major, Wyntoun, Fordun and the anonymous monastic chroniclers of the distant past all live on in Shakespeare's *Macbeth*,
rather more recognisably, in some cases, than the king himself.

The early seventeenth century cannot, of course, be the end
of our story and even the definitive, all-consuming version of
Macbeth penned by William Shakespeare has not succeeded
in putting an end to further reworkings, most particularly within
the genre of romantic fiction. These range from the sexually
charged and politically subversive *The Secret History of Mackbeth,
King of Scotland* (1708) to Dorothy Dunnett's hugely popular
King Hereafter, first published in 1982 and reprinted in 2000.

Both *The Secret History* – supposedly reproduced from 'a very
Ancient Original Manuscript', as was the fashion at the time

---

* The name Stewart – derived from the family's original function as steward
of the royal household – was transformed into 'Stuart', a French version,
during the reign of Mary, Queen of Scots.

– and *King Hereafter* – which was based on extensive historical research – highlight another, more recent, trend: the need
to get at the 'truth' of the 'real' Macbeth's life.[24] Such a desire
is surely a reaction both to the universal popularity of
Shakespeare's play and its indifference to the known facts about
the historical Macbeth. With the advent of modern historical
methods, which emphasise the need to weigh and measure
evidence for potential bias, it has become possible to scrape away
the layers of myth-making to reassess the nature and character
of both Macbeth himself and eleventh-century Scotland.

The renewed interest in the king by professional historians
from the second half of the twentieth century also testifies to
the need for, and the potential of, medieval Scottish history as
a serious academic subject, however frustrating the gaps in this
particular story will continue to be. At the same time, there is
a temptation to go too far the other way. 'This historical revi-
sionism was intended to expose a perceived miscarriage of justice,
right a historical wrong and exonerate Macbeth from the charges
levelled against him over the centuries, thus enabling him to
occupy his proper place in history. But behind this attempted
rehabilitation sometimes lay a thinly veiled nationalism,
attempting to restore the blackened reputation of a good Scottish
king from the libels of an English dramatist.'[25]

How, then, should we judge Macbeth mac Finlay, high king
of Scotland?

It may not seem particularly original or insightful to begin by
saying that Macbeth's story is, in essence, about the nature of
power. However, I am not referring to the perceptive psycho-
logical insights offered by Shakespeare when he presents us

with a decent but weak man, seduced and bullied into seizing the throne by a murderous act that exposes the villainy in him, and, by extension, all of us, if we do not keep our unreasonable ambitions in check.

For a start, the real Macbeth could never undergo such canny profiling for the simple reason that we know so little about him as a person, and must rely instead on assessing his actions, so far as we can, within the context of his own time. But even those few actions and reactions to them, when compared with the behaviour of his contemporaries, can speak volumes about the man. In particular, they serve as pages torn from a book on the nature of secular power at a crucial period in British history. Historians talk these days of the 'sacral nature' of Scottish kingship in this period, by which they are referring to the notion – associated with the Celts, but far from exclusively their preserve – that: 'If the country was ruled by a good king, if he had the power of truth, his personal prosperity would be reflected in the well-being of his subjects. Conversely the bad king would bring war, famine, pestilence and poverty upon his kingdom'.[26]

Here we have a reminder of the reason why hierarchies headed by chiefs or kings replaced more egalitarian social structures in the first place – out of the expectation that the man exalted in this way could intercede with the Divine powers that controlled the cosmos. Christianity, with its emphasis on the will of God, merely recast this ancient relationship in biblical terms, its priests – like their pagan predecessors – retaining their role as the interpreters of Divine pleasure or discontent. This guiding principle, emphasising the essential *function* of the office rather than its outer *form*, which dictated what the king could (and occasionally could not) do, underpinned Pictish/Scottish kingship for the best part of a millennium, long after a particular kin group had come to dominate it.

As a result, and despite the undoubted need for a veneer of legitimacy, the blood coursing through the veins of the king was still less crucial than his approval rating in the eyes of God. Obviously, politics – essentially the approval rating of import-ant individuals much closer to home – was the real arbiter of success, no matter what churchmen might say, but there is no doubt that the ability to rule well and justly, however that was construed in practice, was still a far more important consider-ation than a narrow and rigid blood relationship to one's predecessor.

Unfortunately, as far as Scotland was concerned, relying on God's favour – which often manifested itself as the political manoeuvrings of other credible contenders for the throne – became a short-cut to violent upheaval when there was no external threat to distract attention elsewhere. We can have no idea of the economic cost or the emotional insecurity gener-ated by the regular assassination of the current ruler by his successor in late tenth-century Scotland. All we can do is compare the dearth of literary and artistic endeavour in Alba with the evidence of cultural sophistication displayed, often to the wider world, by the earlier kingdoms of Pictland and Dál Riata.

That everyone – kings, aristocracy and the million or so Scots who supported their endeavours – might wish to see an end to the infighting is surely substantiated by the fact that, across Europe, enduring royal dynasties were emerging to lead their embryonic nation states into a more assured future. Such a trend was often violently instigated and certainly rooted in ambition. However, turning away from the instability of a performance-related system towards one that emphasised the Divine, and therefore immutable, credentials of a single blood-line would at least settle the issue of who should be king and allow everyone to move on.[27] Scotland bit this particular political bullet comparatively late in the day, but, by the end of the tenth century, most of Scotland's great men were no doubt convinced of the need for change – so long as it was their man who ended up as the winner who would take all.

Annexing the throne to a single dynasty took time, a luxury that most Scottish kings after 944 were not permitted. It also took guts and political savvy to tackle the inevitable political fall-out from those who would lose their rights to challenge for the kingship and all those with a vested interest in keeping things exactly as they were, despite the body count and the insecurity. Malcolm II combined unusual longevity with sheer cold-blooded brutality and, probably, popularity to ensure that he was followed on the throne by his daughter's son, an unheard-of proposition in Scotland at the time (though one for which there was a European precedent). He underlined just how serious he was by assassinating at least one of the claimants under the old system, Maelbaethe mac Boite.

To add to this volatile mix of dynastic politics, Scotland itself was not the clear-cut and firmly delineated kingdom that it later became. The acquisition of Lothian, the region south of the Forth appropriated from the former Anglo-Saxon kingdom of Northumbria, had little effect, as yet, on Scottish politics, since it was a discrete addition whose non-Celtic population was required only to knuckle down and accept the new status quo without having to see themselves as Scots. With Moray –

a key component of the former Pictish kingdom of Fortriu – the situation was more complicated. Although it is far from clear exactly how the region evolved after 900, when Alba first comes on record, there is enough evidence to suggest that the Moravians held themselves aloof from this new Scotland, while almost certainly acknowledging its king.

That Moravian and Scottish politics were intertwined is also clear. Scottish kings did intervene directly, though extremely rarely, in the north, though it is harder to discern whether the number of royal murders attributed to the Moravians is genuine or a product of their later reputation as a byword for rebellion and mayhem. Moray's aloofness – or, rather, its rare appearance in the written record – must also have had something to do with Norse attacks in the region. Though the Norwegian earldom of Orkney does not, despite the assertions of the Sagas, seem to have been formally created until the later tenth century, Norse raiding in the area must surely have had an effect on northern politics well before then, if the archaeological record relating to the citadel at Burghead and the monastery at Portmahomack is anything to go by. Though we cannot know for sure that it was the Vikings who caused the fire that destroyed Burghead, for example, it is likely that the later kings of Pictland were increasingly tempted to reside in the south because it was less prone to Norse attack. By the time they had been renamed as kings of the Scots, it was the region focused around Perth in central Scotland that contained the royal residences of choice and the ceremonial centres of kingship in the renamed kingdom. The main monasteries were all there too.

However, even if the rulers of Moray were forced to spend a considerable amount of time fighting off attacks from the Norse, they were still paying attention to the politics of Scotland itself. How could they have failed to do otherwise, when the chances are high that Macbeth's great-grandfather, Ruari, had married a princess of the royal family descended from Kenneth mac Alpin's younger son, Aed? When that line came to an end on the death of King Constantine mac Culen in 997, it seems too much of a coincidence that this is precisely the period when the ruler of Moray reappears in the Irish annals with the title of *ri alban*.

This recognition of Finlay mac Ruari, Macbeth's father, as king of Scotland is thus most easily explained as a reaction to Malcolm II's murder of his own uncle, Kenneth III, where-upon he became king in 1005. Both Malcolm and Kenneth were members of the line of Kenneth mac Alpin's elder son, Constantine. If the friends and relatives of the other line of Aed mac Kenneth did not move quickly, their participation in the succession would soon be a distant memory. These were the powerful nobles and churchmen, deprived of the sporadic access to the power and patronage they enjoyed when their man wore the crown, who must have helped to persuade Finlay – not that he necessarily needed that much persuasion – to activate his claim.

This was politics in the raw, Scotland's own prosperity and, as each protagonist would be quick to point out on his own behalf, God's will cast aside in the struggle for power. But let us not rush too hastily to judge. Even in modern democracies, there is still a perception that vested interests can propel a less than convincing candidate to power, and keep him or her there. We cannot do much to unpick the networks that supported these eleventh-century Scottish kings and their challengers, but we can suppose that they were there.

'Power is like the wind; we cannot see it, but feel its force'.[28] This is often as much to do with the innate qualities – the powerfulness – of a leader, as with the authority that he wields. Such qualities are difficult to pin down and categorise and, while it is possible to improve confidence and assertiveness, real leaders are born rather than created. Unfortunately for Finlay of Moray, he does not seem to have been much of one, though we are admittedly venturing into uncharted waters. We can certainly say that he could not muster enough support to propel him onto the throne of Scotland proper, despite, presumably, having the backing of the supporters of clan Aed mac Constantine.

What makes this even more underwhelming is the fact that Malcolm II's own grip on power quickly began to come unstuck after the disastrous defeat at Durham in 1006. A stronger contender would surely have been able to challenge the king directly, something that Finlay never ventured to do. In the end, his failure to make anything of the claim, which he clearly took seriously, must have been the main factor behind his assassination in 1020 by his nephews, Malcolm and Gillacomgain. With Malcolm II's hand considerably strengthened by his victory at Carham in 1018, this was no time for clan Aed mac Kenneth to be fielding a substandard candidate.

Malcolm of Moray does seem to have displayed more leadership qualities than his uncle, allying himself with the displaced southern heir, Maelbaethe mac Boite, and Echmarchach of Waterford, and hitching their respective causes to the wider political manoeuvrings of Cnut of Denmark and England. At last, too, the ruler of Moray felt strong enough to launch a direct challenge on Scotland with the burning of Dunkeld in

1028. Though this attack did not succeed, it left Malcolm II in no doubt as to the deadly seriousness of those who wished to challenge him.

If Malcolm of Moray had lived longer, that threat might well have intensified. However, his demise in 1029 brought his brother, Gillacomgain, to power. Here, again, we are left with the vague impression of a man whose abilities were not equal to his ambitions. His shortcomings soon led his own people to get rid of him in preference for his cousin, Macbeth.

However romantic or distasteful the autocratic and ostentatious trappings of later medieval and early modern kingship might appear to modern eyes (and Scotland did not go as far in that respect as England or France), we should not forget that they emerged for reasons that were not simply to do with self- and national aggrandisement. Or rather, such an accumulation of power – perceived and actual – was a *consequence* of the heartfelt need to restrict challenges to the throne to the bare, unavoidable minimum. On the other hand, creating a strong, dynastic monarchy did not necessarily reduce the body count; it merely shifted the blame to those perceived as a threat, or a nuisance, or an embarrassment among the wider nobility rather than the royal family itself. However, we should not criticise each generation for dealing with the pressing concerns of its own time, unaware that the solutions might well store up problems for the future.

With the murder of Gillacomgain, Macbeth almost certainly enters the history books. His early years are obscure, though we have a few clues scattered around the literature of the period that hint at early brushes with the Norse, and an exile in Ireland.

So, to be honest, the means – the networks, the arguments, the promises – whereby he, of all his family, managed to supplant the mac Alpins are lost to us. That he was related to clan Aed mac Kenneth in the female line was surely vitally important in helping him to couch his claim to the throne in terms acceptable to Scotland's nobility. But the historians of the period are in no doubt that Macbeth came from a very different lineage to his predecessors.

We can be fairly sure, too, that Macbeth was helped to the throne by the fact that there was no obvious alternative, a result, perhaps, of the ruthless elimination of opponents before and during the reign of Malcolm II. However, such a bold step – bearing in mind that Moray was not part of Scotland and was therefore an unlikely place to look for a king of Scots – is a testament to the impression that Macbeth himself made on those weighing up his credentials. Behind that three-week hiatus between the death of Duncan at Pitgaveny and the new king's inauguration lay tense and delicate negotiations as the Moravian strove to show that he would, among many things, be good for Scotland and its great men. The ability to reward one's friends whilst not keeping everyone else out in the cold is one that Duncan could not master but which Macbeth did.

It is surely right to stress the mythologising that takes place even during a ruler's lifetime, when poets are paid to compliment their patrons in verse with stock allusions to their military prowess and their abundant generosity.[29] Spin-doctors have a very long history. And yet it is a brave man – and a bad poet – who seeks to praise through assertions and analogies that would be recognised as blatantly untrue, not least because such barefaced contentions might ironically reflect the king's inadequacies. Indeed, a 'don't mention the war' attitude perhaps lies behind the eulogies to King Duncan in the *Duan Albanach*, written in the time of his son, Malcolm. Here Macbeth's predecessor is described as 'Duncan the handsome, of lively aspect', 'the wise' and 'of royal countenance', generalised epithets of admiration which tell us very little about the king's character, as opposed to his appearance, perhaps because there was so little to tell.

Macbeth's own spin-doctors, on the other hand, did feel a somewhat defensive need to cast aspersions on the king's predecessor 'of many diseases', emphasising the party line that regime change had been necessary to save Scotland's people from the difficulties into which Duncan had led them. The legitimacy and righteousness of Macbeth's own kingship was then underlined by references to the prosperity that the kingdom enjoyed under his rule – 'Scotland will be brimful, in the west and the east', says the same poet who insulted Duncan; 'and in his reign there were productive seasons' says another, less florid, writer.[30] The fact that this perception of well-being comes from sources likely to be independent of each other strongly suggests that this was a genuinely held belief about this king.

That contemporaries might regard Macbeth's reign as particularly blessed is given added weight by the fact that he found himself able – within only a few years of a fairly serious rebellion – to leave Scotland and go to Rome. Although he was not the only senior figure among the elites of western Europe's outer edge to make the trip, he is certainly the only Scottish king known to have done so. As such, the very fact of his going is significant. The experience also attests to the rather broader vision of what it meant to be king of Scots that Macbeth seems to have developed, again, in comparison to previous kings. Here was a man who could look beyond the traditions of the warband and the need to maintain loyalty through military exploits and booty-collecting to present Scotland's compliments, and its concerns, to the pope himself.

His adventures clearly brought him into contact with interesting men with fascinating ideas. The brief, tragic sojourn of Osbern Pentecost and his fellow Normans in Macbeth's household shows that the Scottish king was both willing to give some of these new ideas a try and sufficiently renowned beyond Scotland to get the support he needed to put them into practice. It is tempting to wonder what else he might have achieved if he had been a much younger man with a long life ahead of him when he became king.

However, Macbeth's ability to guide Scotland along a path of relative peace had relied, to a large extent, on the fact that his southern neighbour, the much more powerful king of England, had his mind firmly chained to domestic matters for the first ten years of his reign. Once those matters had been resolved, England's relationship with Scotland began to deteriorate rapidly. We do not know the cause – actual or ostensible. A cursory reliance on English sources would suggest that the Scottish king had lost the plot, turning to raiding across the border in his old age, presumably in order to prop up his flagging authority. But the reality may have been far more interesting: perhaps it was Macbeth's likely assertion of Scottish ecclesiastical independence from England in Rome and/or Scottish intervention in Strathclyde that brought the northern kingdom to Edward's attention. In any event, the ambitions of Earl Siward of Northumbria now received enthusiastic royal support and an invasion of Scotland was launched in 1054.

Macbeth and his men put up a hard fight against this celebrated warrior but, despite serious casualties on both sides,
including Siward's son, it was the invaders who won the day.
The English seem to have ended up with little to show for the
carnage, though, particularly once Siward had followed his son
into the next life within little over six months. And it surely
says much about the Scottish king's standing that he maintained his grip on power, despite being well into his fifties and
now with a distinctly flawed military record. In these respects,
Macbeth's life resembles that of one of Scotland's greatest early
kings, Constantine II, who was defeated at Brunanburh towards
the end of his long reign. The similarities may not have ended
there, if Macbeth really did resign the kingship to his stepson,
Lulach, perhaps to enter a monastery. Lulach, of course, had
even more royal blood in him, thanks to his mother, Gruoch,
and, just because this new dynasty ended so precipitately, we
should not underestimate the extent to which Scotland had
adjusted to it.

And this was indeed the makings of a dynasty. Even if
Macbeth had to be 'persuaded' to retire by Lulach, their relationship was, in effect, that of a father and son, and the
expectation would certainly have been that Mael Snechta would
eventually take the throne in his turn. Though Macbeth's own
blood would have run but thinly on into this future, it was his
reign that taught the kingdom as a whole that Moray – far
from being a troublesome and barbarous adjunct – could join
with Scotland peacefully and prosperously. It was Macbeth, too,
who emerged as the very antithesis of a parochial northerner,
taking Scotland out into Europe and introducing new ideas
back home on his return.

The gaping crevasses in the evidence will never allow us to understand Macbeth's contribution in full and it is impossible to judge whether Scotland would have turned out a different place if the house of Moray had continued to rule it. The chances are that the marginalisation of Celtic Scotland would still have happened simply because Scottish politics could not have failed to be drawn, one way or another, into the destructive orbit of powerful England, an orbit that eventually fixed the political focus of the northern kingdom firmly south of the Forth.

To understand Macbeth fully, then, we will probably always have to use our imagination at least as much as our intellect. Shakespeare has held his version of the Scottish king to the world as a terrible warning against the flaws in human nature that can turn even decent, honourable men into power-maddened tyrants. Few could do it half as well, and it would be a fool's errand indeed even to consider trying to excise this Macbeth from humanity's conscience. But if, out of this tangled web of deceit, slander and the flimsiest of evidence, another man, more real but perhaps less tangible, emerges from 'the dunnest smoke of hell'[31] to stand alongside his alter ego, then that would be no less than 'the generous king of Fortriu', and Scotland, deserves.

Sources

Contemporary primary sources for the life and times of Macbeth certainly do exist, usually surviving now in chronicles compiled at a later date but with internal clues as to when the original sections were written. Given Scotland's close connection with Ireland in this period, Irish sources provide at least as many illuminating snippets of information about what was happening in the Scottish kingdom as the indigenous Scottish ones. Taken together, this adds up to a considerable body of evidence, including *The Pictish Chronicle*, the *Synchronisms of Flann Mainistreach* (a list of Irish provincial kings 'synchronised' with the monarchs of the whole of the British Isles; Flann died only a year before Macbeth); Irish and Pictish additions to the *Historia Britonum* (History of Britain), which contains within it a poem written no later than the end of Macbeth's reign, the *Duan Albanach* (The Scottish Poem, but probably written in Ireland); the *Chronicle of Marianus Scotus*, written in a monastery on the Rhine by an Irishman keen to record what was going on back home; the *Annals of Tighernac* (originally finished in 1088, but subsequently continued down to 1178); the *Prophecy of St Berchan*, which was written by 1119, but purported – as was the fashion at the time – to be the prophecies of a seventh-century saint; and the *Chronicle of the Scots*, which was written around 1165 and thus begins to show hints of attempts to rewrite the life of Macbeth to fit the needs of his successors. These are followed by somewhat later (thirteenth- and fourteenth-century) sources, such as the *Chronicle of the Picts and Scots* (*c.*1280), another *Chronicle of the Scots* (1333–4), John of Fordun's *Chronica Gentis Scotorum* (*c.*1380), and Walter Bower's *Scotichronicon* (1440s), which do draw on earlier material but already – certainly the Scottish ones – have elements of overt propaganda designed to destroy the reputation of Highland Scotland in general, and Macbeth in particular. The *Annals of Ulster*, although compiled in 1498, also seem to contain reliable earlier information.

The Norse Sagas, which give the most fulsome descriptions of events and flesh out the characters of key historical players to a fantastical degree, are nonetheless also important primary source material. If handled carefully, works such as the *Orkneyinga Saga*, *Njal's Saga* and the *Heimskringla* (Harold Fairhair's Saga) provide evidence not only for particular events and the people involved, but also for wider social conditions, including attitudes towards women and the role of farmers in this warlike society.

Finally, English, Welsh and even Continental primary sources, including the *Anglo-Saxon Chronicle*, the various *Brut* chronicles of Wales and the chronicle of Ralph Glaber, all offer perspectives on Scottish history, as is to be expected, given the extent to which Scotland was integrated into wider British and European politics.

Archaeology also acts as another form of primary evidence, revealing from physical remains major political shifts and the ways in which royal and elite authority was wielded. The sophisticated design of the key power centres of early medieval Scotland, such as the impressive palace at Forteviot, can tell us much about how a Pictish/Scottish king saw himself and the kind of impression he wished to make on others. Though most of the sites of relevance to Macbeth were excavated over thirty years ago, archaeologists such as Steve Driscoll and Sally Foster have recently published pioneering work enhancing our understanding of what these physical remains meant within medieval Scottish society. I was also fortunate that the ten-year excavation at the monastery at Portmahomack culminated with the recent publication of a monograph detailing the finds and their interpretation by the project's director, Marin Carver, in *Portmahomack. Monastery of the Picts* (Edinburgh University Press, 2008).

There have been important advances in the secondary literature too. In particular, our understanding of Scottish kingship and government in the early centuries of the kingdom has been greatly enhanced in the last few years, the result of a new conviction on the part of Scottish historians that such research is worthwhile. Recent works – such as A.A.M. Duncan's well-researched monograph *The Kingship of the Scots* (Edinburgh University Press, 2002); Dauvit Broun's ground-breaking *Scottish Independence and the idea of Britain. From the Picts to Alexander III* (Edinburgh University Press, 2007); an excellent and innovative Ph.D. thesis on the earldom of Moray, Macbeth's homeland, by Alasdair Ross; and, most particularly, Alex Woolf's magisterial work, *From Pictland to Alba. Scotland in the Viking Age, 789–1070* (Edinburgh University Press, 2007) – have revolutionised current thinking on the period. Important articles, such as Alex Woolf's 'The "Moray Question" and the Kingship of Alba in the Tenth and Eleventh Centuries', in the *Scottish Historical Review* (2000) and Dauvit Broun's 'Scotland before 1100: writing Scotland's origins', in B. Harris and A.R.

Macdonald (eds), *Scotland: the Making and Unmaking of the Nation, c.1100–1707*, vol. 1 (Dundee University Press, 2006), have also critically re-examined vital issues, including how the kingdom of Scotland, Alba, evolved in the first place and that kingdom's relationship with provinces such as Moray.

Moving further afield, *Viking Empires*, by Angelo Forte, Richard Oram and Frederik Pederson (CUP, 2005), offers an up-to-date synthesis of the Norse contribution to British, and wider, politics. Barry Cunliffe's book *Facing the Ocean: The Atlantic and its Peoples* (OUP, 2001), which accompanied a Radio 4 series, examines the histories of the seafaring Scots and Irish, as well as the Norse who came to live among them.

Modern scholarship on English history, including recent works such as Emma Mason's *The House of Godwine: The History of a Dynasty* (Hambledon and London, 2004), also help to shed light on the English politics which had a profound effect on Macbeth's own foreign policy and which, ultimately, cost him his life. Finally, there is a wealth of material on wider medieval European history, within which context Macbeth's story must sit, not least in order to provide a radical new Celtic perspective on the crucial developments taking place in the eleventh century.

All of the above sources, both primary and secondary, must be brought to bear to understand the complicated and shifting politics of the British Isles in which Macbeth and his predecessors were certainly not passive players. While the material is, and always will be, frustratingly inadequate for a full analysis of the complexities of politics in this period, I hope that, by digging deep and wide across a range of material, I have managed to bring some life to what would otherwise be condemned for ever as a historical wasteland.

Notes

Abbreviations

ASC – *Anglo-Saxon Chronicle*
AT – *Annals of Tighernach*
AU – *Annals of Ulster*
ESSH – *Early Sources of Scottish History*
PSAS – *Proceedings of the Society of Antiquaries of Scotland*
SHR – *Scottish Historical Review*
Stat. Acc. – *The Statistical Accounts of Scotland*

Introduction

1 M. Barber, *The Two Cities. Medieval Europe 1050–1320* (London and New York: Routledge, 1993), p. 38
2 http://www.dorothydunnett.co.uk/dunnettqa5.htm
3 *All's Well that Ends Well*, Act III, Scene v

Chapter 1: All the King's Men

1 M. Lynch, *Scotland: A New History* (London: Pimlico, 1992), p. 239
2 See, for example, Sir Walter Scott, *Tales of a Grandfather*, Chapter 35
3 Keith M. Brown, 'Reformation to Union, 1560–1707', in R.A. Houston and W. Knox (eds), *The New Penguin History of Scotland* (London: Penguin Books, 2002), p. 234

4 Brown, 'Reformation to Union', p. 195

5 Lynch, *Scotland*, p. 234

6 Lynch, *Scotland*, p. 236

7 Lynch, *Scotland*, p. 237

8 Quoted in M. Magnusson, *Scotland: The Story of a Nation* (London: HarperCollins, 2001), p. 400

9 S. Greenblatt, *Will in the World: How Shakespeare became Shakespeare* (London: Pimlico, 2005), p. 405

10 P. Ackroyd, *Shakespeare: The Biography* (London: Vintage, 2006), p. 444

11 Greenblatt, *Will in the World*, p. 179

12 Lynch, *Scotland*, pp. 239–40

13 N. Aitchison, *Macbeth: Man and Myth* (Stroud: Sutton Publishing, 2000), p. 125

14 Greenblatt, *Will in the World*, p. 346, p. 351

15 Preface to *Daemonologie, In Forme of a Dialogue. Divided into Three Books*. http://www.geocities.com/pagantheology/james/ copied from the 1969 facsimile edition of the copy of the *Daemonologie* held at the Bodleian Library, Oxford, and published by Theatrum Orbis Terrarum and Da Capo Press, Amsterdam.

16 Greenblatt, *Will in the World*, p. 349

17 *Macbeth*, Act I, Scene iii. See Greenblatt, *Will in the World*, for a discussion of this possibility.

18 Lynch, *Scotland*, p. 232, p. 234

19 Brown, 'Reformation to Union', p. 199

20 Lynch, *Scotland*, p. 241

21 Lynch, *Scotland*, pp. 241–2; Brown, 'Reformation to Union', pp. 237–8

22 See Chapter 10, p. 254

Chapter 2: Christendom in 1050

1 The Emperor Constantine supposedly made Pope Sylvester this extraordinary gift in thanks for having brought him to Christianity. The emperor would thus (allegedly) rule only the eastern part of the empire from his new capital at Constantinople. In fact, the edict

was probably concocted three hundred years later, in the mid-eighth century, around the same time as the Donation of Pepin. This bona fide gift brought the popes control of what is known as the papal states, a large swathe of territory extending north-west of the city of Rome, which they acquired in 756 from the Frankish king, Pepin, who in turn had conquered them from the Lombards, as a reward for helping Pepin to his throne.

2 See R. Fletcher, *Bloodfeud* (London: Penguin Books, 2003), p. 90 ff. for a succinct discussion of the evidence for a degree of millennium fever either side of AD 1000.

3 R. Morris, 'Northern Europe invades the Mediterranean', in G. Holmes (ed.), *The Oxford Illustrated History of Medieval Europe* (Oxford: Oxford University Press, 2001), p. 204

4 Morris, 'Northern Europe invades the Mediterranean', p. 206

5 G. V. Irving, 'Description of a Scottish pilgrim in the middle of the twelfth century', *PSAS*, vol. 5 (1862–4), p. 337

6 M. Shaw (trans.), Joinville et Villehardouin, *Chronicles of the Crusades* (Harmondsworth: Penguin, 1963), p. 167

Chapter 3: Light on a Dark Age

1 See http://www.visitscotland.com/aboutscotland/ for the latest version of how Scotland is sold at home and abroad.

2 The phrase comes originally from a poem by Hamish Henderson and was also used in the title of a book on twentieth-century Scottish history by Christopher Harvie, as well as the song from which these words have been quoted. B. McNeill, 'No gods and precious few heroes', *No Gods* (Greentrax Records, 1995); H. Henderson, *Elegies for the Dead of Cyrenaika*, first elegy: 'End of a Campaign' (London: J. Lehman, 1948); C. Harvie, *No Gods and Precious Few Heroes. Scotland since 1914* (Edinburgh University Press, 1993).

3 Tacitus, *The Life and Times of Julius Agricola*, 31

4 K. Forsyth, 'Scotland to 1100', in J. Wormald (ed.), *Scotland. A History* (Oxford University Press, 2005), p. 3

5 See Lynch, *Scotland*, p. 17 for the more outdated version of 'Scotti' history (showing how quickly Scottish history has changed in the

last decade or so). Magnusson, *Scotland*, pp. 32–3 provides a straightforward but more equivocal account of the Scottis' early relationship with Scotland. See also E. Campbell, *Saints and Sea-Kings. The First Kingdom of the Scots* (Edinburgh: Canongate/Historic Scotland, 1999) and Forsyth, 'Scotland to 1100', pp. 14–15.

6 Other Germanic races also flooded into southern Britain at the same time but 'Anglo-Saxon' became the shorthand for all of them, though we should remember that neither Britons nor Anglo-Saxons were single nations (C. Lowe, *Angels, Fools and Tyrants. Britons and Anglo-Saxons in Southern Scotland* [Edinburgh: Canongate, 1999], p. 8, pp. 10–11, p. 7).

7 Lowe, *Angels, Fools and Tyrants*, pp. 39–40

8 E. James, 'The Northern World in the Dark Ages, 400–900', in Holmes (ed.), *The Oxford Illustrated History of Medieval Europe*, p. 75

9 Patrick, credited with bringing the new religion to Ireland in the fifth century and becoming the island's patron saint, is perhaps the most famous, but Finnian (who has probably been mistaken for the earlier saint, Ninian) was also active in Ireland in the mid-sixth century. Kentigern became a bishop in the British kingdom of Strathclyde in the later sixth century and, possibly, the royal-born Run went south to evangelise among the Anglo-Saxons at around the same time (Forsyth, 'Scotland to 1100', p. 7).

10 Forsyth, 'Scotland to 1100', p. 17

11 See Campbell, *Saints and Sea-Kings*; J.A. MacClannahan Hanna, *A History of the Celtic Church from its inception to 1153* (Ann Arbor: Edwards Brothers, 1963), pp. 38–9

12 Adomnan, *Life of Columba*, Chapter 22

13 B. Cunliffe, *Facing the Ocean. The Atlantic and its Peoples* (Oxford University Press, 2001), p. 481

14 See, for example, C. Frayling, *Strange Landscape. A Journey through the Middle Ages* (London: BBC Books, 1995), p. 60

15 Forsyth, 'Scotland to 1100', p. 17

16 Campbell, *Saints and Sea-Kings*, p. 36. Here it is suggested that Adomnan was actually the Ionian scholar in question, but this issue seems far from settled. Cú Chuimne seems to have led an 'interesting' life in his youth, inspiring the following cheerful ditty:

> Cú Chuimne in youth
> Read his way through half the truth.
> He let the other half lie
> While he gave women a try.
> Well for him in old age
> He became a holy sage.
> He gave women the last laugh.
> He read the other half.

(D. Ó Crónín, 'Hiberno-Latin Literature to 1169', in D. Ó Crónín (ed.), *A New History of Ireland*, vol. 1. (Oxford: Clarendon Press, 2005)

17 See, for example, *Chronicle of the Kings of Scotland*, version D 843–858 in *ESSH*, p. 289 right through to *Chronicle of the Kings of Scotland*, version D 1057 in *ESSH*, p. 600 and *Chronicle of the Kings of Scotland*, version D 1057–8 in *ESSH*, p. 603. See also W. Bower, *A History Book for Scots. Selections from Scotichronicon*, ed. D.E.R. Watt, Book I (Edinburgh: Mercat Press, 2007), p. 7. Kings Constantine II (d.952), Culen (d.971) and Kenneth II (d.995) were the exceptions.

18 See S. Foster, 'Before Alba: Pictish and Dál Riata power centres from the fifth to late ninth centuries AD', in S. Foster, A. Macinnes and R. MacInnes (eds.), *Scottish Power Centres. From the early Middle Ages to the twentieth century* (Glasgow: Cruithne Press, 1998), pp. 9–10

19 Forsyth, 'Scotland to 1100', p. 15

20 Just to add to this complicated story, the kindred of Gabráin then split off into two lines, the second of which was the kindred of Comgaill, which gives its name to modern Cowal in central Argyll.

21 A. Woolf, *From Pictland to Alba. Scotland in the Viking Age, 780–1070* (Edinburgh University Press, 2007), p. 221, p. 341; Forsyth, 'Scotland to 1100', p. 17. See Chapter 5, pp. 99–100.

22 Campbell, *Sea-Kings*, p. 20

23 *AT*, 578.2; *AU*, 580.3

24 Woolf, *From Pictland to Alba*, pp. 9–10; see also A. Woolf, 'Dún Nechtáin, Fortriu and the Geography of the Picts', *SHR*, 85 (2006), pp. 182–201

25 James, 'The Northern World in the Dark Ages, 400–900', p. 83

26 Forsyth, 'Scotland to 1100', p. 11

27 See Chapter 5, pp. 109–11

28 I. Armit, *Scotland's Hidden History* (Stroud: Tempus Publishing, 1998), p. 135

29 See Woolf, *From Pictland to Alba*, pp. 64–5; Chapter 5, pp. 96–7

30 G. Donaldson, 'Scottish bishops' sees before the reign of David I', *PSAS*, vol. 87 (1952–3), p. 108; T. O. Clancy, 'Philosopher-King: Nechtan mac Der-Ilei', *SHR*, vol. 83, no. 2, pp. 125–49; Woolf, *From Pictland to Alba*, p. 56. It should be noted that many of these names, including Rígmonaid (St Andrews), are the Gaelic ones which were later attached to these important Pictish sites when they were taken over as part of the new kingdom of Alba/Scotland.

31 *AU*, 736.1; 736.2; 741.10; 761.4; Woolf, *From Pictland to Alba*, p. 9, pp. 28–9; Forsyth, 'Scotland to 1100', p. 22

32 See Woolf, *From Pictland to Alba*, pp. 63–7 for the most recent account of the relationship between the kings of Pictland and Dál Riata which discounts older theories that the latter went on to rule both kingdoms between 789 and 839.

33 Woolf, *From Pictland to Alba*, p. 65

34 N. Aitchison, *Forteviot. A Pictish and Scottish royal centre* (Stroud: Tempus Publishing, 2006), p. 51

35 Woolf, *From Pictland to Alba*, pp. 104–5

36 Aitchison, *Forteviot*, p. 199. See Chapter 9 for a discussion of the architectural context of the arch.

37 A.A.M. Duncan, *The Kingship of the Scots, 842–1292, Succession and Independence* (Edinburgh University Press, 2002), pp. 9–10

38 Woolf, *From Pictland to Alba*, pp. 100–1

39 Woolf, *From Pictland to Alba*, pp. 66–7; J. Anderson, 'Notice of a bronze bell of Celtic type at Forteviot, Perthshire', *PSAS*, vol. 26 (1891–2), pp. 435–6

40 See Woolf, *From Pictland to Alba*, p. 64

Chapter 4: Accidental Birth of a Nation

 1 A. Forte, R. Oram and F. Pederson, *Viking Empires* (Cambridge University Press, 2005), pp. 54–7

2 Woolf, *From Pictland to Alba*, pp. 56–7

3 *AU*, 807.4; see below, p. 69; Woolf, *From Pictland to Alba*, p. 65, pp. 98–101

4 Woolf, *From Pictland to Alba*, p. 66

5 *AU*, 839.9; Forte et al, *Viking Empires*, pp. 81–2

6 Interestingly, the Scots themselves had accepted as king in 1292 a man who was, really, an Englishman, albeit one who held a Scottish title: John Balliol of Barnard Castle in Northumberland and lord of Galloway in Scotland. The new king's mixed ancestry – English father, Scottish mother – allowed the Scots to claim him as their own. But it should come as no surprise that, having endured decades of war with England after 1296, the Scottish parliament refused to accept the notion in 1364 that their childless king, David Bruce, should acknowledge the English king's younger son as his heir.

7 See Forsyth, 'Scotland to 1100', p. 29

8 S. Driscoll, *Alba. The Gaelic Kingdom of Scotland. AD 800–1124* (Edinburgh: Birlinn with Historic Scotland, 2002), pp. 33–4

9 See Woolf, *From Pictland to Alba*, p. 93 ff.

10 Forte et al, *Viking Empires*, pp. 82–3; Woolf, *From Pictland to Alba*, pp. 99–100

11 *ESSH*, p. 288; P. E. Michelli, 'Four Scottish Crosiers and their relation to the Irish tradition', *PSAS*, vol. 116 (1986), p. 389; see below, p. 73

12 *ESSH*, p. 288

13 Fletcher, *Bloodfeud*, p. 16

14 *ESSH*, p. 352. See Duncan, *Kingship of the Scots*, p. 11.

15 See Duncan, *Kingship of the Scots*, p. 12, though this line is not followed by Woolf (see *From Pictland to Alba*, which deals in detail with Giric from p. 117). Duncan also acquiesces in the long-standing tradition that the Picts found matriliny (descent through the female line) perfectly acceptable, unlike the Scots. See also Chapter 5, pp. 104–5.

16 *ESSH*, pp. 364, 366

17 Duncan, *Kingship of the Scots*, p. 13

18 *ESSH*, p. 364; Duncan, *Kingship of the Scots*, p. 13

19 See above, Chapter 3, pp. 59–61

20 See Woolf, *From Pictland to Alba*, pp. 136–7 for discussion of an

earlier English meeting, which also laid down certain ecclesiastical privileges, showing that the Picts were certainly not alone in experiencing this kind of pressure.

21 A.A.M. Duncan, *Scotland. The Making of the Kingdom*. (Edinburgh: Mercat Press, 1992), p. 111

22 See Chapter 5, p. 105

23 *AU*, 900; W.J. Watson, *The History of the Celtic Place-Names of Scotland* (Edinburgh: Birlinn, 2005), pp. 10–13; Forsyth, 'Scotland to 1100', p. 31. The issue of 'Alba' is explored most fully and effectively in D. Broun, *Scottish Independence and the Idea of Britain. From the Picts to Alexander III* (Edinburgh University Press, 2007), Chapter 2.

24 *ESSH*, pp. 444–6

25 *Fragmentary Annals*, 429

26 *ESSH*, pp. 444–6; Woolf, *From Pictland to Alba*, pp. 134–8

27 Forte et al, *Viking Empires*, pp. 101–2; *AU*, 917.4. See Woolf, *From Pictland to Alba*, p. 144.

28 *AU*, 918.4; Woolf, *From Pictland to Alba*, p. 142 ff.

29 Woolf, *From Pictland to Alba*, p. 145

30 *ASC*, Chronicle A, 920. The year date had been changed to 923 then 924 in other hands, but that would have been impossible because Ragnall was already dead.

31 *ASC*, Chonicle D, 926

32 Fletcher, *Bloodfeud*, p. 20

33 Forte et al, *Viking Empires*, p. 104

34 *ESSH*, pp. 91–2

35 See Duncan, *Making of the Kingdom*, p. 92 ff; Woolf, *From Pictland to Alba*, p. 146 ff.

36 See Chapter 3, p. 56

37 Forte et al, *Viking Empires*, pp. 99–100. See also Woolf, *From Pictland to Alba*, p. 158 ff.

38 See Duncan, *Making of the Kingdom*, p. 91

39 *AU*, 937.6

40 Woolf, *From Pictland to Alba*, p. 175

41 *ESSH*, pp. 452–3

42 Duncan, *Kingship of the Scots*, p. 24

43 See Duncan, *Kingship of the Scots*, pp. 23–5 for a discussion of Anglo-Scottish relations up to the reign of Kenneth I.

44 Forsyth, 'Scotland to 1100', p. 32

45 Forsyth, 'Scotland to 1100', p. 32

46 Woolf, *From Pictland to Alba*, pp. 316–20

47 A. Woolf, 'The "Moray Question" and the Kingship of Alba in the Tenth and Eleventh Centuries', *SHR*, 79, 2, no. 208 (October 2000), p. 153

48 Woolf, 'The "Moray Question"', p. 154

49 W. D. Simpson, 'The early castles of Mar', *PSAS*, vol. 63 (1928–9), p. 119

50 It is striking that neither Mar and Buchan (there is some dispute as to whether or not Buchan was actually separate from Mar in this period) north of the Mounth, nor Atholl south of it, are given mythical Irish antecedents in a document of AD *c.*1000 to help explain how the various mormaers were related to the royal family, though the northern branch of the descendants of Conaing remained unallocated (see Woolf, *From Alba to Pictland*, pp. 226–7). In other words, the omitted regions might well be the homelands of the two branches of the royal family. Interestingly, too, a grant of lands in Buchan to the abbey of Deer was made by 'Malcolm, Culen's son' (*ESSH*, p. 470; *ESSH*, vol. 2, pp.175–8), perhaps indicating that King Culen (d. 970/1), though of the southern branch of the royal family, was marrying his sons around the country. The evidence, which can be summarised as follows, is certainly not clear-cut, but, on balance, can support the north–south hypothesis presented here. So far as deaths are concerned, we should ignore Giric, who came from a different dynasty altogether, as well as places where kings were fighting an external threat, i.e. the Norse:

877 Constantine, Kenneth's son, fought a battle against the Danes at Dollar and was driven into Ach cochlam (to Atholl?); slain by Norwegians at **Inverdovat**

878 Aed, Kenneth's son, killed by Giric at **Nrurim/Strathallan** (south)

889 Giric (different dynasty), killed at **Dundurn**

900 Donald, Constantine's son, died in **Forres**, killed because of his daughter (north)

952 Constantine, Aed's son, held meeting at Hill of Belief,

Scone; Battle of Tinemore against the Norse; Battle of Brunanburh against the English; died a monk at St Andrews (all south)

954 Malcolm, Donald's son, took an army into Moray; plundered English as far as Tees; killed at Fetteresso by men of the Mearns (borderline north/south) or in Ulnem/Vlurn by men of Moray (north)

962 Indulf, Constantine's son, killed by Norwegians at Invercullen

966/7 Dubh, Malcolm's son, fought a battle against Culen, Indulf's son, upon the ridge of Crup (Duncrub near Dunning?) in which fell the abbot of Dunkeld and the lord of Atholl (south); killed in Forres (north)

970/1 Culen, Indulf's son, killed in a burning house in Ybandonia by Amdarch, Donald's son (a Briton of Strathclyde), for his daughter who had been killed (south)

995 Kenneth, Malcolm's son, plundered into Northumbria and was defeated, possibly in Lothian; walled the banks of the ford of Forthin (Forth?) (south); was killed at Fettercairn by men of the Mearns (borderline north/south); also said to be at Dunsinane (south)

977 Olaf, Indulf's son, killed by Kenneth, Malcolm's son

997 Constantine, Culen's son, killed at Rathinveralmon (south)

51 Duncan, *Kingship of the Scots*, p. 20

52 See Duncan, *Making of the Kingdom*, p. 97 and *Kingship of the Scots*, p. 22. Richard Fletcher, an expert on the subject, also describes this murderous cycle as a bloodfeud; see *Bloodfeud*, pp. 73–4.

53 Fletcher, *Bloodfeud*, p. 9. See p. 7 ff. for a discussion of the nature of bloodfeuds.

54 In 964 King Dubh defeated a challenger (Culen) in a battle that claimed the lives of both the abbot of Dunkeld and the lord of Atholl (in which Dunkeld is situated). However, two years later Culen successfully overthrew Dubh (*ESSH*, pp. 471–4). Kenneth II was ousted, temporarily, by Culen's brother, Olaf, though the latter was killed before he could try again to take the throne (see Duncan, *Kingship of the Scots*, p. 21).

55 See Woolf, *From Pictland to Alba*, p. 197
56 *Annals of the Four Masters*, 998.14

Chapter 5: View from the North

1 Some in the region have recently and laudably taken steps to address the huge discrepancy between the man and his reputation, including the truth about his origins and life before becoming king: see http://www.kingmacbeth.com

2 Both John Major and Hector Boece's histories of Scotland (1521 and 1527 respectively) provide the same version of Macbeth's origins ultimately handed down to Shakespeare.

3 The earliest known description of the medieval earldom of Moray dates to 1312, but almost certainly harks back to at least 1130. See A. Ross, 'The Province of Moray, *c.*1000–1232', unpublished Ph.D. thesis, University of Aberdeen (2003), pp. 38–40

4 http://www.moray.gov.uk/LocalHeritage/Assets/html_pages/morayheritage.html

5 L. Shaw, *The History of the Province of Moray*, enlarged and brought down to the Present time by J.F.S. Gordon, vol 1 (Glasgow: Thomas D. Morison, 1882), p. 28

6 Adomnan, *Life of Columba*, Book Two, Chapter 28 and Book One, Chapter 29; Bede, *Historia Ecclesiastica Gentis Anglorum*, Book Three, Chapter 4. *AU* 693.1. The date of this expedition is not given, but it must have taken place sometime after 563, when Columba came to Iona, and *c.*584, when Bridei died.

7 See Chapter 3, p. 58

8 http://www.york.ac.uk/depts/arch/staff/sites/tarbat/bulletins/datareports/2006.html; M. Carver, *Portmahomack. Monastery of the Picts* (Edinburgh University Press, 2008), Chapter 6

9 Carver, *Portmahomack*, p. 127, p. 128

10 R. Oram, *Moray and Badenoch. A Historical Guide* (Edinburgh: Birlinn, 1996) pp. 60–1

11 Foster, 'Before Alba', p. 11

12 See Chapter 3, p. 57

13 K. I. Edwards and I. Ralston, 'New dating and environmental

evidence from Burghead Fort, Moray', *PSAS*, vol. 109 (1977–8), pp. 207–8

14 See Chapter 3, p. 54

15 See Chapter 4, p. 65

16 Carver, *Portmahomack*, p. 80, p. 64

17 Woolf, *From Pictland to Alba*, pp. 99–100, p. 201

18 See Woolf, *From Pictland to Alba*, p. 99, p. 101 for an alternative reading of this problematic period, but one which, nevertheless, first postulates an alliance between Kenneth and Fortriu.

19 See *AU*, 839.9, cf. *AU*, 858.2

20 See Chapter 4, p. 69; Chapter 3, p. 58; *AU*, 865.6

21 See Chapter 4, p. 70; *AU*, 866.1, 871.2; *ESSH*, p.292; Forte et al, *Viking Empires*, p. 88

22 *ESSH*, p. 351. See Chapter 4, pp. 71–2. See also the confusing entry in the *Chronicle of the Kings of Alba*, *ESSH*, p. 352.

23 See Woolf, *From Pictland to Alba*, p. 321

24 See Woolf, *From Pictland to Alba*, p. 227

25 *ESSH*, p. 366

26 Forte et al, *Viking Empires*, p. 90

27 Forte et al, *Viking Empires*, pp. 91–2

28 *ESSH*, pp. 371–2

29 J. Anderson (ed.), *The Orkneyinga Saga* (Edinburgh: Mercat Press, 1999), p. 2

30 Carver, *Portmahomack*, p. 142, p.147

31 Forte et al, *Viking Empires*, p. 268

32 Forte et al, *Viking Empires*, p. 92 ff. See Chapter 4, p. 75

33 *AU*, 904.4

34 See Woolf, *From Pictland to Alba*, pp. 289–93, p. 300 ff.

35 In this context we can, unfortunately, only talk about southern Fortriu, i.e. Moray, since it is the only part of Scotland whose medieval landscape has been reconstructed in this way. See Ross, *The Province of Moray*, pp. 42–51 and 228–9. The fact that this farming unit was given a Gaelic name, but one which did not exist in the original 'Scottish' Gaelic homeland of Dál Riata, suggests that this landscape revolution had taken place before the Gaels took over Pictland. The Gaelic word *dabhach* was thus a renaming of the original Pictish agricultural unit.

36 Ross, *The Province of Moray*, p. 204
37 See Chapter 3, p. 59 ff.
38 See Chapter 4, pp. 83–4
39 Broun, *Scottish Independence*, p. 8
40 *AU*, 904.4; *Chronicon Scotorum*, 904. See Broun, *Scottish Independence*, pp. 81–4 for the reason why the Gaelic word 'Alba' was used for Pictland, later becoming Scotland, and the Gaelic '*Cruithentuaithe*', also effectively meaning Pictland, was not.
41 We do not know where the bishopric held by Cellach, who stood with King Constantine on the Hill of Belief and reiterated Giric's promise to liberate the Pictish Church, actually was, though later traditions suggest that it was St Andrews, or perhaps Abernethy, both in the south (Woolf, *From Pictland to Alba*, pp. 134–5).
42 W.F. Skene (ed.), *Chronicles of the Picts, Chronicles of the Scots and other early memorials of Scottish history* (Edinburgh: T. Constable, 1867), p. 10
43 Woolf, *From Pictland to Alba*, p. 201
44 *ESSH*, pp. 451–5
45 The next king from Dubh's side of the family was, unusually, his brother, Kenneth, who may well have decided to draw a permanent line under his older sibling's career. One version of the *Chronicle of the Kings of Scotland* states only that Dubh was 'driven from the kingdom', while other versions are explicit that he died in Forres (*ESSH*, pp. 472–4). The *Annals of Ulster* also state that he was killed by Scots, a term which may have been used by contemporaries to describe the Moravians (*AU*, 967.1).
46 *ESSH*, pp. 511–13
47 I am happy to note once again my gratitude to Dauvit Broun for helping me through this and for providing me with the genealogy of David I in the *Book of Lecan* which contains the fullest account of these connections.
48 See, for example, Woolf, 'The "Moray Question"' and Ross, *The Province of Moray*, p. 230; Broun, *Scottish Independence*, p. 8, pp. 10–11
49 *ESSH*, vol. 2, pp. 175–8. I am again very grateful to Dauvit Broun for pointing out to me the potential significance of this entry. Donald and Malcolm need not necessarily have made the grant of their

respective bits of Biffie at the same time, but it is at least as likely that they did. Malcolm II later gave the 'king's portion' of Biffie to Deer, perhaps providing evidence that the line of Constantine mac Kenneth was muscling in on territory once controlled by the (by then) defunct line of Aed mac Kenneth.

50 See Woolf, *From Pictland to Alba*, p. 242 ff., p. 300 ff.

51 See Forte et al, *Viking Empires*, p. 221

52 Forte et al, *Viking Empires*, pp. 225–6; D. Ó Corráin, 'Ireland, Wales, Man and the Hebrides', in P. Sawyer (ed.), *The Oxford Illustrated History of the Vikings* (Oxford University Press, 1997), p. 101. See Chapter 6, pp. 136–7

53 R. Cook (ed.), *Njal's Saga* (London: Penguin Classics, 1997), verse 86

54 Cook (ed.), *Njal's Saga*, verse 85

55 Anderson *Orkneyinga Saga*, p. 209, p. 4

Chapter 6: Murder as Usual

1 The eleventh-century Gaelic poem, 'The Birth of Aedan mac Gabrain', is essentially based around the need for sons and the implicit expectation on a wife to provide them. T. O. Clancy (ed.), *The Triumph Tree. Scotland's earliest poetry AD 550–1350* (Edinburgh: Canongate, 1998), pp. 178–82.

2 There were later attempts to identify her as Donada, a daughter of the future Scottish king, Malcolm II (1005–34). Such a match was not impossible, but it was unlikely. The relationship between Malcolm – whose accession to the throne signified the crown's retention by the descendants of Constantine mac Kenneth – and Finlay, a competitor from the ousted line of Aed mac Kenneth, could hardly have been easy. And why would Malcolm, who was, if anything, the younger man, invest the house of Moray with even more royal blood?

3 Ross, *The Province of Moray*, p. 230

4 *Stat. Acc.* of 1791–9, vol. 12, p. 390: Nairn, County of Elgin. Shakespeare's Macbeth is, of course, named as 'thane of Cawdor' by the three witches, having just been promoted to that office for his recent military service to King Duncan (Act I, Scene iii). As

we will see, however, this appellation was the result of a transmogrification of the earlier 'thane of Cromarty'.

5 G. Anderson, 'On certain Vitrified (and Unvitrified) Forts in the neighbourhood of Loch Ness and the Moray Firth', *PSAS*, vol. 4 (1860–2), pp. 196–7. For a discussion of Malcolm's Tower see E. Henderson, *The Annals of Dunfermline and Vicinity from the earliest authentic period to the present time* AD 1069–1878 (Glasgow: 1879), pp. 2–3.

6 The first volume of the *Annals of Ulster* covers the period from 431 to 1201 and the name occurs only four times, including our king.

7 'The Birth of Aedan mac Gabrain'; 'The Life of St Catroe', *ESSH*, pp. 432–3; K. Meyer (trans.), 'The wooing of Emer', in *Archaeological Review* (London), vol. 1 (1888), p. 74

8 'The wooing of Emer', p. 70, p. 74

9 Broun, *Scottish Independence*, p. 58

10 See Chapter 4, p. 83

11 The description of these events, originally written down by a monk of Durham some sixty years later, can be found translated into English in C. J. Morris, *Marriage and murder in eleventh-century Northumbria: a study of the 'De Obsessione Dunelmi'* (Borthwick Papers, no. 82, York, 1992), pp. 1–5. See also B. Hudson, *Kings of Celtic Scotland* (Westport/London: Greenwood Press, 1994), p. 112 and Woolf, *From Pictland to Alba*, p. 233.

12 See Broun, *Scottish Independence*, pp. 39–40 for a discussion of how the eleventh and twelfth centuries in Britain and Ireland witnessed the rise of a new phenomenon in the writing of history, the articulation of a continuous narrative of kingship, which 'represents one of the most significant examples of the increasing prominence of kingdoms in the mental landscape'.

13 This issue was dealt with explicitly by Alex Woolf as recently as 2007 in his book *From Pictland to Alba*, p. 241

14 *AU*, 1020.6

15 *ESSH*, pp. 500–1, pp. 529–30; *Orkneyinga Saga*, pp. 209–10

16 B. Crawford, 'Medieval Strathnaver', in J.R. Baldwin (ed.), *The Province of Strathnaver* (Edinburgh: Scottish Society for Northern Studies, 2000), p. 2

17 *Orkneyinga Saga*, p. 209

18 The Battle of Skitten Mire is reported in a number of Sagas for different periods and reputedly involved both an Earl Finlay and an Earl Macbeth as leaders on the Scottish side, the latter fighting against a previous earl, Liot, rather than Sigurd. However, it is possible that this was just one misremembered event and a youthful Macbeth (who eventually did become earl of Moray) was working in conjunction with his father who, as already mentioned, merits the description in the Sagas as 'the Scottish king' (*ESSH*, pp. 483–4; 500–2). Earl Sigurd was probably the first proper *jarl* of Orkney, though skirmishes between Norse and Scots before his time were likely. Pinning precise dates on the Sagas is a notoriously frustrating exercise.

19 *Orkneyinga Saga*, p. 210

20 *War of the Gaedhil with the Gaill*, p. 191

21 *AU*, 1014; *Annals of the Four Masters*, 1014; *Annals of Loch Cé*, 1014.4

22 *Njal's Saga*, pp. 301–3, for a description of the battle and Earl Sigurd's death

23 There is a continuing debate, for reasons that will become apparent, as to whether the Malcolm, king of Scots whose daughter married Earl Sigurd was Malcolm (II) mac Kenneth, as described here, or Macbeth's cousin, Malcolm, son of Maelbrigde (Finlay's brother), who has yet to enter our story (see, for example, A.B. Taylor, 'Karl Hundason, King of Scots', *PSAS*, vol. 17 [1936–7], pp. 339–41). The son of that marriage was Earl Thorfinn of Orkney, whose life was also interwoven with that of Macbeth. Given that the marriage was reputed to have taken place *c.*1005 (i.e. five to ten years before Earl Sigurd's death in 1014), my own view is that Malcolm of Moray was too young to have produced a daughter of marriageable age, even though he was likely to have been at least ten years older than Macbeth (so born *c.*985/990). It is also not clear what strategic advantage this would have brought Earl Sigurd, since Malcolm was not at that time a member of the ruling Moray family, though closely connected to it. The Leinster connection supposedly shared by Malcolm II and Earl Sigurd also lends more weight to the idea that these two were father- and son-in-law, even though the latter was surely older than the former.

24 See Hudson, *Kings of Celtic Scotland*, p. 114

25 *Orkneyinga Saga*, p. 4 (and also p. 16 for a description of the youthful
   Thorfinn). Once again, placing any faith on the dates or chronology
   of the Sagas is probably going too far; certainly, the incredible deeds
   ascribed to Earl Thorfinn when he first began his military and political career are still only marginally believable if he was born no later
   than 1005/6 rather than 1009.

26 See Chapter 5, p. 93. By the time the story got to Shakespeare,
   'Cromarty', 'Moray' and 'king' had been transformed into 'Cawdor',
   'Glamis' and 'king' (Act I, Scene iii).

27 Cromarty – which lies between the Moray and Cromarty Firths –
   does not feature on any list of later medieval thanages, but it is
   possibly that it was one (R. Oram, 'David I and the Scottish conquest
   and colonisation of Moray', *Northern Scotland*, xix [1999], 1–19).

28 See Woolf, *From Pictland to Alba*, pp. 346–8, compared with A.
   Grant, 'Thanes and Thanages, from the Eleventh to the Fourteenth
   Centuries', in A. Grant and K. Stringer (eds), *Medieval Scotland:
   Crown, Lordship and Community* (Edinburgh University Press, 1993),
   pp. 39–81; Foster, 'Before Alba'; S. Driscoll, 'Formalising the mechanisms of state power', in S. Foster, A. Macinnes and R. MacInnes
   (eds), *Scottish Power Centres. From the early Middle Ages to the twentieth century* (Glasgow: Cruithne Press, 1998).

29 See Fletcher, *Bloodfeud*, p. 111, Woolf, *From Pictland to Alba*, pp.
   236–40, Duncan, *Kingdom of the Scots*, pp. 28–9 for some of the
   conflicting views on the protagonists in this battle, thanks to the
   difficulties with the sources.

30 *ESSH*, p. 544

31 Quoted in Fletcher, *Bloodfeud*, p. 111

32 Woolf, *From Pictland to Alba*, p. 240

33 Fletcher, *Bloodfeud*, p. 114

34 *ESSH*, p. 545

35 See Chapter 5, p. 120

36 See Woolf, *From Pictland to Alba*, pp. 230–2; Fletcher, *Bloodfeud*, pp.
   101–3 for a discussion of aspects of the life of Cnut.

37 *ESSH*, pp. 545–9. See below for the reason why we know that
   Malcolm's son – if this is indeed correct – cannot have lived for
   long.

38 *ESSH*, p. 551

Chapter 7: Kings in Waiting

1 See Fletcher, *Bloodfeud*, pp. 7–12 for a concise discussion of the current understanding of both the historical and contemporary blood-feud.

2 The similarity with the name of the subject of this book is un-mistakable and may have been responsible for the unusual representation of this young man's name by the scribe responsible for noting his death in the *Annals of Ulster*. His first name has been reduced merely to an 'M' – M. m. Boite m. Cinaedha – perhaps because the scribe intended to go and check that he had got it right and never finished the job. See Duncan, *Kingship of the Scots*, p. 32 for a discussion of the likelihood that the first 'M' is a name, rather than implying that he was a grandson of Boete (*mic mac* – 'son of the son of').

3 See Chapter 4, p. 90

4 His great-grandfather, King Dubh, seems to have been the pro-genitor of the house of Fife, giving it its surname, Macduff, a name of profound resonance to the Shakespearian version of Macbeth's life and death. See J. Bannerman, 'MacDuff of Fife', in Grant and Stringer (eds), *Medieval Scotland*, pp. 20–38. There is also the fact that Maelbaethe's sister, Gruoch, later gave away lands in West Fife to the monastery of St Serf's (see Chapter 8, pp. 201–3).

5 *ESSH*, pp. 573–5; Woolf, *From Pictland to Alba*, pp. 253–4

6 Forte et al, *Viking Empires*, pp. 196–7

7 See *ESSH*, pp. 545–9 for the various sources commenting on these events. Traditionally the Malcolm of these sources has been presumed to be Malcolm II, but the description of the meeting, implying as it does obsequiousness on the part of those who sought Cnut out from the north, does not fit at all with the upper hand in cross-border politics then enjoyed by the victor of Carham. It also contra-dicts the agreement already made between Cnut and Malcolm II in Ralph Glaber's account.

8 J. A. Graham-Campbell, 'The Viking-age silver and gold hoards of Scandinavian character from Scotland', *PSAS*, vol. 107 (1975–6), p. 115; *Stat. Acc.*, 1834–45, vol. 9, pp. 51–2

9 Forte et al, *Viking Empires*, p. 228
10 Forte et al, *Viking Empires*, pp. 197–8
11 Fife (together with its western part, Forthriff) was one of the former Pictish kingdoms. However, the earldom of Fife, as it emerged in the documents in the late eleventh century, was quite unlike the other mormaerdoms. 'We cannot envisage the earldom of Fife as a compact territory in which the earl's sway was undivided, as, for example, Buchan or Strathearn probably were. It consisted rather of a group of scattered fiefs' (G.W.S. Barrow, 'The earls of Fife in the twelfth century', *PSAS*, vol. 87 [1952–3], p. 56). This strongly suggests that it had been forfeited to the crown and, eventually, restored to its earls in a much reduced and haphazard state (see also Chapter 9, pp. 237–8)
12 *AU*, 1029.7; *AT*, 1029.5
13 *ESSH*, pp. 569–70
14 *Orkneyinga Saga*, Chapters 5 and 6. The Oykel runs through the Black Isle, in Ross, just above Moray.
15 *ESSH*, pp. 576–7. See Chapter 7, pp. 159–60 for references to the possibility that Thorfinn had been given lands in Fife.
16 *The Prophecy of St Berchan* does note that Macbeth took Scotland 'after slaughter of Gaels', which may refer to the role he played in his cousin's demise (*ESSH*, p. 601).
17 *AU*, 1032.2
18 *AU*, 1033.7. 'In the older, A or Trinity College, Dublin copy of the Annals of Ulster a line is drawn from the notice of the murder [of Maelbaethe, described here as M.m. Boite m. Cinaedha] to the *obit* of Mael Coluim, to ensure that there was no mistake about the identity of the man responsible' (Hudson, *Kings of Celtic Scotland*, p. 120).
19 Hudson, *Kings of Celtic Scotland*, p. 120
20 *ESSH*, p. 573
21 *ESSH*, pp. 573–5. See *Prophecy of St Berchan* in Skene, *Chronicles*, p. 100
22 Duncan describes Macbeth as 'valiant cousin! Worthy gentleman!' (Act I, Scene ii).
23 The wars between Scotland and England broke out in the final decade of the thirteenth century because the long line of kings

descended from Macbeth's successor, Malcolm III, finally ran out on the death of Alexander III. Edward I of England, who claimed overlordship of Scotland, initially went through the tortuous legal process of identifying the rightful heir, who turned out to be John Balliol, in 1292. This is, in essence, what Archie Duncan's *Kingship of the Scots* is about and anyone interested in this issue should look there. Four years later, Edward deposed King John and took over the kingdom directly. Ten years after that, Robert Bruce, whose family's claim had been deemed less 'rightful' than Balliol's, seized the throne, proving once again that the ability to lead and – perhaps above all – maintain power could still, in exceptional circumstances, prove more important than a superior quality or quantity of royal blood.

24 *AU*, 1034.9
25 Woolf, *From Pictland to Alba*, p. 254
26 Berchan says that Macbeth became king 'After slaughter of Gaels [of which more anon], after slaughter of Foreigners', implying that he had engaged in at least one successful campaign against the Norse (*ESSH*, p. 601).
27 *ESSH*, pp. 584–5.
28 Symeon of Durham, *Libellus De Exordio*, III.ix

Chapter 8: Macbeth the King

1 D. Broun, *The Irish Identity of the Kingdom of the Scots in the twelfth and thirteenth centuries* (Woodbridge: The Boydell Press, 1999), p. 173
2 *ESSH*, p. 579. Macbeth is here described as Malcolm II's *nepos*, which is more usually translated as 'grandson' rather than the more literal meaning of 'nephew'.
3 It does, of course, depend on how you define the term, but I am thinking here of William I, Henry IV, Edward IV, Richard III and Henry VII. Scotland, interestingly, endured only one – Robert Bruce – in exceptional circumstances, a product, perhaps, of having a less taxing monarchy (literally).
4 P. Croft, *King James* (Basingstoke and New York: Palgrave Macmillan, 2003), pp. 50–1; *Macbeth*, Act 1, Scene vii. Arabella Stewart's father

was brother of King James's father, Henry, Lord Darnley. Though a woman, she at least had the virtue of being born and brought up in England.

5 *ESSH*, p. 579

6 Woolf, *From Pictland to Alba*, p. 258

7 Broun, *Scottish Independence*, p. 7

8 Broun, *The Irish Identity of the Kingdom of the Scots*, p. 173 n.36

9 See Broun, *Scottish Independence* for a revolutionary new understanding of the whole identity of Scotland leading up to the outbreak of the wars with England at the end of the thirteenth century. Chapters 1 to 3 form the basis of this discussion, along with Chapters 7 and 8 of his equally startling, but more challenging *The Irish Identity of the Kingdom of the Scots*.

10 *ESSH*, p. 579, p. 602. Marianus Scotus, the only contemporary chronicler to give dates for the events in question (presumably written up from notes taken when he was still in Ireland), seems to have tripped up over which Feast of the Virgin (Assumption, 15 August or Nativity, 8 September) the reigns of Duncan and Macbeth came to a beginning and an end on, an unlikely mistake for a scholarly monk to make. However, the explanation may lie with the brief gap between the death of Duncan on 15 August and the inauguration of Macbeth on 8 September, just as Duncan's reign began five days after his grandfather's death.

11 Broun, *Scottish Independence*, p. 60

12 'The Birth of Aedan mac Gabran' in Clancy (ed.), *The Triumph Tree*, p. 182. This poem may be slightly later than the reign of Macbeth (*c.*1060), and is the first reference to the infamous Stone.

13 The Brecbennoch is now known as the Monymusk reliquary. It was a portable shrine that must have contained a relic – perhaps a bone or two – of St Columba, one of many brought to Dunkeld by Kenneth mac Alpin around 849 after the evacuation of Iona. For discussions on the Monymusk reliquary, see J. Anderson, 'Notice of an ancient Celtic reliquary exhibited to the society by Sir Archibald Grant, Bart. of Monymusk', *PSAS*, vol. 14 (1879–80); J. Anderson, 'The architecturally shaped shrines and other reliquaries of the early Celtic Church in Scotland and Ireland', *PSAS*, vol. 44 (1909–10); F. Eeles, 'The Monymusk Reliquary or Brecbennoch of Columba',

PSAS, vol. 68 (1933–4). It is even tempting to suggest that a relic of significance in the north was brought for the occasion to replace the Brecbennoch. A likely candidate would be a relic of St Moluag, whose body supposedly lay at Rosemarkie. Moluag had probably become popular in the north because he had once lived and worked in Lismore, off the west coast, falling within the territory of the Cenel Loarn, from whom Macbeth's family now claimed descent. See A. Woolf, 'The cult of Moluag, the see of Mortlach and church organisation in northern Scotland in the eleventh and twelfth centuries', in S. Arbuthnot and K. Hollo (eds), *Fil suil nglais – A Grey Eye Looks Back: A Festschrift for Colm O' Baoill* (Clann Tuirc, 2007), pp. 311–12.

14 See J. Bannerman, 'The king's poet and the inauguration of Alexander III', *SHR*, vol. lxviii, 2, no. 186 (1989), pp. 120–45; Broun, *Scottish Independence*, pp. 55–8. Unfortunately this description properly belongs in the thirteenth century, some two hundred years after Macbeth's own inauguration. However, it is generally agreed that the ceremony has much older origins and the process of declaiming the royal genealogy, together with the participation of Scotland's bishops, must, at the very least, have formed a part of earlier inaugurations.

15 See Chapter 5, p. 102

16 Nick Aitchison argues convincingly that the *Prophecy of St Berchan* contains within it a poem composed for Macbeth himself (*Macbeth*, pp. 46–7).

17 *ESSH*, p. 601, p. 582

18 For a discussion of Crinan's possible origins and career, see Woolf, *From Pictland to Alba*, pp. 249–52. For a supposed intervention by Siward himself in Scotland in 1046, see Aitchison, *Macbeth*, p. 72. It is, in fact, entirely likely that the chronicler got confused with the Northumbrian earl's undoubted expedition against Macbeth in 1054.

19 The description of the eventual conflict in the Irish annals states that 'A battle [was fought] between Scots, upon a united expedition' (*ESSH*, p. 583). This last phrase has been interpreted as meaning 'an expedition led by several kings for one object', in effect a conjoining of different interests in one army.

20 Macduff became the family name of the earls of Fife, most likely

as descendants of King Dubh (see Bannerman, 'Macduff of Fife', p. 21).

21 Like the now-missing *Cath Bhuaidh* (Yellow Battler), the Brecbennoch was required, in the interests of victory, to accompany the Scottish army.

22 *ESSH*, p. 583

23 *Continuations of Flann Mainistreach*, 1119 in Skene (ed.), *Chronicles*, p. 105

24 *ESSH*, pp. 600–1

25 *ASC*, AD 1046; *AU*, 1047.1. This may refer to the same weather conditions.

26 Sir Archibald C. Lawrie (ed.), *Early Scottish Charters Prior to AD 1153* (Glasgow: MacLehose and sons, 1905), nos 5–6. Technically, the lands granted by both the royal couple and the bishop were in Forthriff, which was the western portion of Fife.

27 See A. Kerr, 'Description of the ecclesiastical remains existing upon St Serf's island, Lochleven, at 6th July 1881', *PSAS*, vol. 16 (1881–2), p. 162, p. 165.

28 See Chapter 7, pp. 159–60 for Thorfinn's apparent liking for Fife, though this may just be a chronicler's way of showing how daring the Orcadian fleets could be.

29 The boundary between Fife proper and Forthriff was said to follow 'an imaginary line drawn from the mouth of the Leven, on the Firth of Forth, to Macduff's Cross, near Newburgh' (E. Henderson, *The Annals of Kinross-shire* [1870], 1426). See D. Broun, 'The Seven Kingdoms in De Situ Albanie', in E.J. Cowan and R. Andrew MacDonald (eds), *Alba: Celtic Scotland in the Medieval Era* (Edinburgh: John Donald, 2000), p. 37.

30 J.M. Leighton and J. Stewart, *History of the County of Fife*, vol. 3 (Glasgow: Joseph Swan, 1840), p. 196. 'Bal' in this context does not mean town in an urban sense, but 'tounship' or large farm.

31 Aitchison, *Macbeth*, p. 76

32 J. Jamieson, *An historical account of the ancient Culdees of Iona and of their settlements in Scotland, England and Ireland* (Edinburgh: John Ballantyne and Company, 1811), p. 375

33 The later references to these grants do not make any mention of the date. However, the most likely point in their lives at which the

royal couple might have made such a gift was surely in preparation for the pilgrimage and, in this respect, they were no different from other pilgrims except in the scale of their offering.

Chapter 9: The Testing Time

1 *Chronicle of Huntingdon*, 198
2 D. J. Birch, *Pilgrimage to Rome in the Middle Ages: Continuity and Change* (Woodbridge: The Boydell Press, 1998), pp. 45–7 and 55–8 for a discussion of the routes to Rome from northern Europe and the problems of timing.
3 *Annals of the Four Masters*, 1051.11
4 Birch, *Pilgrimage to Rome*, pp. 61, 65, 69
5 *Rex Scottiae Macbethad Romae argentum pauperibus seminando distribuit.* The *Chronicle of Marianus Scotus*, in *ESSH*, p. 588. Marianus wrote his chronicle from his new home in the monastery of Mainz on the Rhine.
6 Birch, *Pilgrimage to Rome*, pp. 29–33
7 Birch, *Pilgrimage to Rome*, p. 92, pp. 133–4
8 R. Krautheimer, *Rome: profile of a city, 312–1308* (Chichester: Princeton University Press, 2000); Fletcher, *Bloodfeud*, p. 48
9 J. Osborne, 'Exorcising the demons: Rome's ancient monuments in the experience of medieval pilgrims', International Conference on *Pilgrimage: Jerusalem, Rome, Santiago*, Cork, Ireland (2000). Abstract: http://www.ucc.ie/acad/classics/pilgrimage/abstracts.html#osborne
10 A. Graftan, quoted in A.M.H. Schuster, 'Rome 1–1000', *Archaeology*, vol. 53 no. 1, January/February 2000
11 Since none of these charters are dated, it is possible that the bishop's gift was made independently of those of Macbeth and Gruoch, but it probably makes more sense to imagine that they were linked to this period immediately prior to the king's pilgrimage.
12 *AT*, 1055.2
13 Woolf, *From Pictland to Alba*, p. 260
14 See Chapter 2, p. 31
15 Broun, *Scottish Independence*, p. 109
16 Cnut seems to have instigated a fashion among the British and

Irish (including the Gall-Gaedhil, Scandinavian Gaels) to go on pilgrimage, which might seem to diminish the significance of Macbeth's own foray to Rome. However, there was surely a political distinction between the average noble and a king, however remote his kingdom, making the same journey.

17 Forte et al, *Viking Empires*, p. 276

18 Forte et al, *Viking Empires*, p. 140

19 See E. Mason, *The House of Godwine: The History of a Dynasty* (London and New York: Hambledon and London, 2004), pp. 74–5

20 R. Lomas, *County of Conflict: Northumberland from Conquest to Civil War* (East Linton: Tuckwell Press, 1996), p. 8

21 http://www.archaeologists.tv/content/view/15/30/

22 Mason, *The House of Godwine*, p. 75

23 Aitchison, *Macbeth*, p. 84

24 P. Contamine, *War in the Middle Ages*, trans. M. Jones (Oxford: Basil Blackwell, 1984), p. 52

25 *AU*, 1052.8; *Annals of the Four Masters*, 1052.8. See Chapter 7, pp. 158–9

26 Forte et al, *Viking Empires*, pp. 228–9

27 The poem tells the story of how the Picts came to Ireland before moving on, finally, to Scotland. 'They are described as landing in the territory of the Ui Chennselaig.' Since Diarmait was 'the first Ui Chennselaig king of Leinster for many centuries', we can read this as 'a desire to bring to mind a link between Mac Bethad and [Diarmait] mac Maíl na mBó' (Broun, *Scottish Independence*, p. 58).

28 *Lebor Bretnach*, p. 166; Broun, *Scottish Independence*, p. 57

29 Skene, *Chronicles*, pp. 57–64

30 Duncan, *Kingship of the Scots*, p. 39

31 As mentioned earlier, Edward was described as having 'the wrath of a lion'. In the later Middle Ages, the crown of England was represented by the leopard (symbol of the Plantagenets), while Scotland's kings sported the lion.

32 Fletcher, *Bloodfeud*, p. 137; Mason, *The House of Godwine*, p. 88

33 Duncan, *Kingdom of the Scots*, p. 39

34 E. J. Cowan, 'The Historical Macbeth', in W.D.H. Sellar (ed.), *Moray, Province and People* (Scottish Society for Northern Studies, 1993), p. 124

35 See Chapter 4, p. 80

36 This may be another indication of the connection between Northumberland and the house of Atholl, given that Crinan's son by his first marriage, Maldred, had married Ealdgyth of the Anglo-Saxon family of Bernicia, who was also King Edward's niece (see Chapter 8, p. 196). Crinan's second marriage to Bethoc, daughter of Malcolm, king of Scots, brought him both the abbacy of Dunkeld and a relationship by marriage with the royal house of Atholl. Earl Siward had also married into the same family, Ealdgyth being his wife's aunt.

37 *AU*, 1054.6 See Duncan, *Kingship of the Scots*, pp. 37–41 and Woolf, *From Pictland to Alba*, pp. 261–2 for discussions of the tortuous process whereby history – and Shakespeare – came to believe that it was Duncan's son, Malcolm, who was meant by the term 'son of the king of the Cumbrians'.

38 Mason, *The House of Godwine*, p. 88

39 See Woolf, *From Pictland to Alba*, p. 263 ff. for a full rendition of this entirely different account of how Malcolm III won his throne.

40 See A. Low, 'Notices of the localities in a grant of the lands of Keig and Monymusk, by Malcolm, King of Scots, to the church of St Andrews; and a sketch or history of the priory of Monymusk', *PSAS*, vol. 6 (1864–6), p. 223. Though the story related here of Macduff putting down a rebellion in Moray (in which he does not exactly cover himself in glory) is found in a much later source, it may contain an echo of his involvement in the events of 1058.

41 *ESSH*, p. 601

Chapter 10: From Death to Demonisation

1 'En ma Fin gît mon Commencement'. A cloth of estate hangs behind the person in the place of honour, especially a throne. For an excellent overview of the literary elements of the creation of the Macbeth myth, see Aitchison, *Macbeth*, Chapter 4.

2 Walter Bower, *Scotichronicon*, Chapter 42. This work was a continuation of John of Fordun's chronicle of the previous century.

3 See Chapter 8, p. 193

4   *ESSH*, pp. 602–3. See Broun, *Scottish Independence*, pp. 59–60 for a discussion of the *Duan Albanach* and the context in which it was composed.

5   *ESSH*, p. 603

6   *Rawlinson B502*: 1697; Ross, *The Province of Moray*, p. 19; *AU*, 1085.1

7   *AU*, 1093.5

8   Ross, *The Province of Moray*, p. 225, p. 186, p. 225

9   Broun, *Scottish Independence*, p. 273, p. 61

10 Ross, *The Province of Moray*, p. 187

11 Ross, *The Province of Moray*, p. 225

12 *Chronicle of Lanercost*, pp. 40–1

13 Ross, *The Province of Moray*, pp. 215–23. The origin legend is first found in John of Fordun's *Chronica Gentis Scotorum*, a fourteenth-century text, but Dr Ross argues convincingly that it is likely to have come from an earlier source.

14 Cowan, 'The Historical Macbeth', p. 132

15 *ESSH*, pp. 600–1, p. 603

16 Andrew of Wyntoun, vol. 4, p. 276, p. 256

17 For a discussion of a lost romance used by both Fordun and Wyntoun, see Duncan, *Kingship of the Scots*, pp. 35–8.

18 Broun, *Scottish Independence*, pp. 277–8

19 Broun, *Scottish Independence*, p. 6

20 John of Fordun, *Chronica Gentis Scotorum*, ed. W.F. Skene (Edinburgh: 1871), p. 188, p. 189; see Ross, *The Province of Moray*, p. 148

21 Cowan, 'The Historical Macbeth', pp. 134–5

22 Aitchison, *Macbeth*, p. 122

23 Hector Boece, *Scotorum Historiae*, vol 2, p. 144

24 Quoted in Aitchison, *Macbeth*, p. 130; http://www.dorothydun nett.co.uk/dunnettqa5.htm

25 Aitchison, *Macbeth*, p. 134

26 See, for example, Cowan, 'The Historical Macbeth', p. 135; Aitchison, *Macbeth*, p. 102

27 Of course, primogeniture, which eventually became the norm in western Europe, settles the issue of the succession only until the bloodline runs out – as it will do, especially if it is reliant on only the male line. Once that happens, conflict among potential claimants

will almost certainly break out, as it did in England on the death of Henry I (1135) and in France on the death of Charles IV (1328). Scotland, to its credit, avoided the horror of civil war after the death of Alexander III in 1286, but perhaps unity was assured (apart from the Bruce faction) because of the threat from England.

28 D. Cannadine, 'Introduction: divine rites of kings', in D. Cannadine and S. Price (eds), *Rituals of Royalty, Power and Ceremonialism in Traditional Societies* (Cambridge University Press, 1987), p. 1

29 Aitchison, *Macbeth*, p. 103, p. 137

30 *ESSH*, p. 582, pp. 600–1. In both cases, the chronicles in which these statements can be found seem to be incorporating earlier material which may – certainly in the case of Berchan's *Prophecy* – be more or less contemporary with Macbeth himself.

31 *Macbeth*, Act I, Scene v

Bibliography

Primary Sources

I would like to express my gratitude to the scholars of CELT (Corpus of Electronic Texts) at University College, Cork. Thanks to them, the following chronicles essential to any study of Macbeth and his times are available online in both the original language (usually Gaelic) and in translation. (See http://www.ucc.ie/celt/captured.html for the list of texts.)

Annals of the Four Masters
Annals of Loch Cé
Annals of Tighernach
Annals of Ulster
Chronicon Scotorum
Fragmentary Annals
Lebor Bretnach
Rawlinson B502.
War of the Gaedhil with the Gaill

The following are the main sources of primary material consulted in addition.

Adomnan, *Life of Columba* – http://www.fordham.edu/halsall/basis/columba-e.html
The Anglo-Saxon Chronicle – http://omacl.org/Anglo/ (*ASC*)

Bede, *Historia Ecclesiastica Gentis Anglorum* (London: Penguin Classics 1990)

Hector Boece, *Scotorum Historiae*, Batho, E.C. and Husbands, H.W. (eds). *The Chronicles of Scotland, Compiled by Hector Boece, Translated into Scots by John Bellenden, 1531*. 2 vols (Edinburgh: Scottish Text Society, 1938)

Walter Bower, *A History Book for Scots. Selections from Scotichronicon*, Book I, Watt, D.E.R. (ed.) (Edinburgh: Mercat Press, 2007)

Chronicle of Huntingdon, Forester, Thomas T. (trans.) (London: George Bell and Sons, 1876)

Chronicles of the Picts, Chronicles of the Scots and other early memorials of Scottish history, Skene, W.F. (ed.) (Edinburgh: T. Constable, 1867)

Early Scottish Charters Prior to AD 1153, Lawrie, A.C. (ed.) (Glasgow: MacLehose and sons, 1905)

Early Sources of Scottish History AD 500 to 1286, Thomson, A.O. (ed.) (Edinburgh: Oliver and Boyd, 1922) (*ESSH*)

John of Fordun, *Chronica Gentis Scotorum*, Skene, W.F. (ed.) (Edinburgh: 1871)

John of Fordun and Walter Bower, *Scotichronicon* (Edinburgh: Mercat Press, 1993)

Njal's Saga, Cook, R. (ed. and trans.) (London: Penguin Classics, 1997)

The Orkneyinga Saga, Anderson, J. (ed.) (Edinburgh: Mercat Press, 1999)

The First (Old) Statistical Account, Sinclair, J. (ed.) (1791–9), vol. 12 (Edinburgh: printed and sold by William Creech)

The Second (New) Statistical Account (1834–45), vol. 9 (Edinburgh: William Blackwood)

Symeonis monachi Opera omnia, Arnold, T. (ed.), *Rolls Series*, lxxv; 2 vols (1882–5), vol. 1

Andrew of Wyntoun, *The Orygynale Cronykil*, Laing, D. (ed.) (Edinburgh: Edmonston and Douglas, 1872)

Bibliography

Secondary Sources

Ackroyd, P., *Shakespeare: The Biography* (London: Vintage, 2006)

Aitchison, N., *Macbeth: Man and Myth* (Stroud: Sutton Publishing, 2000)

Forteviot. A Pictish and Scottish royal centre (Stroud: Tempus Publishing, 2006)

Anderson, G., 'On certain Vitrified (and Unvitrified) Forts in the neighbourhood of Loch Ness and the Moray Firth', *PSAS*, vol. 4 (1860–2)

Anderson, J., 'Notice of a bronze bell of Celtic type at Forteviot, Perthshire', *PSAS*, vol. 26 (1891–2)

'Notice of an ancient Celtic reliquary exhibited to the society by Sir Archibald Grant, Bart. of Monymusk', *PSAS*, vol. 14 (1879–80)

'The architecturally shaped shrines and other reliquaries of the early Celtic Church in Scotland and Ireland', *PSAS*, vol. 44 (1909–10)

Arbuthnot, S. and Hollo, K. (eds), *Fil suil nglais – A Grey Eye Looks Back: A Festschrift for Colm O' Baoill* (Clann Tuirc, 2007)

Armit, I., *Scotland's Hidden History* (Stroud: Tempus Publishing, 1998)

Bannerman, J., 'MacDuff of Fife', in Grant, A. and Stringer, K. (eds), *Medieval Scotland: Crown, Lordship and Community* (Edinburgh University Press, 1993)

'The king's poet and the inauguration of Alexander III', *SHR*, vol. 68, 2, no. 186 (1989)

Barber, M., *The Two Cities. Medieval Europe 1050–1320* (London and New York: Routledge, 1993)

Barrow, G.W.S., 'The earls of Fife in the twelfth century', *PSAS*, vol. 87 (1952–3)

Birch, D.J., *Pilgrimage to Rome in the Middle Ages: Continuity and Change* (Woodbridge: The Boydell Press, 1998)

Broun, D., *Scottish Independence and the idea of Britain. From the Picts to Alexander III* (Edinburgh University Press, 2007)

The Irish Identity of the Kingdom of the Scots in the twelfth and thirteenth centuries (Woodbridge: The Boydell Press, 1999)

'Scotland before 1100: writing Scotland's origins', in Harris, B. and Macdonald, A.R. (eds), *Scotland: the Making and Unmaking of the Nation, c.1100–1707*, vol, 1 (Dundee University Press, 2006)

'The Seven Kingdoms in De Situ Albanie' in Cowan, E.J. and MacDonald, R.A. (eds), *Alba: Celtic Scotland in the Medieval Era* (Edinburgh: John Donald, 2000)

Brown, Keith M., 'Reformation to Union, 1560–1707', in Houston, R.A. and Knox, W. (eds), *The New Penguin History of Scotland* (London: Penguin Books, 2002)

Campbell, E., *Saints and Sea-Kings. The First Kingdom of the Scots* (Edinburgh: Canongate/Historic Scotland, 1999)

Cannadine, D., 'Introduction: divine rites of kings', in Cannadine, D. and Price, S. (eds), *Rituals of Royalty, Power and Ceremonialism in Traditional Societies* (Cambridge University Press, 1987)

Carver, M., *Portmahomack. Monastery of the Picts* (Edinburgh University Press, 2008)

Clancy, T.O., 'Philosopher-King: Nechtan mac Der-Ilei', *SHR*, vol. 83, no. 2 (2004)

The Triumph Tree. Scotland's earliest poetry AD 550–1350 (Edinburgh: Canongate, 1998)

Contamine, P., *War in the Middle Ages*, trans. M. Jones (Oxford: Basil Blackwell 1984)

Cowan, E.J., 'The Historical Macbeth', in Sellar, W.D.H. (ed.), *Moray, Province and People* (Edinburgh: Scottish Society for Northern Studies, 1993)

Crawford, B., 'Medieval Strathnaver', in Baldwin, J.R. (ed.), *The Province of Strathnaver* (Edinburgh: Scottish Society for Northern Studies, 2000)

Croft, P., *King James* (Basingstoke and New York: Palgrave Macmillan 2003)

Cunliffe, B., *Facing the Ocean. The Atlantic and its Peoples* (Oxford University Press, 2001)

Donaldson, G., 'Scottish bishops' sees before the reign of David I', *PSAS*, vol. 87 (1952–3)

Driscoll, S., 'Formalising the mechanisms of state power', in Foster, S., Macinnes, A. and MacInnes, R. (eds), *Scottish Power Centres. From the early Middle Ages to the twentieth century* (Glasgow: Cruithne Press, 1998)

Alba. The Gaelic Kingdom of Scotland. AD 800–1124 (Edinburgh: Birlinn with Historic Scotland, 2002)

Duncan, A.A.M., *The Kingship of the Scots, 842–1292, Succession and Independence* (Edinburgh University Press, 2002)

Scotland. The Making of the Kingdom (Edinburgh: Mercat Press, 1992)

Edwards, K.I. and Ralston, I., 'New dating and environmental evidence from Burghead Fort, Moray', *PSAS*, vol. 109 (1977–8)

Eeles, F., 'The Monymusk Reliquary or Brecbennoch of Columba', *PSAS*, vol. 68 (1933–4)

Fletcher, R., *Bloodfeud* (London: Penguin Books, 2003)

Forsyth, K., 'Scotland to 1100', inWormald, J. (ed.), *Scotland, A History* (Oxford University Press, 2005)

Forte, A., Oram, R. and Pederson, F., *Viking Empires* (Cambridge University Press, 2005)

Foster, S., 'Before Alba: Pictish and Dál Riata power centres from the fifth to late ninth centuries AD', in Foster, S., Macinnes, A. and MacInnes, R. (eds), *Scottish Power Centres. From the early Middle Ages to the twentieth century* (Glasgow: Cruithne Press, 1998)

Frayling, C., *Strange Landscape. A Journey through the Middle Ages* (London: BBC Books, 1995)

Graftan, A., quoted in Schuster, A.M.H., 'Rome 1–1000',
Archaeology, vol. 53, no. 1 (2000)

Graham-Campbell, J.A., 'The Viking-age silver and gold hoards
of Scandinavian character from Scotland', *PSAS*, vol. 107
(1975–6)

Grant, A., 'Thanes and Thanages, from the Eleventh to the
Fourteenth Centuries', in Grant, A., and Stringer, K. (eds),
Medieval Scotland: Crown, Lordship and Community (Edinburgh
University Press, 1993)

Greenblatt, S., *Will in the World: How Shakespeare became
Shakespeare* (London: Pimlico, 2005)

Hanna, J.A. MacClannahan, *A History of the Celtic Church from its
inception to 1153* (Ann Arbor: Edwards Brothers, 1963)

Harvie, C., *No Gods and Precious Few Heroes. Scotland since 1914*
(Edinburgh University Press, 1993)

Henderson, E., *The Annals of Dunfermline and Vicinity from the
earliest authentic period to the present time* AD 1069–1878,
(Glasgow: 1879)
The Annals of Kinross-shire (1870)

Henderson, H., *Elegies for the Dead of Cyrenaika*, first elegy: 'End
of a Campaign' (London: J. Lehman, 1948)

Hudson, B., *Kings of Celtic Scotland* (Westport/London:
Greenwood Press, 1994)

Irving, G.V., 'Description of a Scottish pilgrim in the middle of
the twelfth century', *PSAS*, vol. 5 (1862–4)

James, E., 'The Northern World in the Dark Ages, 400–900', in
Holmes, G. (ed.), *The Oxford Illustrated History of Medieval
Europe* (Oxford University Press, 2001)

Jamieson, J., *An historical account of the ancient Culdees of Iona and
of their settlements in Scotland, England and Ireland* (Edinburgh:
John Ballantyne and Company, 1811)

Kerr, A., 'Description of the ecclesiastical remains existing upon

St Serf's island, Lochleven, at 6th July 1881', *PSAS*, vol. 16 (1881–2)

Krautheimer, R., *Rome: profile of a city, 312–1308* (Chichester: Princeton University Press, 2000)

Leighton, J.M. and Stewart, J., *History of the County of Fife*, vol. 3 (Glasgow: Joseph Swan, 1840)

Lomas, R., *County of Conflict: Northumberland from Conquest to Civil War* (East Linton: Tuckwell Press, 1996)

Low, A., 'Notices of the localities in a grant of the lands of Keig and Monymusk, by Malcolm, King of Scots, to the church of St Andrews; and a sketch or history of the priory of Monymusk', *PSAS*, vol. 6 (1864–6)

Lowe, C., *Angels, Fools and Tyrants. Britons and Anglo-Saxons in Southern Scotland* (Edinburgh: Canongate, 1999)

Lynch, M., *Scotland: A New History* (London: Pimlico, 1992)

McNeill, B., 'No gods and precious few heroes', *No Gods* (Greentrax Records, 1995)

Magnusson, M., *Scotland: The Story of a Nation* (London: Harper Collins, 2001)

Mason, E., *The House of Godwine: The History of a Dynasty* (London and New York: Hambledon and London, 2004)

Meyer, K. (trans.), 'The wooing of Emer', *Archaeological Review* (London), vol. 1 (1888)

Michelli, P.E., 'Four Scottish Crosiers and their relation to the Irish tradition', *PSAS*, vol. 116 (1986)

Morris, C.J., *Marriage and murder in eleventh-century Northumbria: a study of the 'De Obsessione Dunelmi'* (Borthwick Papers, no. 82, York, 1992)

Morris, R., 'Northern Europe invades the Mediterranean', in Holmes, G. (ed.), *The Oxford Illustrated History of Medieval Europe* (Oxford University Press, 2001)

Ó Corráin, D., 'Ireland, Wales, Man and the Hebrides', in Sawyer,

P. (ed.), *The Oxford Illustrated History of the Vikings* (Oxford University Press, 1997)

Ó Crónín, D., 'Hiberno-Latin Literature to 1169', in Ó Crónín, D. (ed.), *A New History of Ireland*, vol. 1 (Oxford University Press, 2005)

Oram, R., *Moray and Badenoch. A Historical Guide* (Edinburgh: Birlinn 1996)

'David I and the Scottish conquest and colonisation of Moray', *Northern Scotland*, xix (1999)

Osborne, J., 'Exorcising the demons: Rome's ancient monuments in the experience of medieval pilgrims': International Conference on *Pilgrimage: Jerusalem, Rome, Santiago*, Cork, Ireland (2000). Abstract: http://www.ucc.ie/acad/classics/pilgrimage/abstracts.html#osborne

Ross, A., 'The Province of Moray, *c.*1000–1232', unpublished Ph.D. thesis, University of Aberdeen (2003)

Scott, Sir Walter, *Tales of a Grandfather* (London: T. Werner Laurie Ltd)

Shaw, L., *The History of the Province of Moray*, enlarged and brought down to the Present time by J.F.S. Gordon, vol. 1 (Glasgow: Thomas D. Morison, 1882)

Shaw, M. (trans.), Joinville et Villehardouin, *Chronicles of the Crusades* (Harmondsworth: Penguin, 1963)

Simpson, W. D., 'The early castles of Mar', *PSAS*, vol. 63 (1928–9)

Taylor, A.B., 'Karl Hundason, King of Scots', *PSAS*, vol. 17 (1936–7)

Watson, W.J., *The History of the Celtic Place-Names of Scotland* (Edinburgh: Birlinn, 2005)

Woolf, A., *From Pictland to Alba. Scotland in the Viking Age, 780–1070* (Edinburgh University Press, 2007)

'Dún Nechtáin, Fortriu and the Geography of the Picts', *SHR*, 85 (2006)

Bibliography

'The "Moray Question" and the Kingship of Alba in the Tenth and Eleventh Centuries', *SHR*, 79, 2, no. 208 (2000)

The *Proceedings of the Society of Antiquaries of Scotland* can all be found online at: http://ads.ahds.ac.uk/catalogue/ARCHway/volumeSelector.cfm?rcn=1340

Index

Index